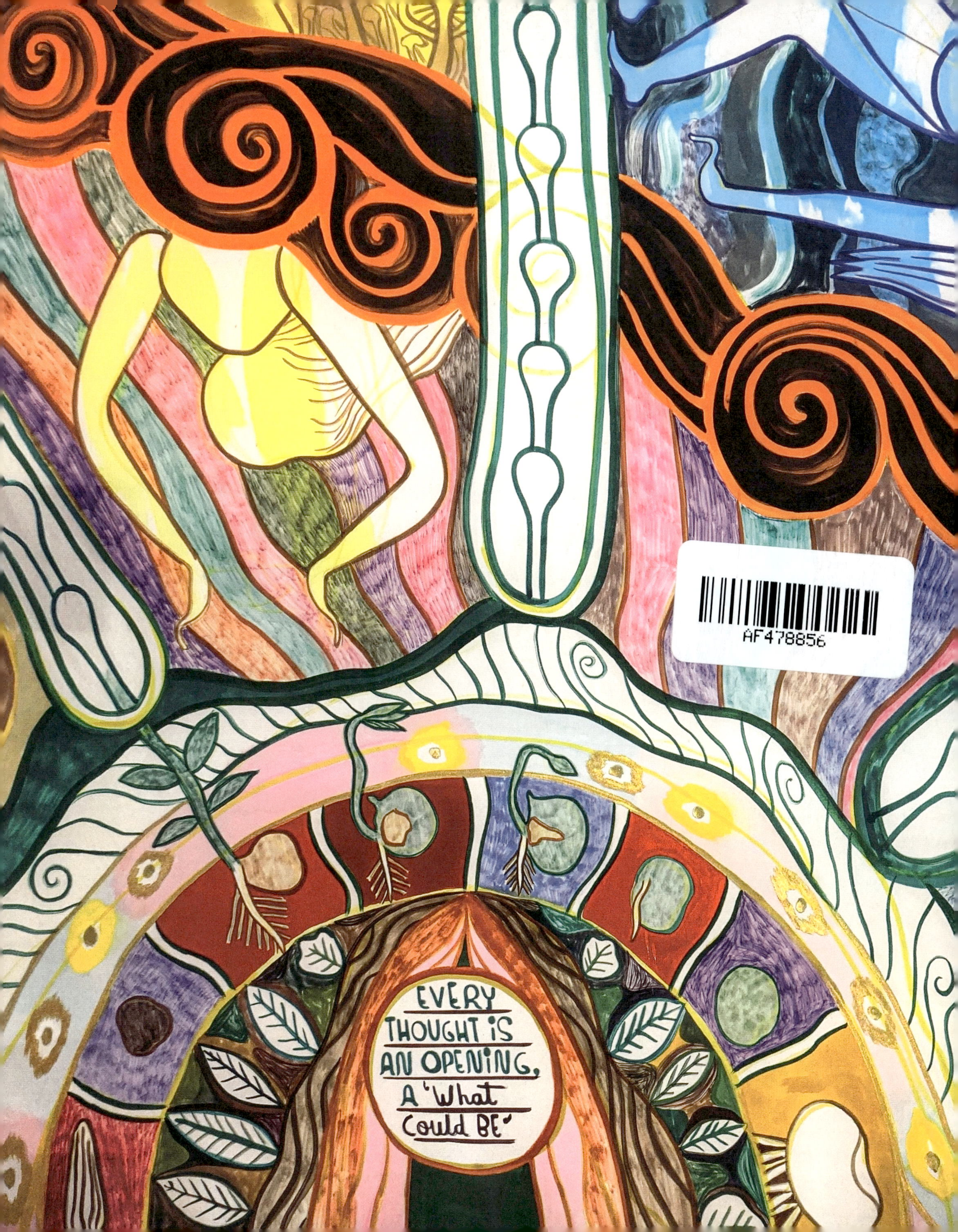

EVERY THOUGHT IS AN OPENING, A "WHAT COULD BE"

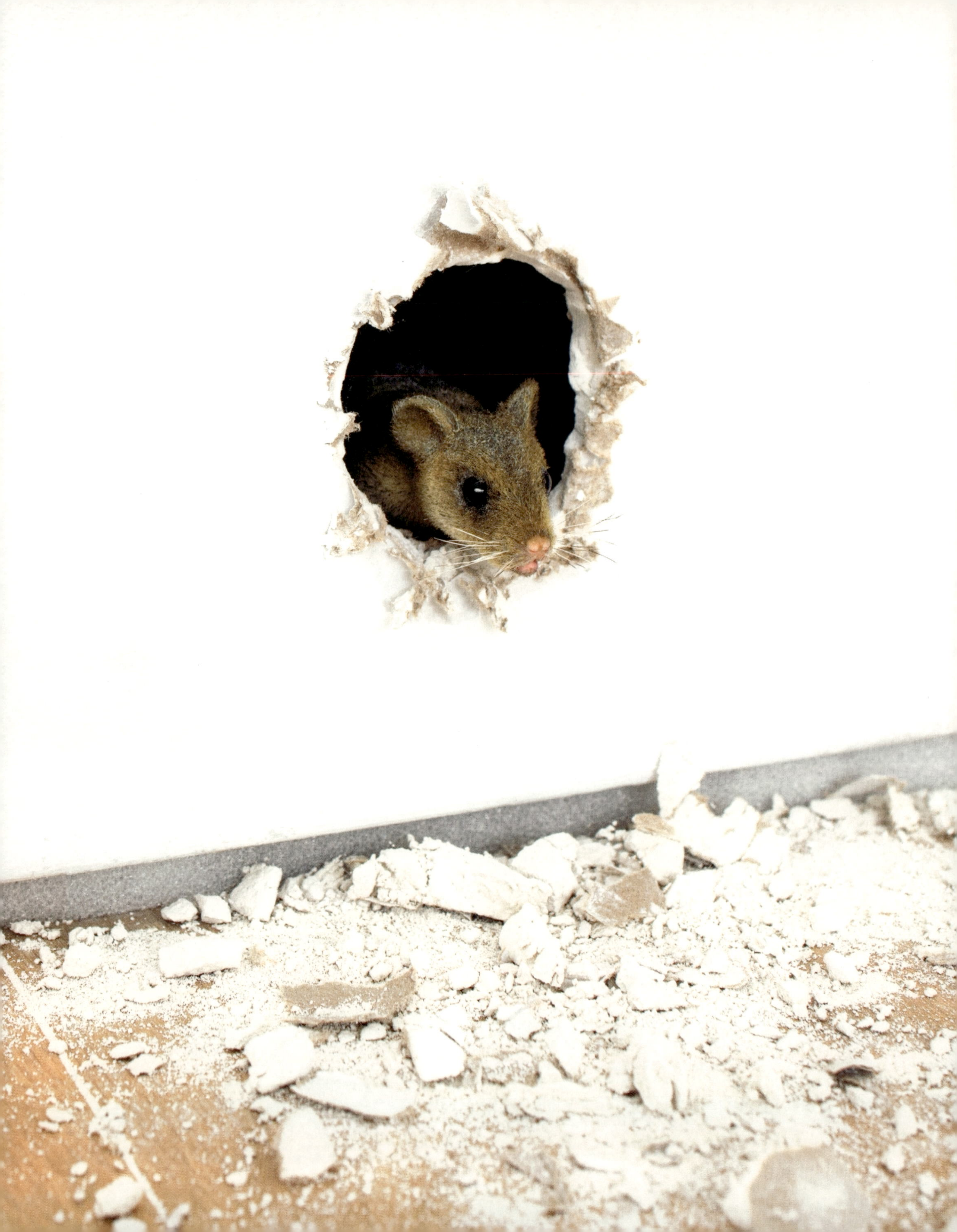

The Irreplaceable Human

– Conditions of Creativity in the Age of AI

Louisiana Museum of Modern Art

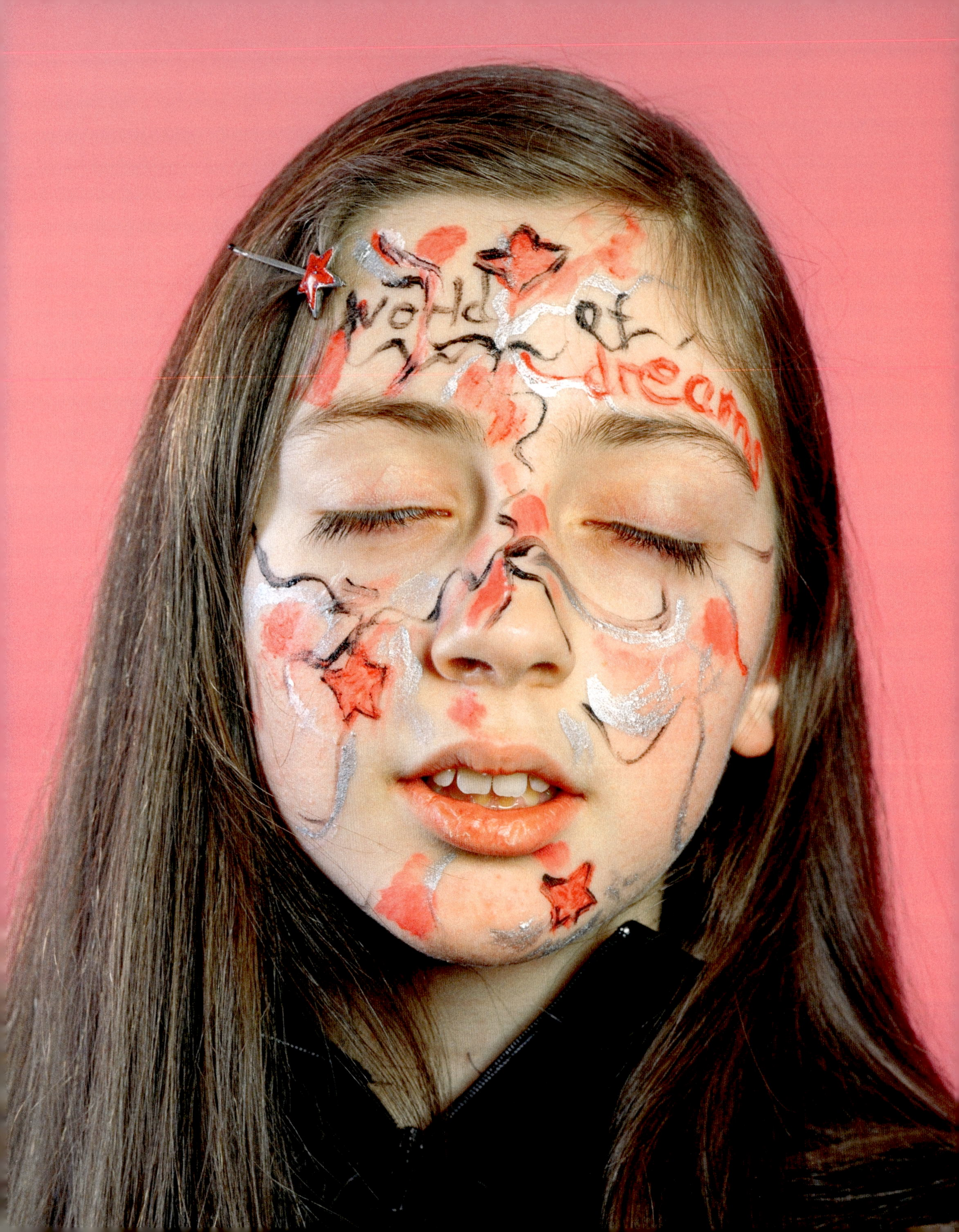

world
of
dreams

Aura Rosenberg
Jutta Koether/Karla, 1996

Foreword

The exhibition *The Irreplaceable Human* deals with the conditions for creativity at a time when the debate about artificial intelligence is once again making us consider what is unique about humanity. What can we do that computers can't? What about the human is irreplaceable?

Creativity is a central concept in our culture, and it has many meanings. It is used in very different contexts – being creative can, for example, mean being able to do something with your hands or being a little too 'smart', bordering on the criminal – *creative accounting*. But regardless of the way it is used, at heart the concept means being good at inventing, being good at making something valuable and new. The extent to which anything is creative is therefore also a question of what we consider to be valuable. We can associate the use of the term with human evolution. History and archeology have demonstrated the ways we have constantly reinvented ourselves, changing our ways of life and reshaping ourselves and our needs. But the word itself only came into widespread English usage in the 1940s and 1950s. So although humanity has always created, it is striking that this ability has only been revered in the way that it is currently from the second half of the 20th century, a period in which machines have gained immense ground in society.

There is actually a direct link between the development of the computer and the usage of the term. As the decades have passed and computers have conquered more and more aspects of existence, creativity as a term has come into more frequent use. The emergence of the word can be seen as an expression of concern that a part of our existence has come under siege, and its usage thus insists on there being something distinctive about us humans that cannot be represented in any other way. Creativity is part of the narrative we tell about ourselves. But today, as computers are becoming ever more advanced, the realm of humanity's uniqueness seems to be shrinking. Is humanity on the retreat towards a point where, eventually, creativity is only negatively defined – namely as what a computer or machine cannot do?

The Irreplaceable Human deals with the conditions for creativity and therefore inevitably with value and valuation. What really has value for society – and for the individual? What is innovation, original thinking, renewal?

We are at a moment in history where the leaps and bounds of artificial intelligence demand that we reconsider who we are and what we are doing. It has become clear in light of these technological breakthroughs that uniformity plays a major role in our relationship with values. Our education system has become predominantly geared towards standardization, rapid completion, and a culture of testing and measurement. This is good news for the computer because it deals with predictability better than we do. But is it good news for us? We pose this question with the help of artists, scientists and writers in this major exhibition, which, in terms of format, follows in the footsteps of three Louisiana exhibitions *Arctic, The Moon* and *Mother!*, which set out to blend art and cultural history into one grand narrative.

We readily admit that this exhibition arose out of a concern about the structural imbalances in modern society. And we hope that our concern – and our engagement – comes through in the catalogue and the exhibition. The title *The Irreplaceable Human* paraphrases a quote from the French writer André Gide, who addresses every individual's need to cultivate those aspects of the self that are only to be found within them, "and create out of yourself, impatiently or patiently, ah! that most irreplaceable of beings".

We believe that creativity is a fundamentally human attribute – and not just an industry or a sociological category reserved for what was once called "the creative class". Creativity is within us all – so, welcome to your own world, now at the Louisiana.

Poul Erik Tøjner
Director

Mathias Ussing Seeberg
Curator

Trevor Paglen
The Treachery of Object Recognition, 2019

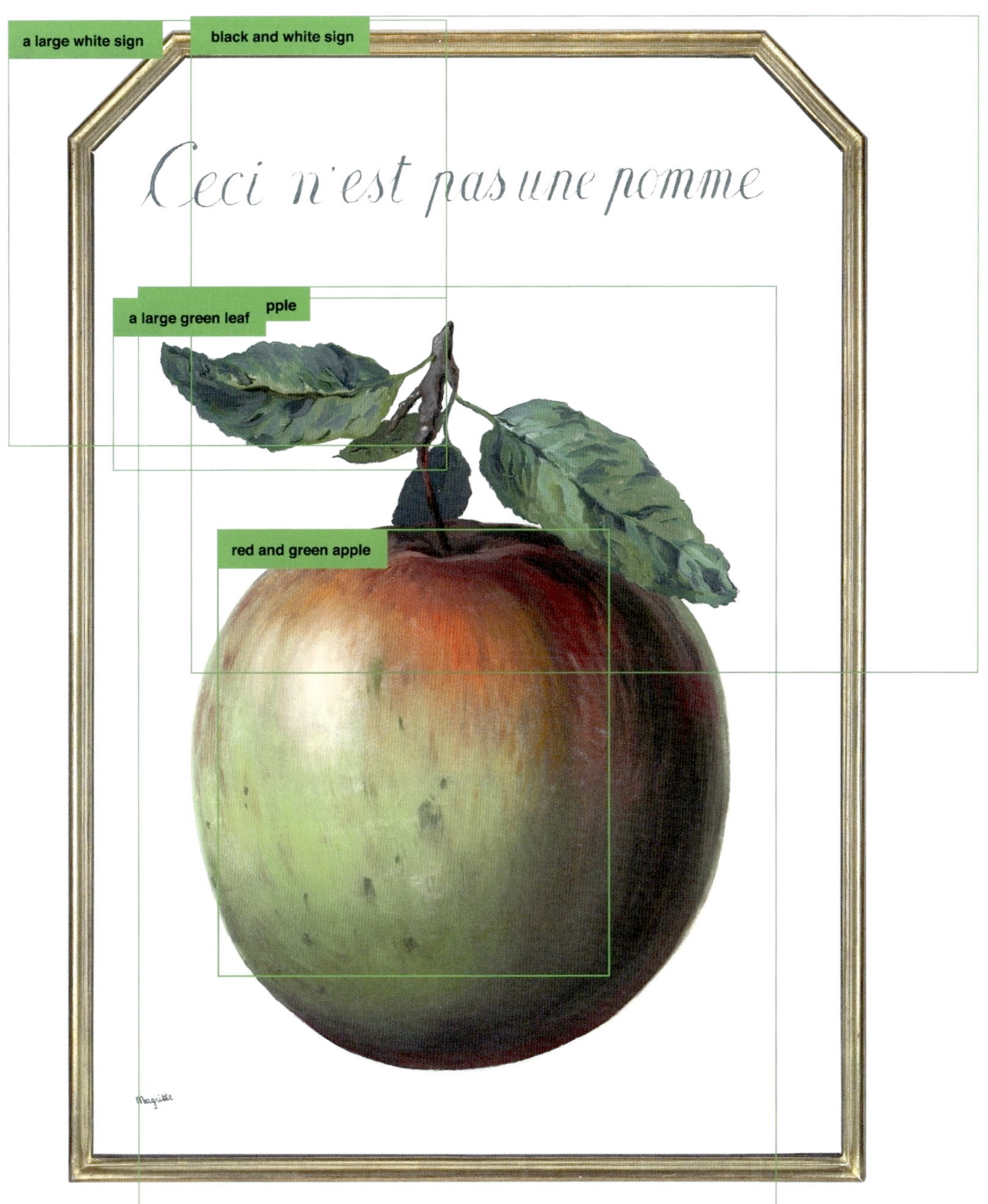

a large white sign
black and white sign
Ceci n'est pas une pomme
a large green leaf
pple
red and green apple
Magritte

<u>Thanks</u>

A big thank you to the A.P. Møller and Chastine Mc-Kinney Møller Foundation for supporting the exhibition.

And a big thank you to Aage and Johanne Louis-Hansen Foundation and the Obel Family Foundation, which have supported the exhibition trilogy *Mother!* (2021), *The Irreplaceable Human* (2023) and *The Ocean* (2024).

Thank you to the artists we have
worked with for this exhibition:
Yuji Agematsu
Trisha Baga
Bertille Bak
Brian Belott
Louisiana Bendolph
Tega Brain and Sam Lavigne
Andrea Büttner
Nick Cave
Ian Cheng
Chicks on Speed & collaborators
Tony Cokes
Joost Conijn
Tacita Dean
Jeremy Deller
Agnes Denes
Simon Denny
Rineke Dijkstra
Mia Edelgart
Ryan Gander
Flavia Gandolfo
Ben Grosser
Andreas Gursky
Marguerite Humeau
Josh Kline
Agnieszka Kurant
Candice Lin
Jumana Manna
Henrik Olesen
Trevor Paglen
Dawn Parsonage
Yuri Pattison
Huang Po-Chih
Pope.L
Jon Rafman
Aura Rosenberg
Nastja Säde Rönkkö
Qiu Shihua
Lily van der Stokker
Tavares Strachan
Pilvi Takala
Emma Talbot
Tourmaline
Lee Wan

Thanks also go to:
Cory Arcangel
Lawrence B. Benenson
Sasha Bergstrom-Katz
Malthe Kouassi Bjerregaard and colleagues at Medicinsk Museion
Anne Boyer
Norman Brosterman
Natascha Burger
Kornelia Cepok
Tony Conrad Estate
Bo Dalsgaard
Jennifer DiGioia
Henry Van Dusen
Heike Eipeldauer
Samuel W. Franklin
Félix Gonzélez Torres Foundation
Douglas Gordon
Ralf Haensel
The family of Tetsuya Ishida
Isolated Labs
Sarah Jaffe
Christian Joas
Leslie Johnson
Raina Lampkins-Fielder
Steen Nepper Larsen
Jack Lawler
Todd Lubart
Phil Mayer and everyone else at Ryan Gander Studio
Marilyn McCully
Mismatch Media
Thomas Meldgaard
Helly Nahmad
Daniel Neves and everyone else at Trevor Paglen Studio
Amy F. Ogata
Tony Oursler
Romy Peires
Marc Porter
Olga Ravn
David Rych
Miguel Sicart
Nick Simunovic
Branka Stipančić
Robert James Sunderland
Lene Tanggaard
Dame Marina Warner
Erin C. Westgate
Robert Wiesenberger
James Wilson Williams

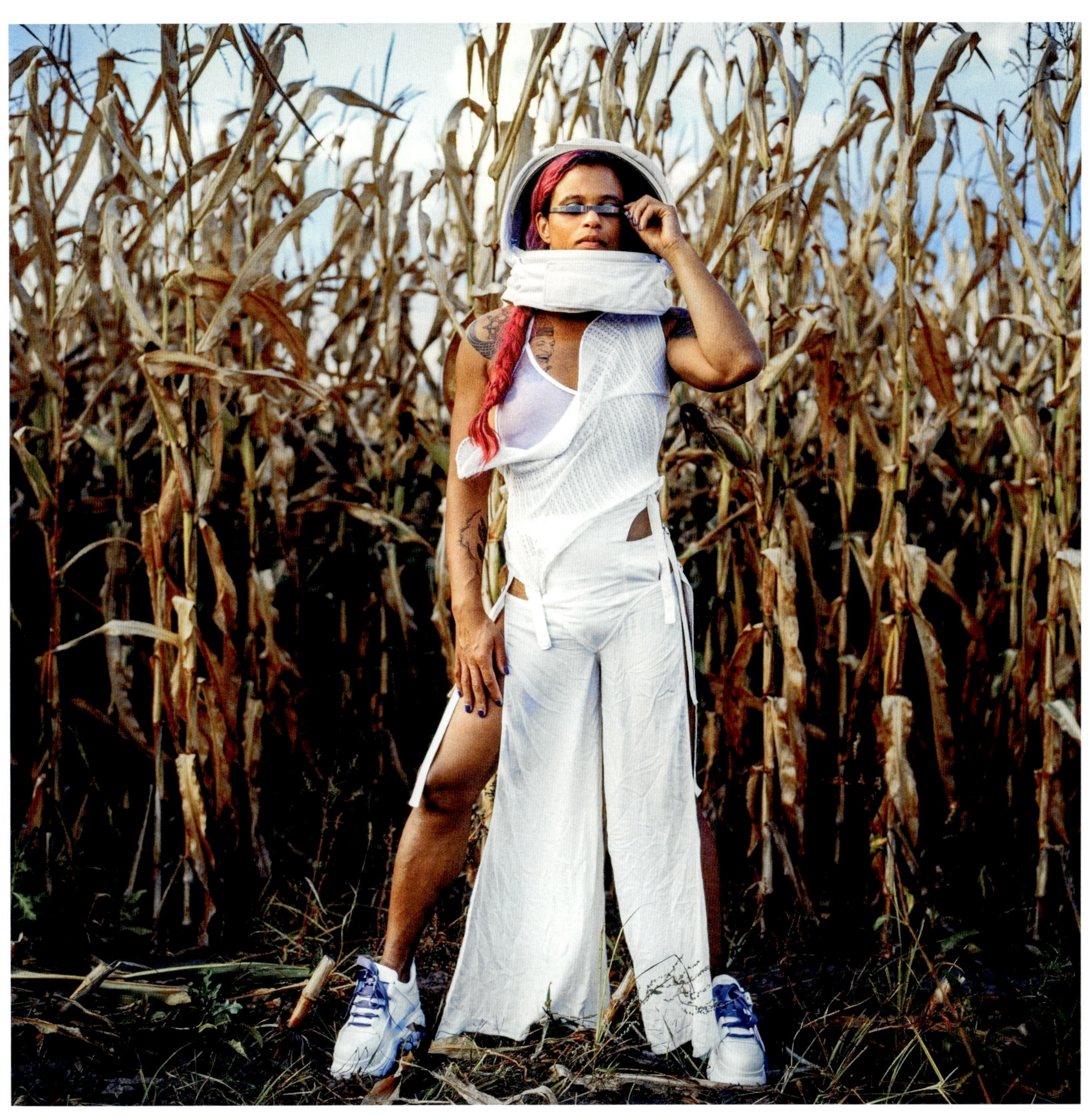

Tourmaline
Coral Hairstreak, 2020

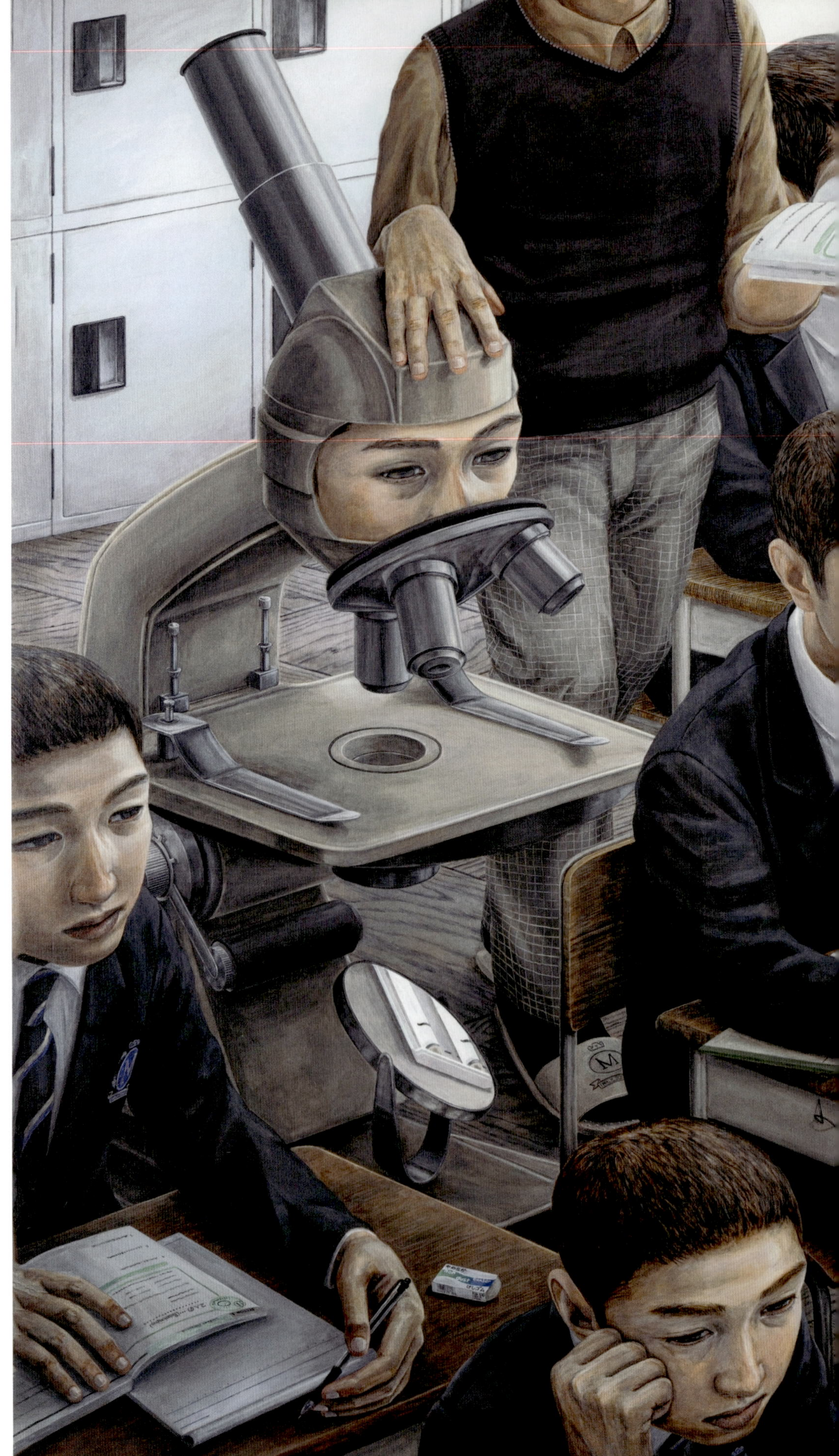

Tetsuya Ishida
Mebae (Awakening), 1998

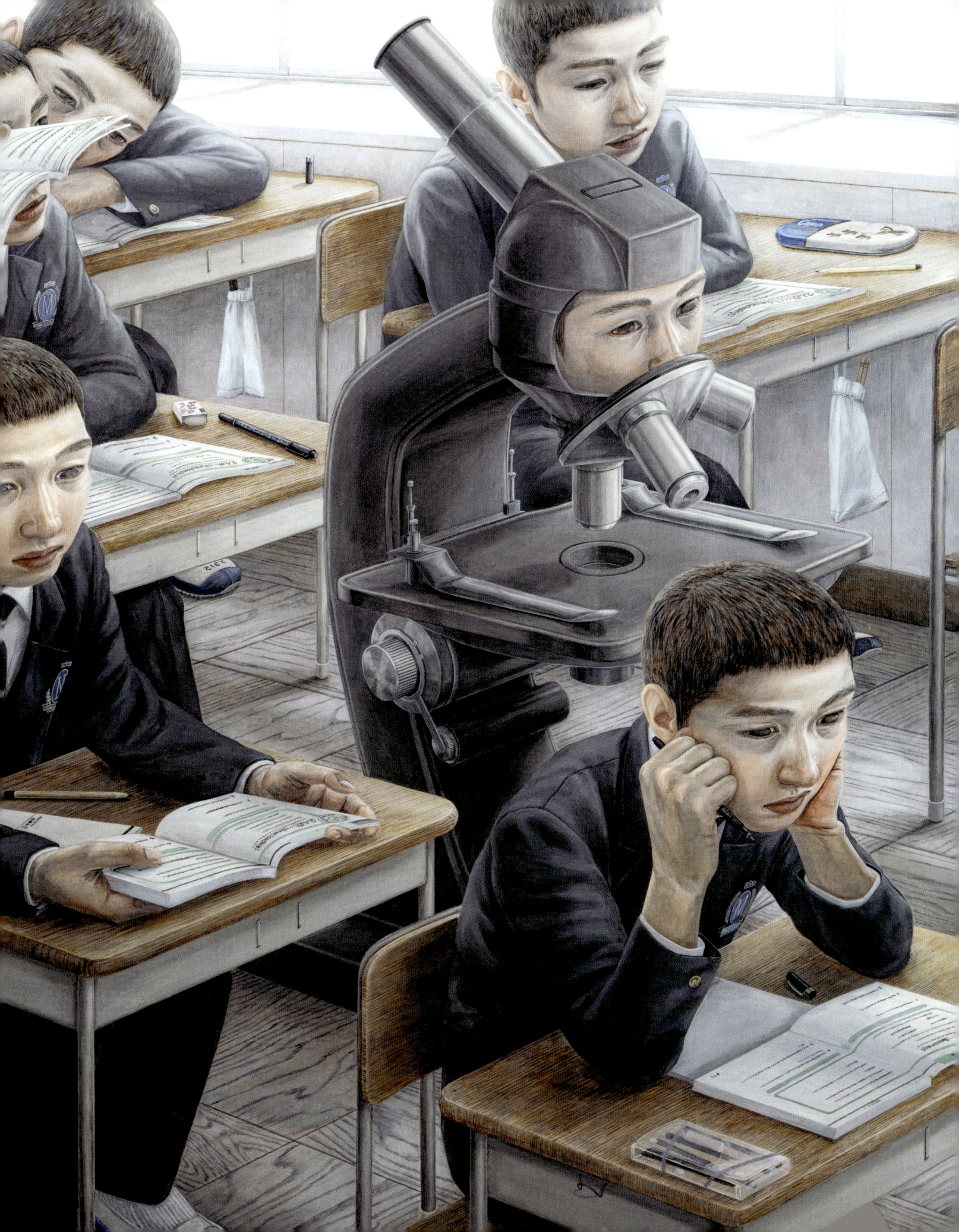

Mathias Ussing Seeberg
The Irreplaceable Human: A Brief Guide to the Exhibition

The Irreplaceable Human is about the time we live in. Examining creativity in the light of the rapid incursion of artificial intelligence into all aspects of our lives, the exhibition asks: are we on the right track? With the climate crisis and war looming large in our minds, the answer, in many ways, is clearly no. Moreover, the implicit question may be whether we have organized our society in the best way to find answers and solutions to the problems that threaten our existence. If creativity has helped ensure our survival and continuing development (for better or worse) does creativity have adequate conditions to thrive in today's world?

The Louisiana's exhibition has two parts. The first part, introducing three concepts central to the potential exercise of creativity, presents an image of where we are. The second part looks at how to cultivate what is uniquely human.

At the heart of the exhibition is art of the last two decades, with samplings of cultural history, science and literature. A recurring motif is people under pressure. People who are reduced to their functionality in a system or squeezed into a mould. The Japanese artist Tetsuya Ishida's painting *Mebae* (Awakening, 1998, pp. 8-9) shows identical schoolboys seated in straight rows, a few boys even morphing into classroom microscopes. The instrumentalization of children, depicted so literally in this painting, is a central point of criticism for the artist. In general, Ishida's images of humans patently lay bare a formulation of the individual as *replaceable*, reduced to a flesh machine to be swapped for another when it breaks down. This is a critique of capitalism. Ishida's works appear in three of the exhibition's five chapters.

Viewers may reasonably contend that the works by Ishida and other artists in the first part of the exhibition are too bombastic and heavy-handed. Whether the art accurately reflects the state of the world or simply asks questions like, "Is this really where we want to go?" is up to you. Similar to what the German curator Yvette Mutumba argued at a conference at the Louisiana in February 2023, the aim of this exhibition is not to end a conversation but to start one.

PART 1: CONDITIONS OF CREATIVITY: CHILDHOOD / WORK / ARTIFICIAL INTELLIGENCE

The first chapter of the exhibition looks at childhood. Children, more than anybody, are associated with the common narrative of creativity. In a European context, the French philosopher Jean-Jacques Rousseau's 1762 *Emile, or On Education* introduced the conception that children are very different beings to adults, and need freedom, not coercion, in their formative years. This notion influenced progressive pedagogy in the following centuries up to the present day. Many of the qualities that are considered creative virtues, including in the neoliberal business world, are associated with children and freedom: imagination, play, spontaneity, etc. In art, children are mostly represented as either possessing or being entirely devoid of these virtues (as with Ishida). It is at this tension that the first part of the exhibition begins, somewhere between dream and reality – again, which is which is up to the viewer. *Kaputtes Kind* (Broken Child, 1984, p. 11), a weird, pre-digital work by the German artist Martin Kippenberger, anticipates the online world's nonstop opinionating, familiar from social media likes. A picture of a child sticking out its tongue, swiped from the Austrian-Irish artist Gottfried Helnwein, has been augmented with an array of stickers with statements about loving everything from dyslexia to Nicaragua to peace and money. The work is intriguing as a

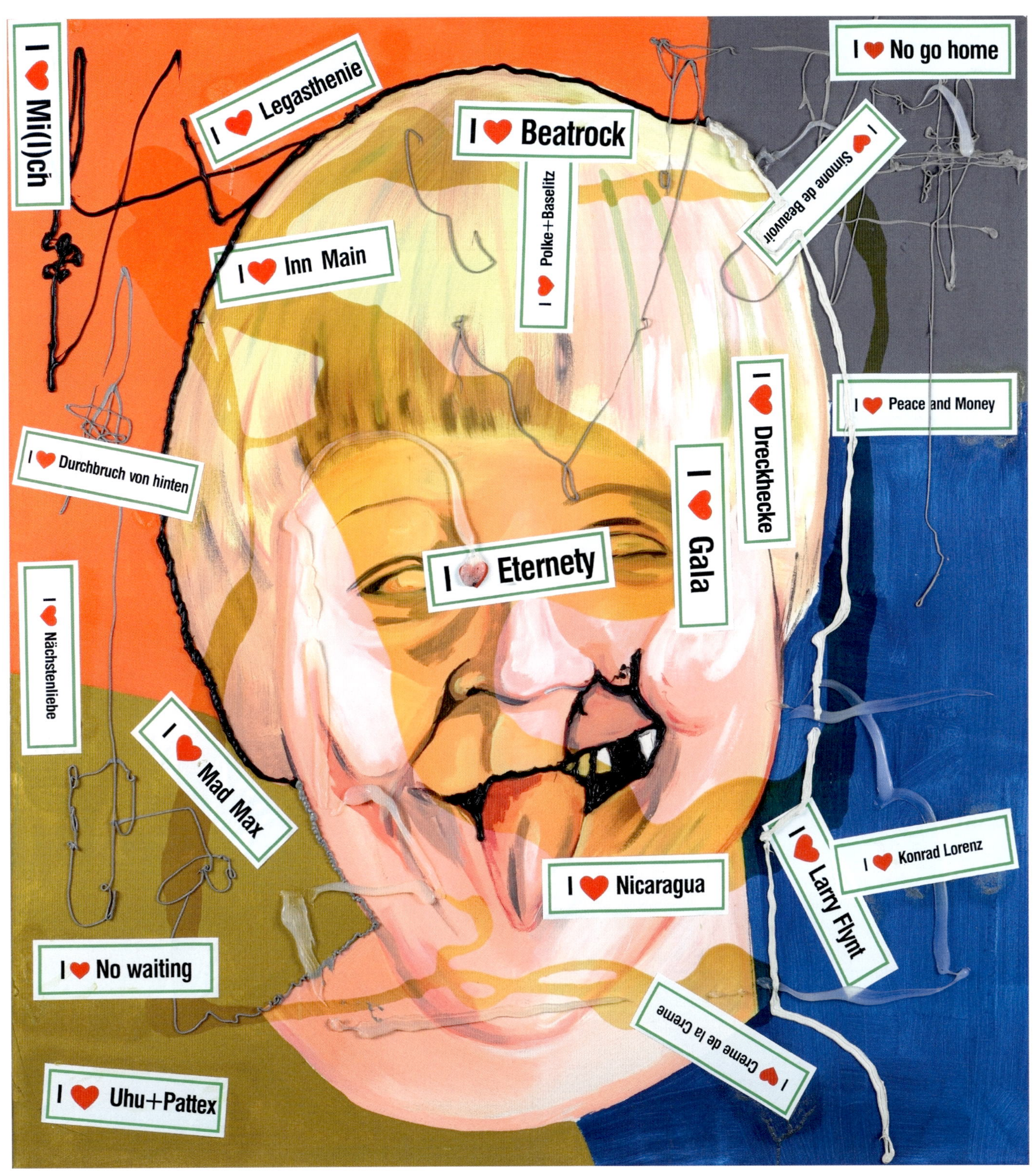

Martin Kippenberger
Kaputtes Kind (Broken Child), 1985

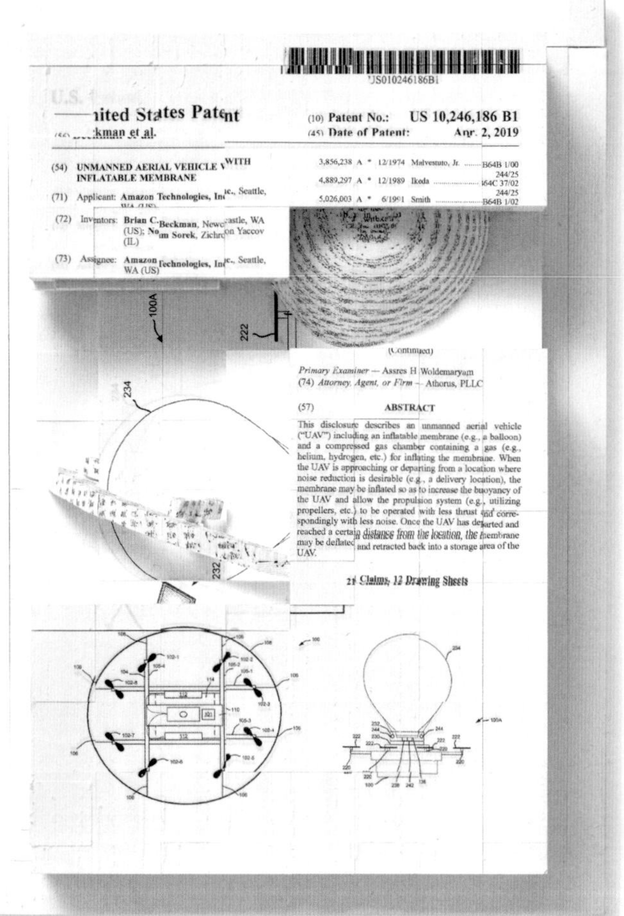

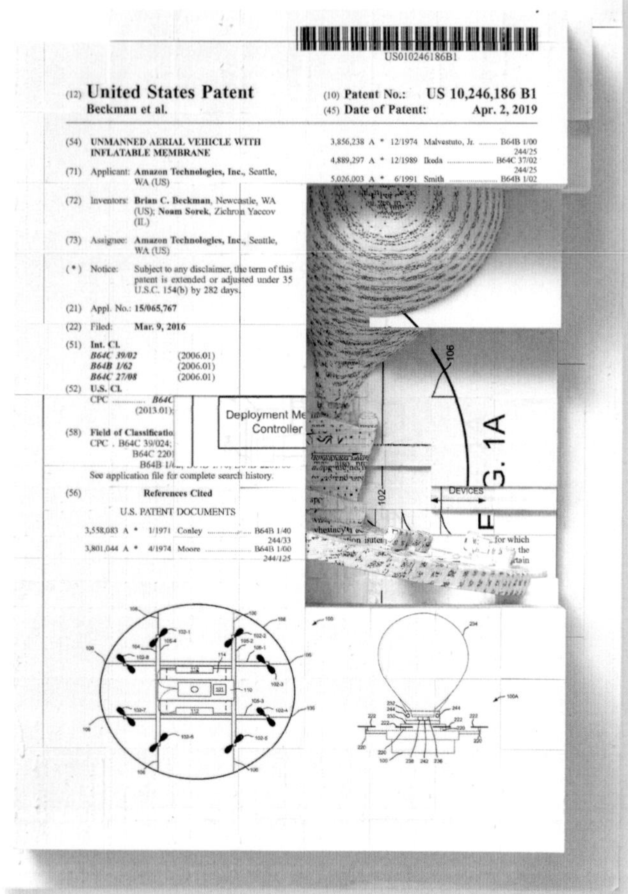

Simon Denny
Document Relief 27, 2020

Simon Denny
Document Relief 28, 2021

precursor to online culture – the world of children today – and because the concept of a broken child is important here as a useful starting point for asking "What should a real child be like?" When is a child whole and not broken? Childhood is a biological stage; as a concept it needs to be articulated and implemented. A child can be anything. Even a miner, as in the French artist Bertille Bak's poetic *Mineur Mineur* (2022, pp. 26-27), punning on the dual meaning in French of "minor" and "miner". The opposition between the two terms emerges from our narrative of the child, not from any particular essence. It is simply a matter, then, of which narrative we want to believe.

The most obvious answer to the question "What is a broken child?" is a grownup. We are familiar with the expression that someone has grown up too fast, typically because they were robbed of their innocence early in life. Adulthood can arrive at different times, just as childhood, in principle, can be extended. The exhibition's second chapter includes a lot of broken children. Looking at existence as a spectrum defined by human activity, freedom and play are found at one end and the rigid, repetitive and machine-like at the other. Arriving at the Louisiana, visitors are greeted by a flag made by the British artist Jeremy Deller, hanging above the main entrance. The flag is manufactured by the same company in London that makes flags for the British labour movement. But the message is different. In awkward English, the flag's white-on-dark lettering reads, "Hello, today you have day off". The words are from a text message informing workers on zero-hour contracts that they will not be working that day. Such contracts are uniquely beneficial to the employer, who can decide from one day to the next whether an employee will be working or not. Inside the museum, we see Deller's *Motorola WT4000 Wearable Terminal* (2013, p. 43), a computer worn by workers in low-paying warehouse jobs, for instance at Amazon, enabling the employer to monitor their productivity and reduce errors. This short step from human to machine reveals the ultimate dream of a capital-driven society: replacing people with much more reliable machines that do not get sick, pregnant or stressed. This chapter also features a project by New Zealander artist Simon Denny examining Amazon patent applications aiming to reduce worker freedom and increase efficiency, even replace workers.

While the notion of machines replacing humans has existed as long as industrialisation itself, it used to be associated chiefly with repetitive work. That is no longer the case. In recent years, a number of tools have appeared (with more coming out every week) that many have proclaimed will replace writers, artists, graphic designers, musicians and architects – in fact, all the professions that are generally considered creative. ChatGPT, Midjourney and Dall-E are some of these AI services that, in record time, can generate a product resembling art, literature or jokes. Naturally, similar tools exist for other occupations, to replace lawyers, accountants and computer programmers. Practically no one can feel secure about the irreplaceability of their profession. All these formats are based on large data sets that define the outer limits of an artificial intelligence, what it "knows". The more data a computer can access, the more possible combinations of content it can create. American Trevor Paglen's monumental installation *From 'Apple' to 'Abomination'* (2023, pp. 62-63) unpacks such a data set to reveal its limitations and dangers. At the end of the day, it is a question of interpretation. Who decides what an image means or what a computer knows? What does a criminal look like? Is an apple always an apple? The exhibition's third chapter looks beyond the fascination with artificial intelligence, though there is much to be fascinated with, to highlight artworks and stories exploring the conditions of artificial intelligence, data sets and the myth that everything is "made" by computers.

The work of the Polish artist Agnieszka Kurant points out how many people it takes to make artificial intelligence. Her 2017 series *Artificial Artificial Intelligence* (A.A.I.) (pp. 64-65) is based on a quote by Amazon founder Jeff Bezos referring to tasks that were too complex for algorithms and had to be done by humans, specifically Amazon's Mechanical Turk department. Kurant produces her work through a different kind of outsourcing. Enlisting termites to build mounds of coloured sand, glitter and crystals, the artist interrogates copyright, collective intelligence and the exploitation of cheap labour. *Aggregated Ghost* (2020, p. 14) is an image based on portraits of thousands of otherwise invisible online workers whose anonymous labour maintains the illusion of artificial intelligence as taking place in the "cloud", without blood, sweat and tears.

The three chapters in the exhibition's first part all look at the society in which we live. We seem to be in a paradoxical place. On the one hand, there is the ubiquitous streamlining of education and work, which is predicated on a spreadsheet manoeuvre. There is no ideology or vision behind it. It simply involves an insistence that anything can be done faster, with fewer people, and more efficiently. Then, it all magically adds up. On the other hand, there is the tech industry's fantasy of making a machine that is like a playful (unbroken) child: free, spontaneous, imaginative – creative. Ultimately, even if it is not consciously processed or articulated, this dream involves definitively switching the roles between human and machine, and having the computer do the dreaming.

If the first part of the exhibition presents a pointed image, and a critique, of where we are, the second part suggests what we are missing or, at least, underemphasising. It involves a wish to assign value to things that the most money- and success-driven parts of our society maybe consider weak or superfluous or insignificant or bad for business or whose value may just be hard to measure. The second part of the exhibition has two chapters: Time and Cross-Pollination.

Time was already a central motif in the first part of the exhibition. The chapter on work features a broken clock in Ryan Gander's *School of Languages* (2023, p. 40-41), an installation that also includes a gorilla under a desk trying to count. Lee Wan's *Proper Time* (2017, p. 52) consists of clocks moving at different speeds, depending on your occupation. The chapter on time, however, focuses less on work time and more on leisure time and how we spend it. The chapter opens with three prints from *Phone Etchings* (2015, pp. 72-73), a series by the German artist Andrea Büttner that tracks fingers moving across the screen of a phone. A different kind of clock or marker of time, these are representations of how most people in the Western world today spend their spare moments. Because of smartphones, we have lost a lot of the time that used to be spent doing nothing. To some it may sound exaggerated to say that we have lost something – as if we were incapable of putting down our phones and going for a walk in the woods. But powerful forces are at work – the more time we spend on our phones, the more profits are generated for giant corporations. In the exhibition's first part, Ben Grosser puts a point on this in his supercut of Mark Zuckerberg saying "more", a word the Facebook founder seems to use a lot.

Profound boredom has vanished from most people's lives as smartphones have remade society. There is always something to spend or – perhaps more accurately – consume time on. Today, we almost incessantly inhabit privately owned digital spaces, where we have signed away a great number of basic rights. The owners of these spaces are entitled to harvest our images and information, and sell them to companies that use them to train artificial intelligence or target ads to us. Our attention has been colonised and mined. Even if, at first glance, we may seem to be getting a lot for free, boredom and other states of inactivity are a huge loss. Not least for children, whose initiative and ability to make things up are nurtured and sustained by profound boredom.

So boredom, pastimes and slowness are at the core of this chapter, as is sleep, arguably our last stronghold. Sleep may be the only remaining time when we are not buying or selling something. *Sleep Synthesis* (2023, pp. 82-83), a video installation by the band and artist collective Chicks on Speed, stages sleep not just as a human need but as a lab for creativity. Two sleepers (from Chicks on Speed), dressed in the costumes in which they usually perform, sleep in a bed across whose covers course neurological data gathered during sleep testing in a lab. The work represents the creative process as never-ending and tied as much to inactivity, here in its ultimate form, as to anything else. *The Trainee* (2008, pp. 78-79), by the Finnish artist Pilvi Takala, shows modern human alienation to processes of inactivity. A corporate trainee, the artist sits at a desk in front of a computer, doing nothing, to the great frustration, even stress, of her new coworkers.

The final chapter of the exhibition is centred on cross-pollination, a biological concept describing the interdependence of species. An example is the tree that needs to be pollinated by a bee to bear fruit and propagate. The concept of cross-pollination stands in opposition to another quality, specialisation. Not because there is anything wrong with specialisation per se, but because it is an often-celebrated quality in society; being the best in one's field is an ingredient in the conventional narrative of success. Too little, however, is said about the importance, including to creativity, of reaching a goal by roundabout ways, or slowness in general, and input from unforeseen angles.

In this exhibition, cross-pollination is conceived as a form of empathy, something computers do not possess, the ability to put yourself in someone else's place and understand circumstances different from your own. Cross-pollination includes understanding the limitations of your own system, the insufficiency and fallibility of your worldview. Cross-pollinations are transgressions of various kinds – of disciplines, borders, etc. They involve the belief that ideas emerge between people and species, and that openness to the world lets in more good than bad. Cross-pollination is opposed to cultural monoculture and conceives of sustainability beyond the political system. Quite simply, it is about contaminating your world and letting "impurities" of all kinds populate your vision. It involves a healthy and productive questioning of existing conceptions of facts and truth. *Six Thousand Years* (2018, pp. 104-105), an installation by the Bahamian artist Tavares Strachan based on his sculptural work *Encyclopedia of Invisibility*, seeks to challenge the Western narrative by creating a counterpart to *Encyclopedia Britannica*, which bills itself as the ultimate survey of important people and events in history. For his alternative encyclopedia, Strachan, over eight years, gathered 15,000 entries on people,

Agnieszka Kurant
Aggregated Ghost, 2020

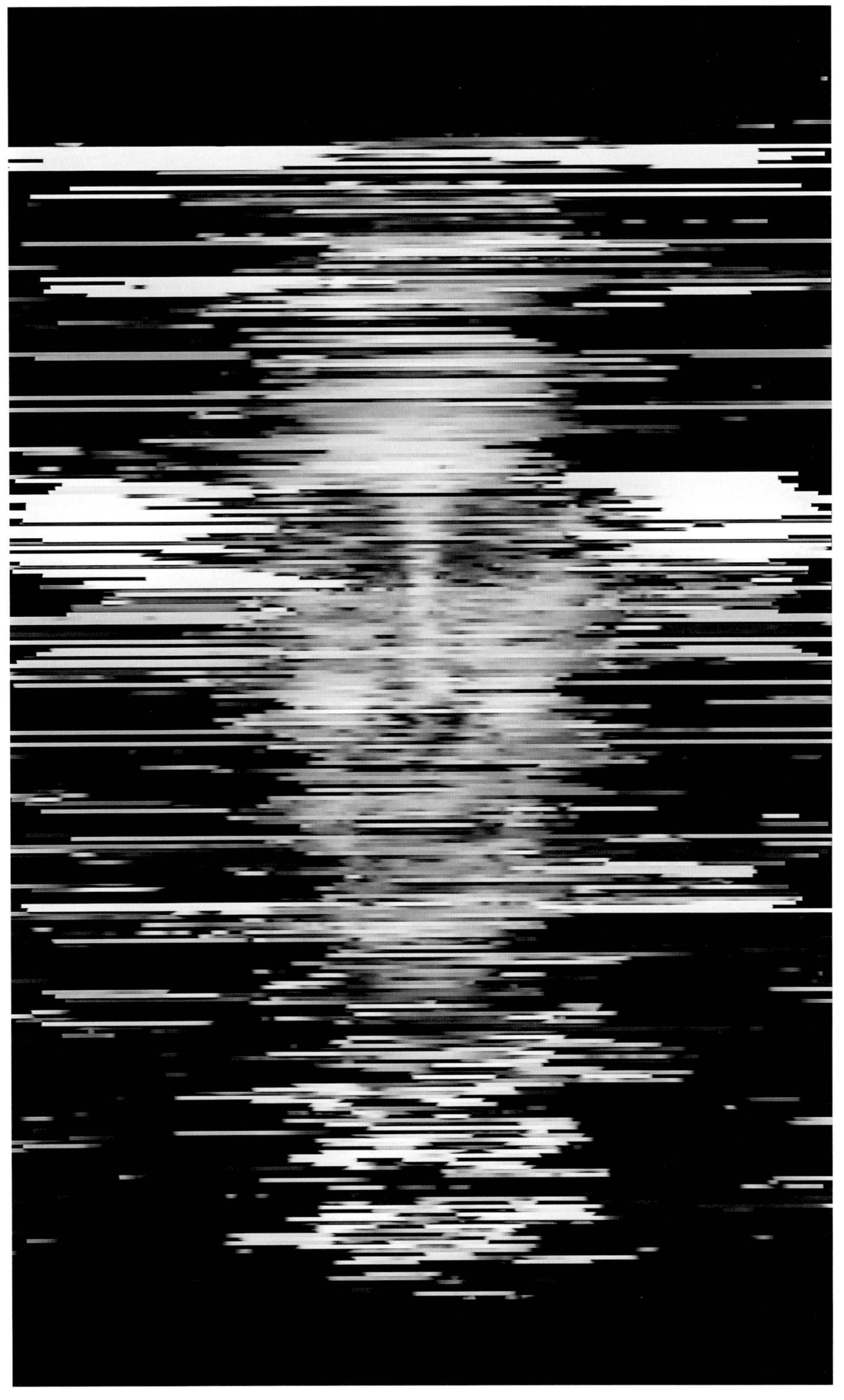

places, objects and concepts that do not appear in the *Britannica* to both challenge its criteria for inclusion and at the same time show how much knowledge has been excluded for one reason or another.

Embracing a wealth of works and narratives that question our perceived entitlement, the chapter points to the importance of – to use a hackneyed term – thinking and acting outside the box, regardless of what box you are in. A few years ago, my research for the Louisiana's exhibition of the Austrian artist Birgit Jürgenssen alerted me to a brief entry she wrote in her journal – in English, amongst the German. It reads, in quotes, "Be really creative refuse your role" (p. 17). This was a strategy in the artist's work, which in so many ways strove to tear down and avoid the roles assigned to women in Austria – and the rest of the world, too, for that matter. Jürgenssen's note also reveals something very important about creativity that is rarely mentioned, since creativity is widely associated with commercial products and economic growth. Her statement points out that challenging the existing roles, including established gender roles, is also a creative act. Another version of non-materialistic creativity is found in the words of the American-Vietnamese writer Ocean Vuong (who appeared at the 2022 Louisiana Literature festival), who often elevates refugees and survival under difficult circumstances into an act of creativity. Thinking beyond the status quo and imagining a different world is being creative. Cross-pollination is essential for conceiving the new.

The Irreplaceable Human aims to create a foundation for discussing the conditions of creativity in our society. Accordingly, the exhibition does not attempt to present examples of creativity but, instead, images or situations, which could be classified either as barren or fertile for the sprouting of creativity. Quite obviously, the exhibition presupposes that creativity is important to our well-being and survival. Whether we are replaceable or not, is not simply a question of what a machine can do, but just as much about what we decide to do as individuals and as a society – what we deem as important and indispensable values. As a whole, the exhibition advocates fertilising the soil beyond what seems immediately profitable, daring to believe that something new and valuable will grow forth. In truth, we have no idea where the new will come from or what it will look like.

Mathias Ussing Seeberg is curator and Head of Research at the Louisiana. In addition to *The Irreplaceable Human*, he has curated exhibitions with artists including William Kentridge, Birgit Jürgenssen, Arthur Jafa, Alex Da Corte and Firelei Báez as well as the group show *Being There*.

Birgit Jürgenssen
Page from notebook, early 1990s

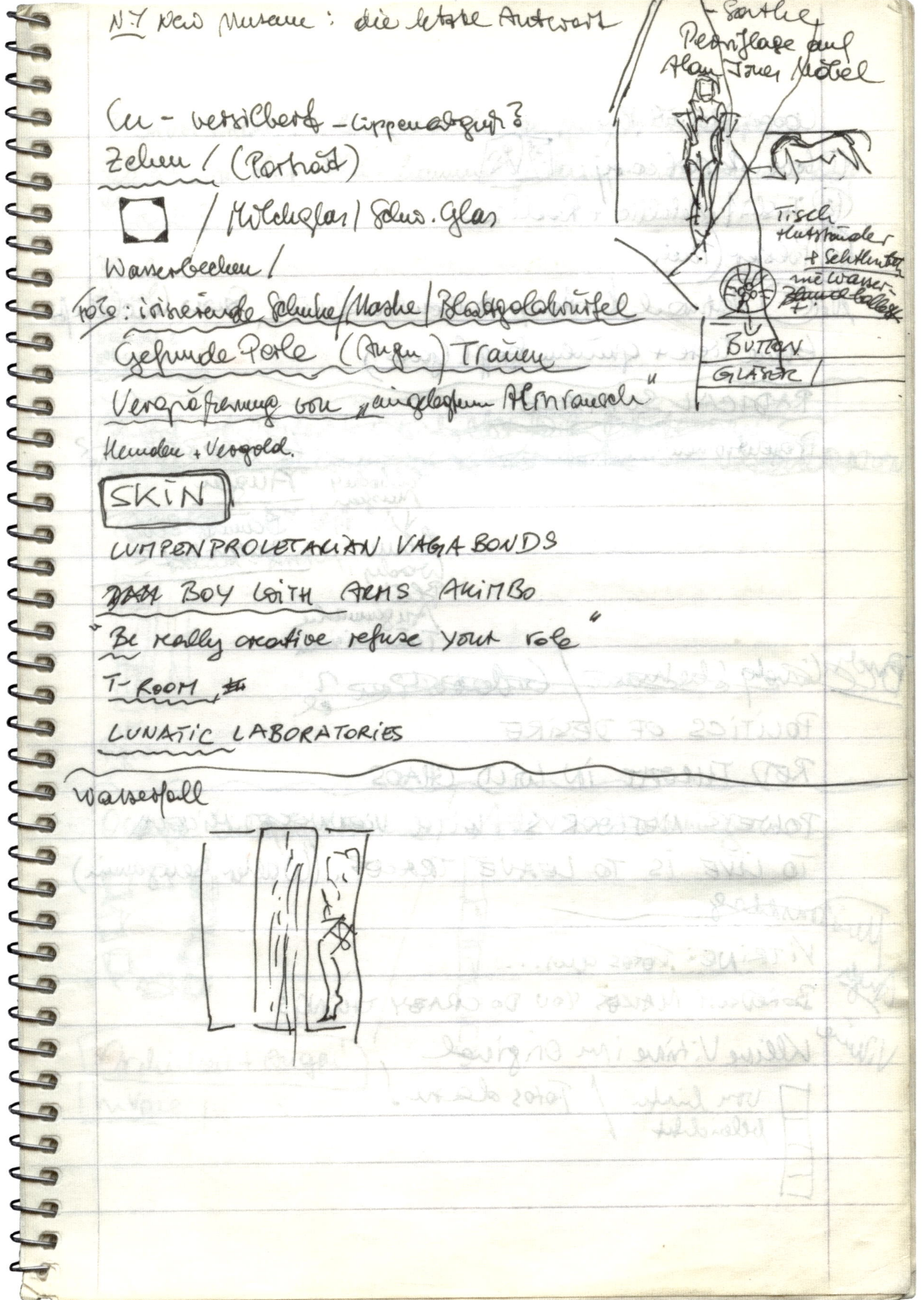

N.Y New Museum : die letzte Antwort

Cu - versichert - Lippenabguß?
Zellen / (Porträt)

▢ / Milchglas / Schw. Glas

Wasserbecken /

Foto : irisierende Schuhe / Maske / Blattgoldwürfel

Gefundene Perle (Augen) Tränen

Vergrößerung von angelegtem Altmrausch

Hemden + Vergold.

SKIN

LUMPENPROLETARIAN VAGABONDS

DAM BOY WITH ARMS AKIMBO

"Be really creative refuse your role"

T-ROOM

LUNATIC LABORATORIES

Wasserfall

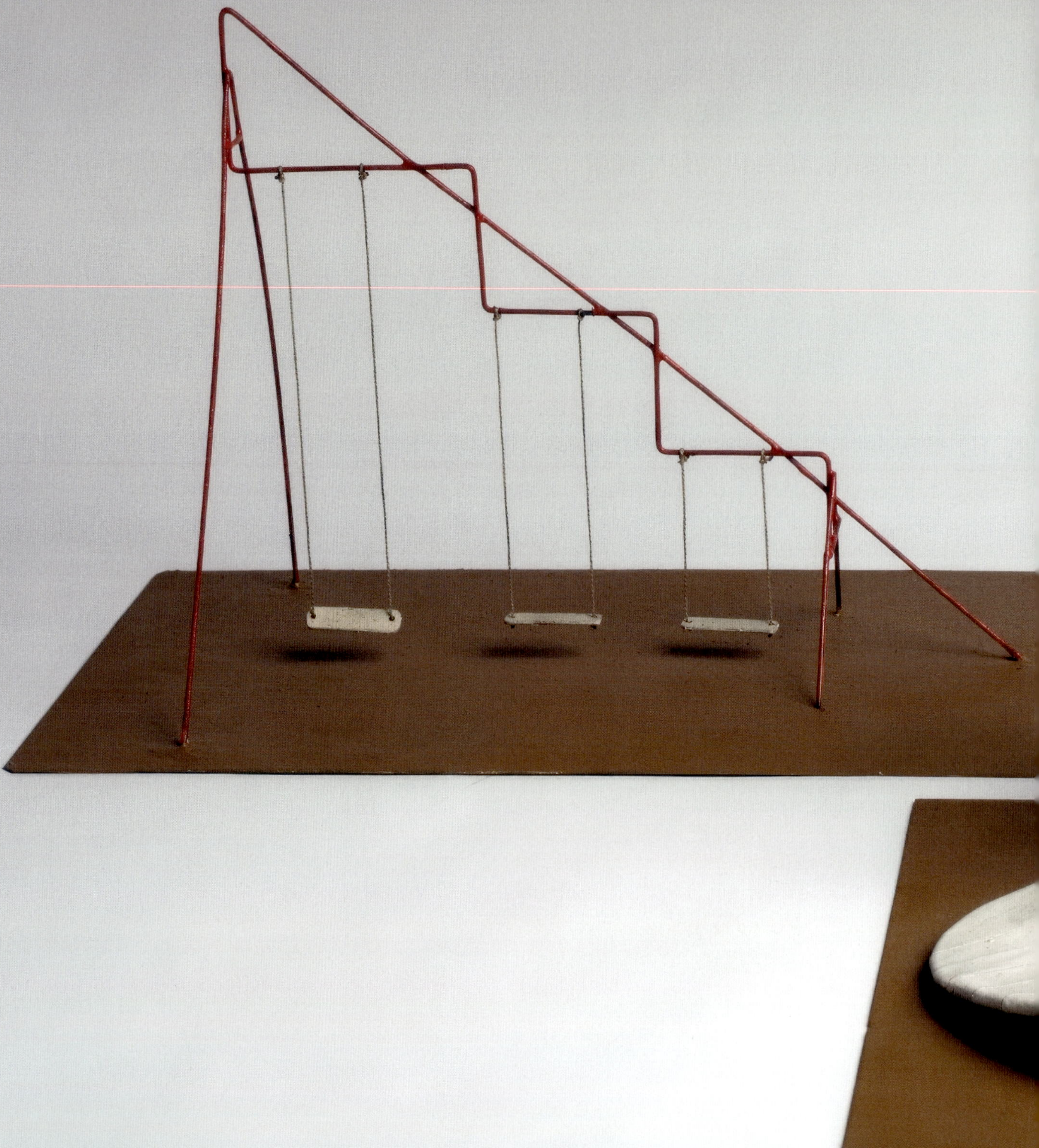

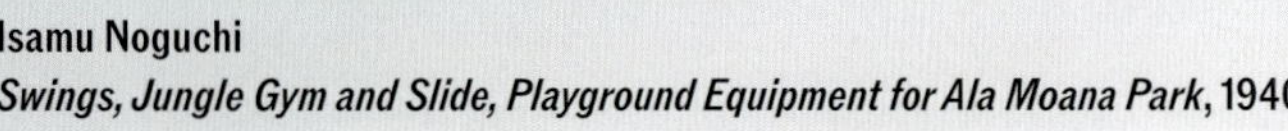

Isamu Noguchi
Swings, Jungle Gym and Slide, Playground Equipment for Ala Moana Park, 1940

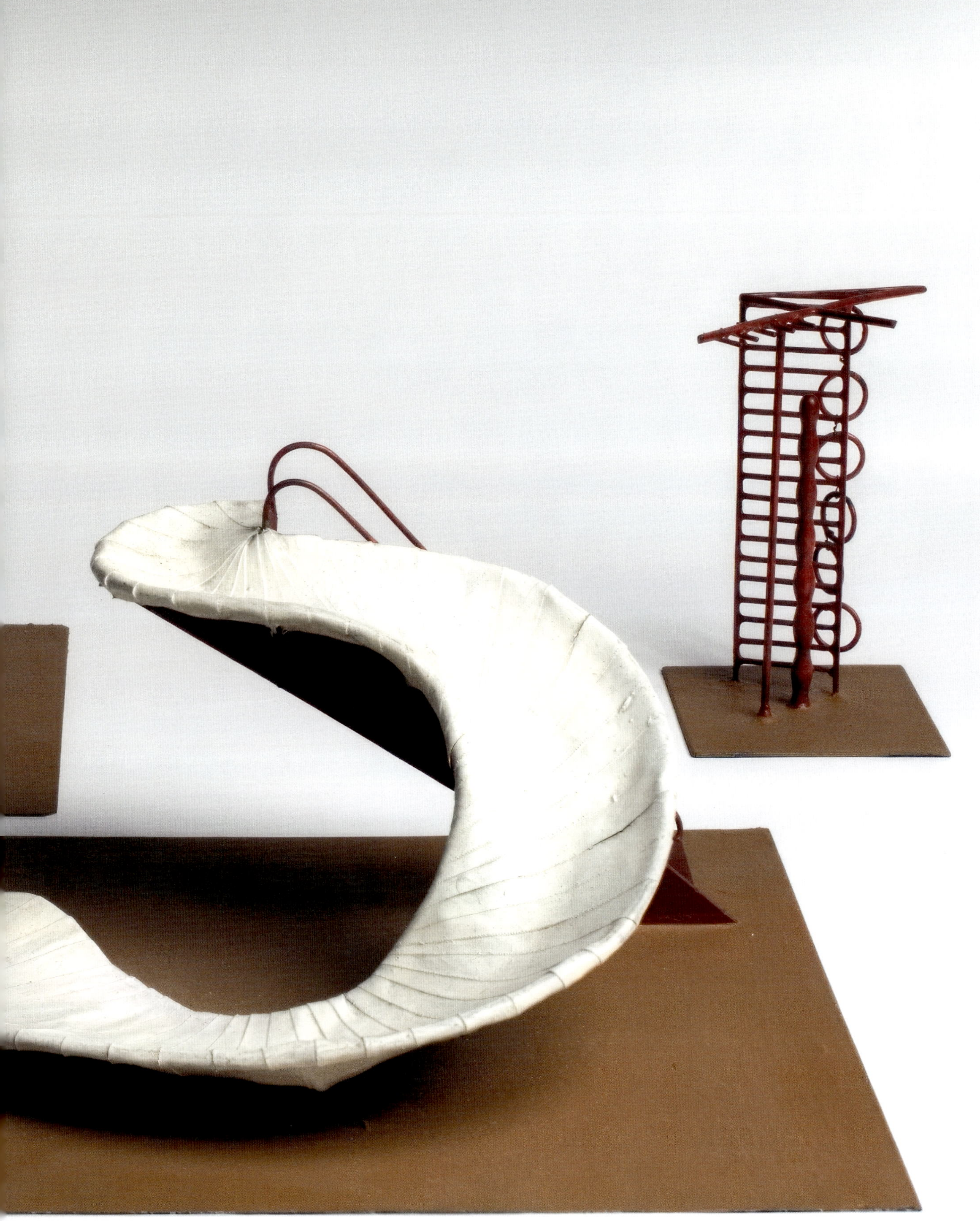

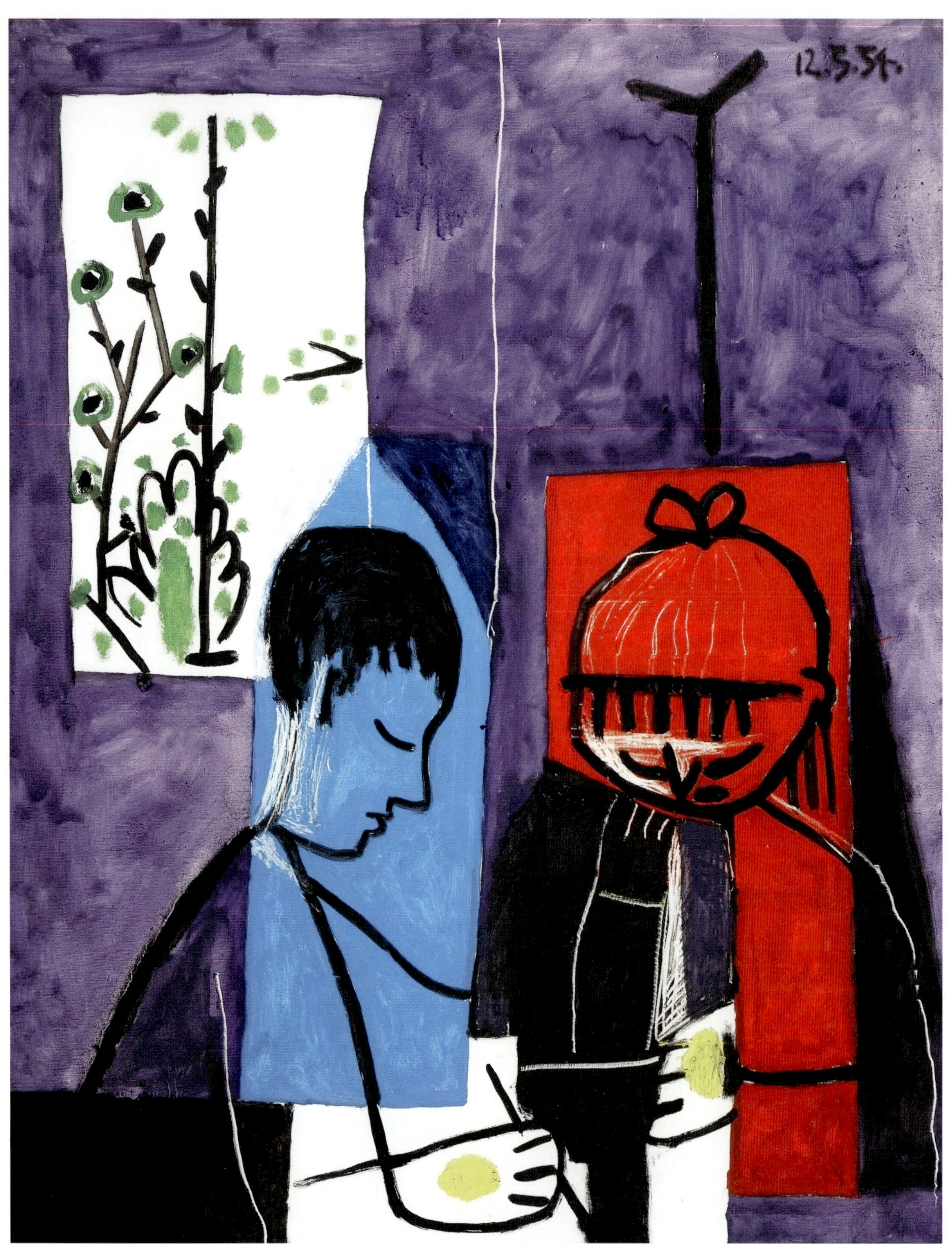

Pablo Picasso
Enfants dessinant (Children Drawing), 1954

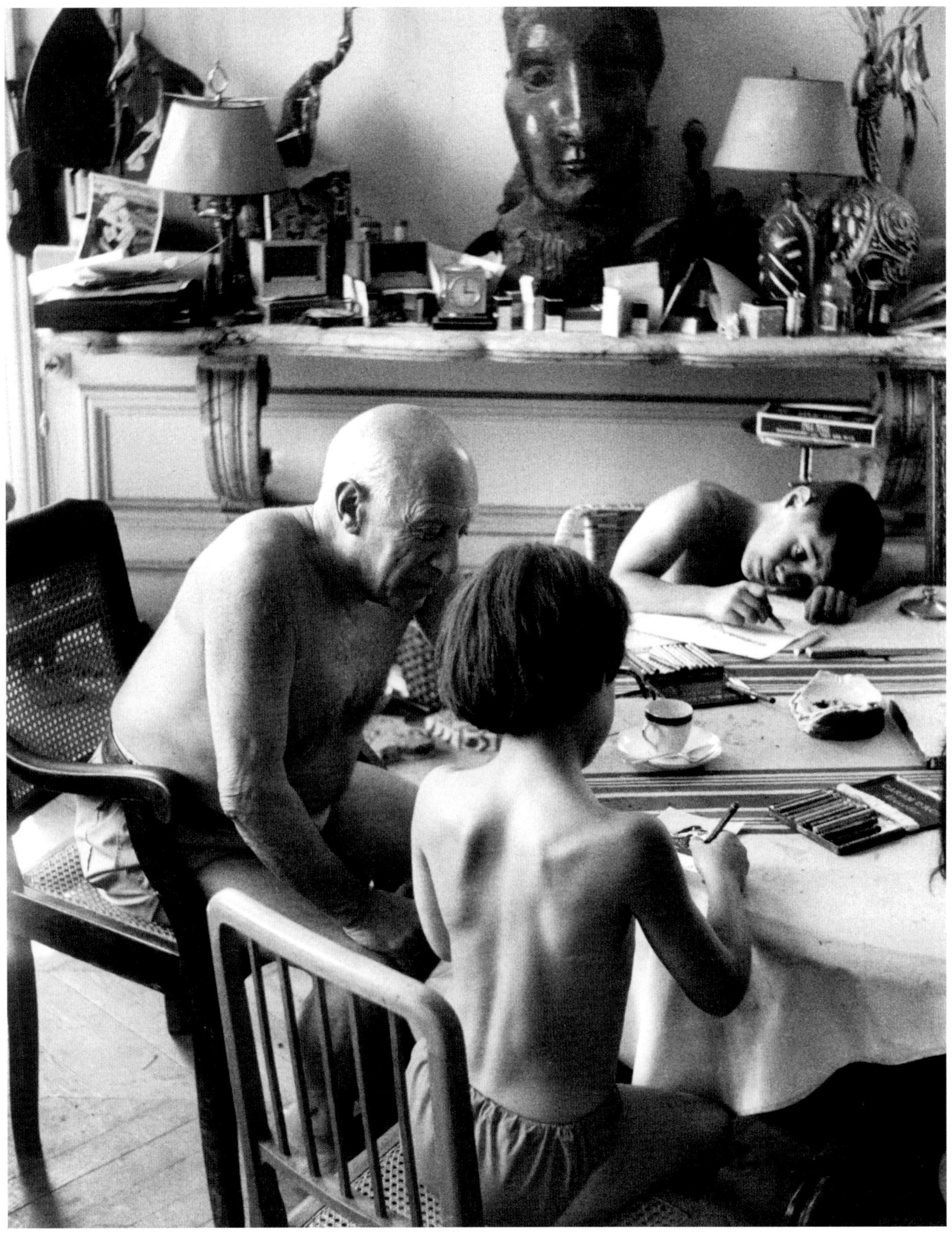

David Douglas Duncan
Picasso, Claude et Paloma au travail
(Picasso, Claude and Paloma at work), 1957

Next spread (from left to right):
Aura Rosenberg
Ann Craven/Chelsea, 1996-1998, *John Miller/Joe (Homer)*, 1996-1998

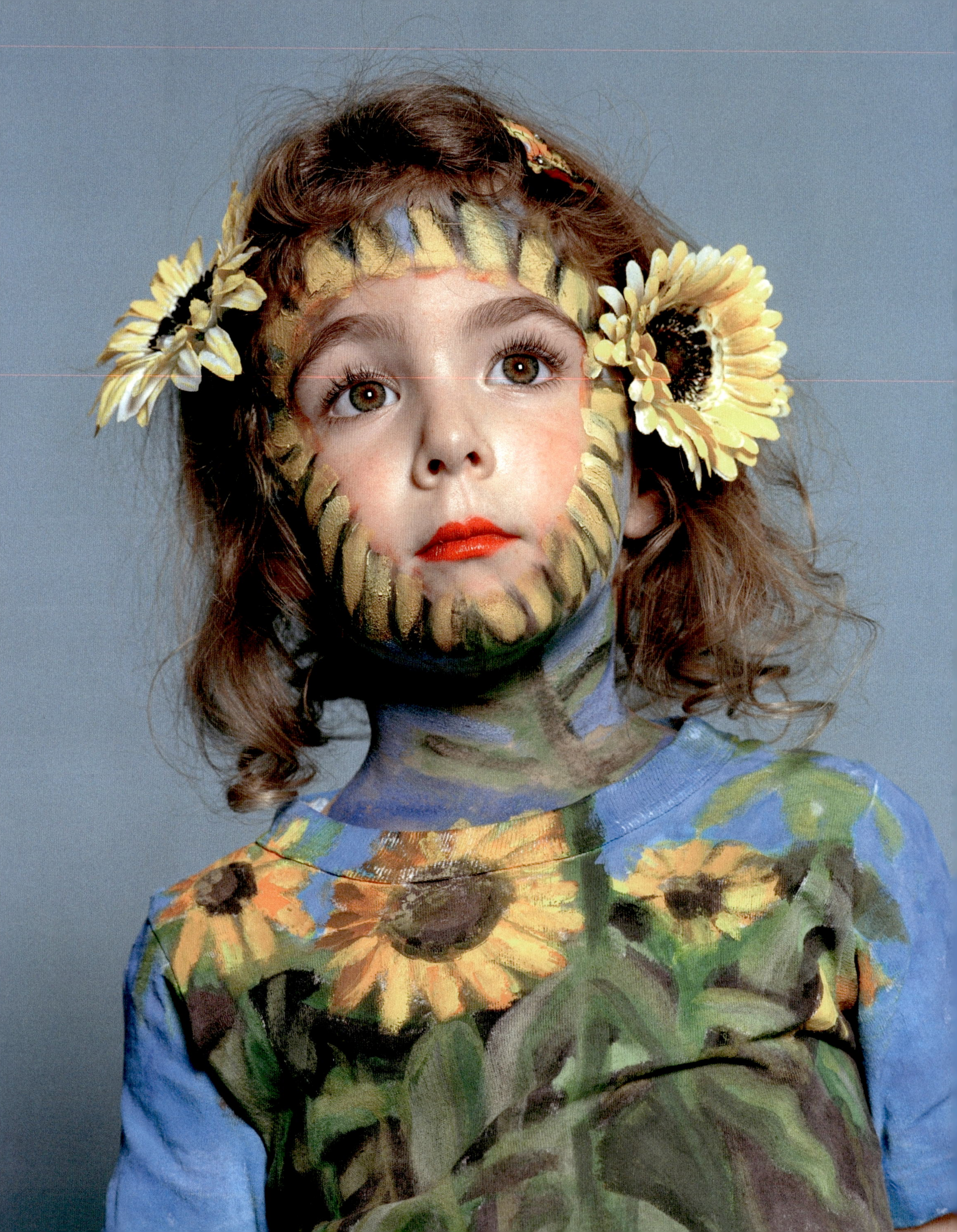

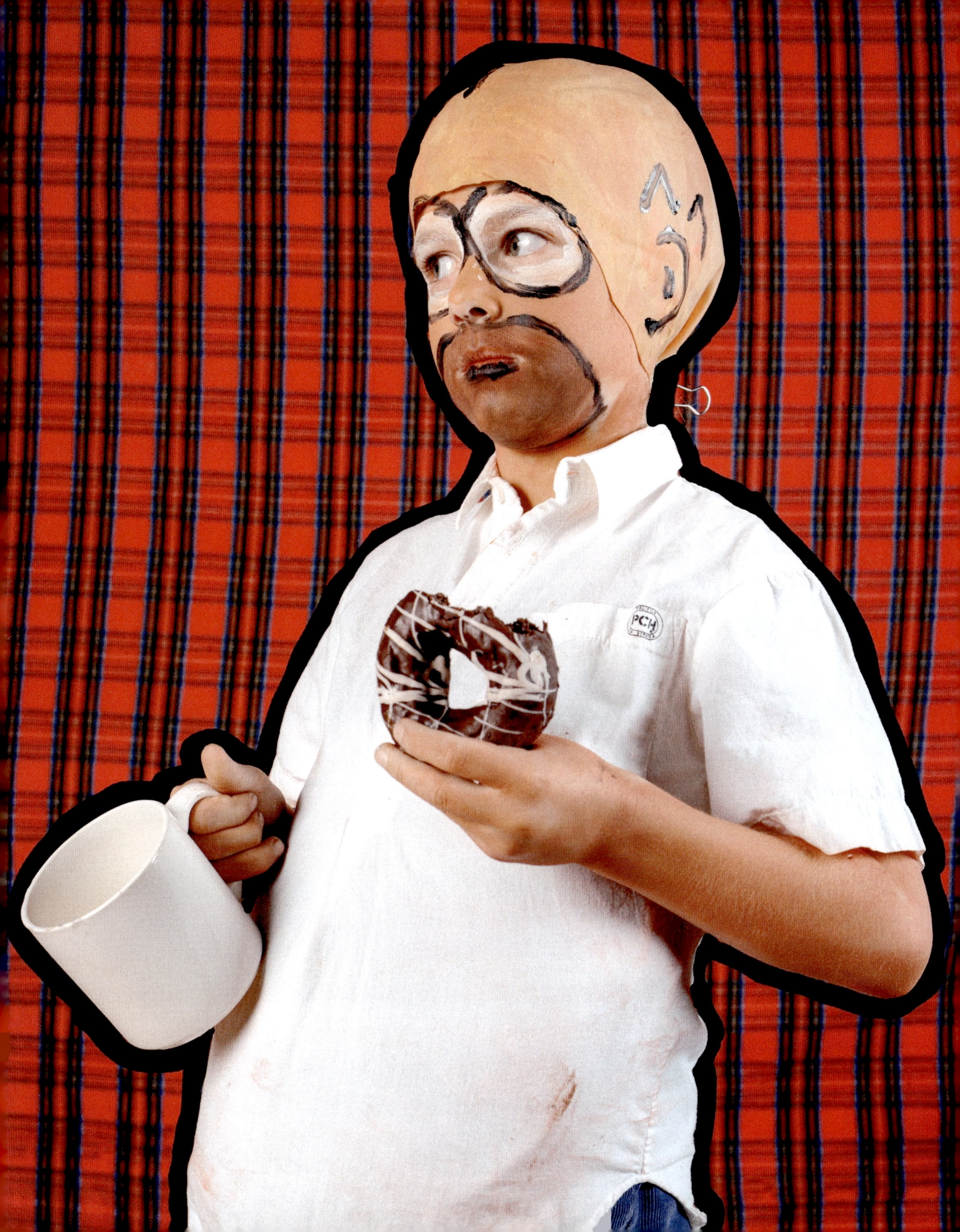

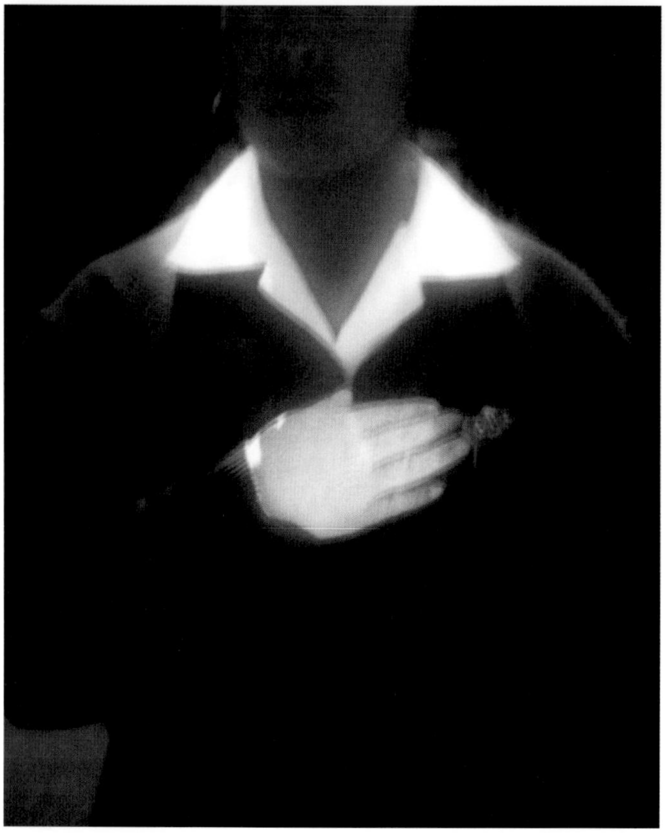

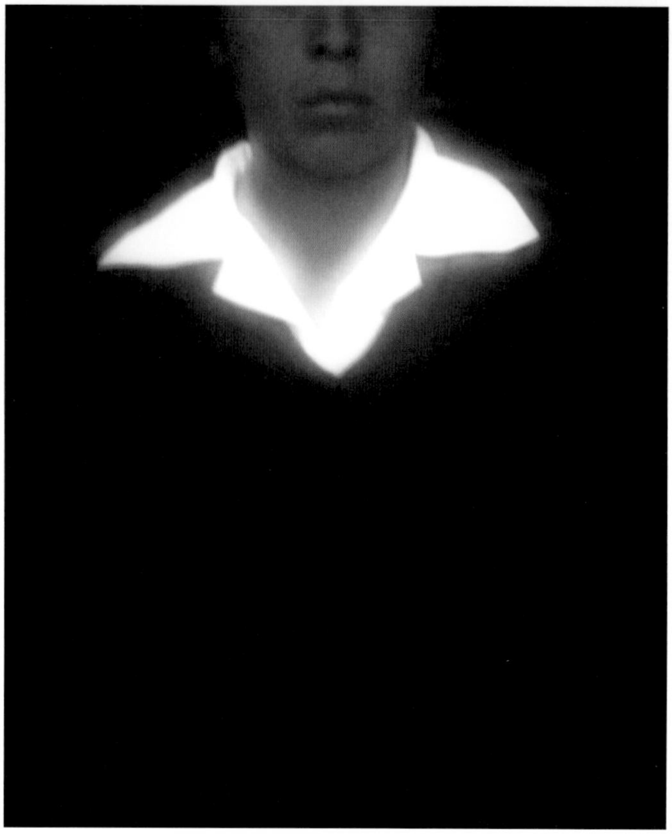

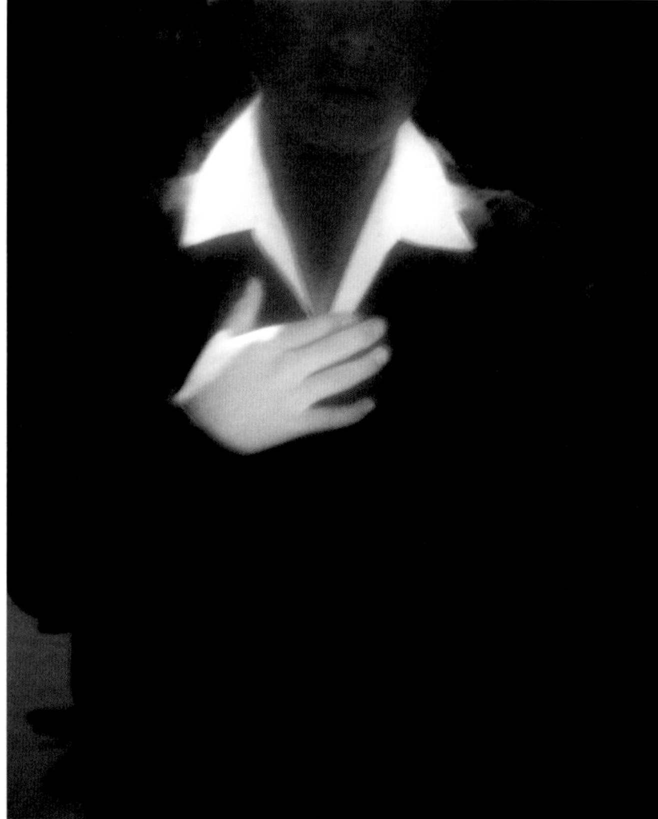

Flavia Gandolfo
Los alumnus (The Students), 1996-1998

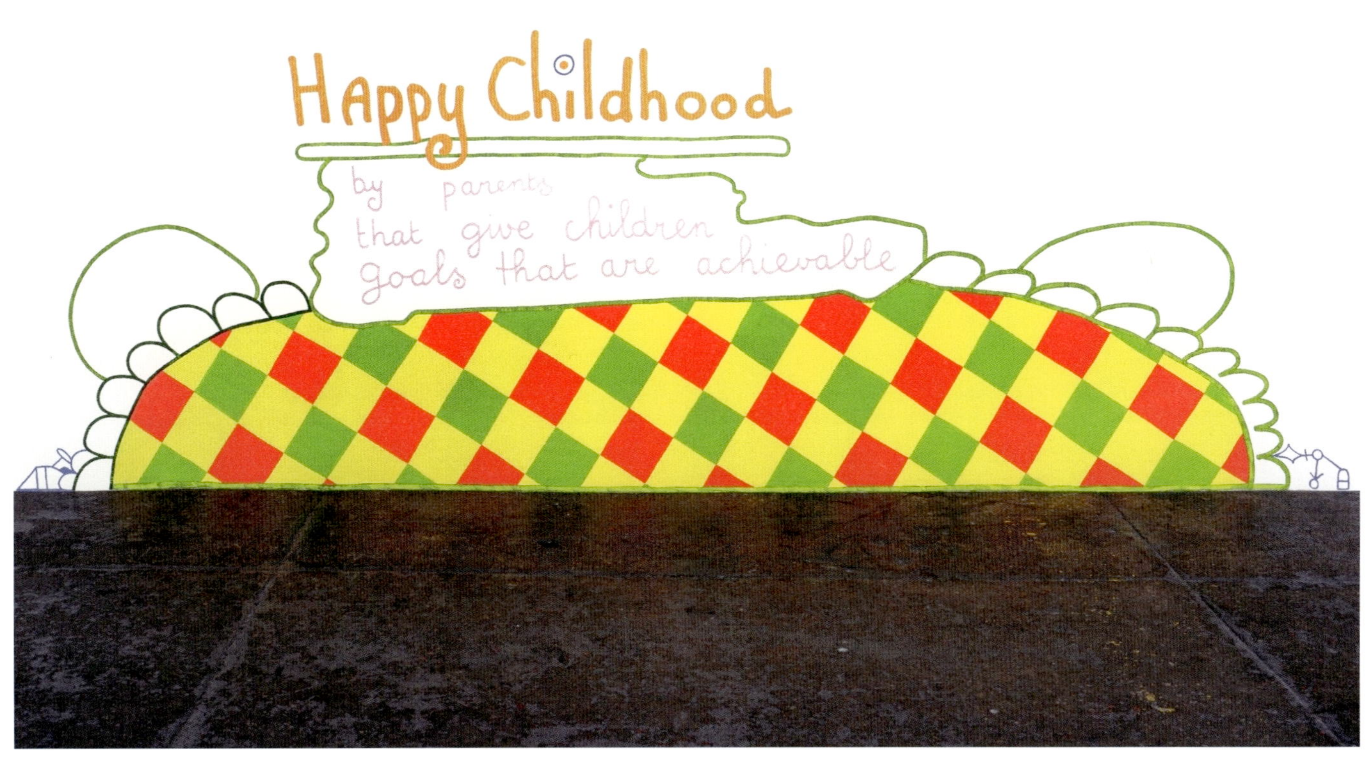

Lily van der Stokker
All kind of good advice (Happy Childhood), 2004-2023

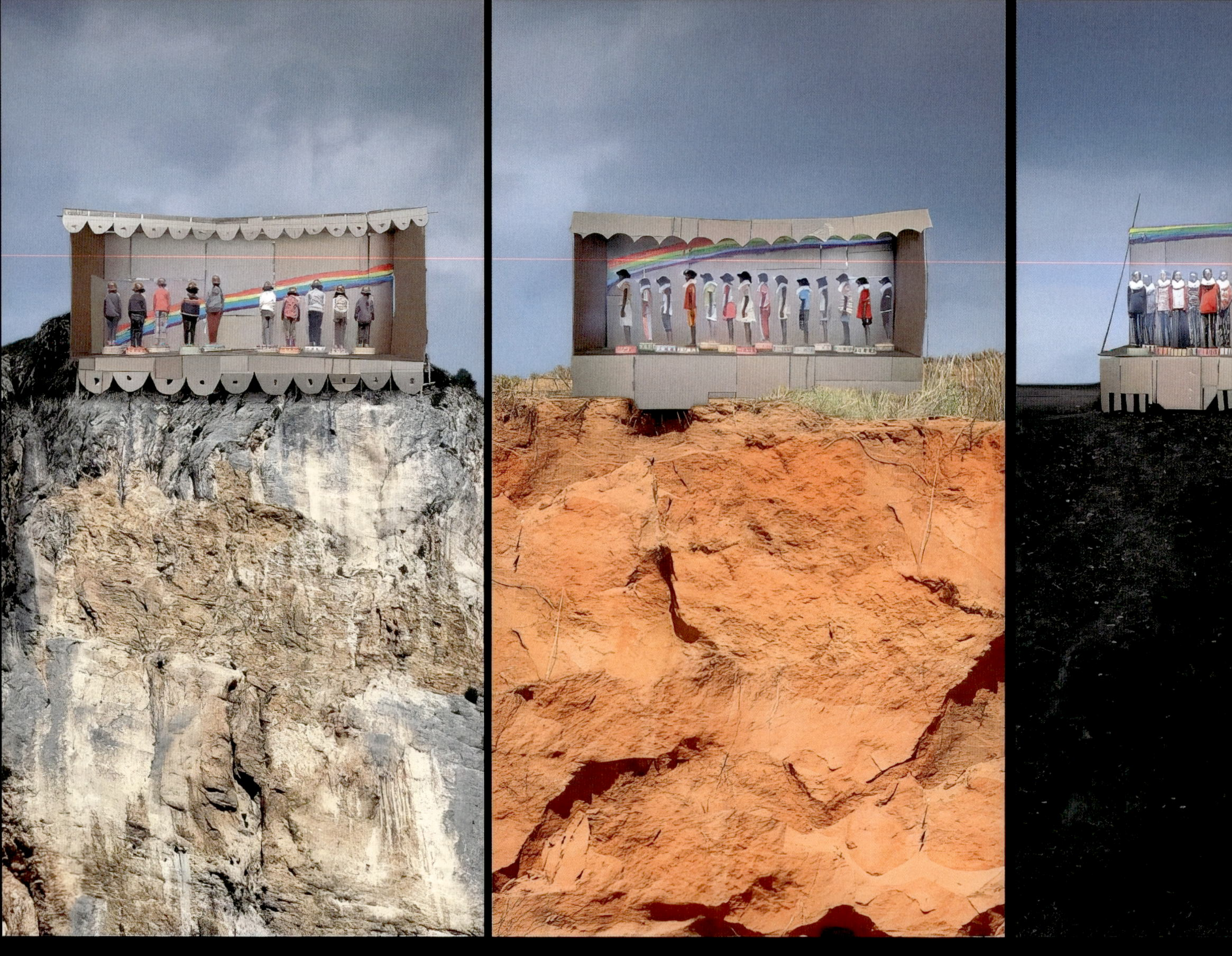

Bertille Bak
Still from *Mineur Mineur,* 2022

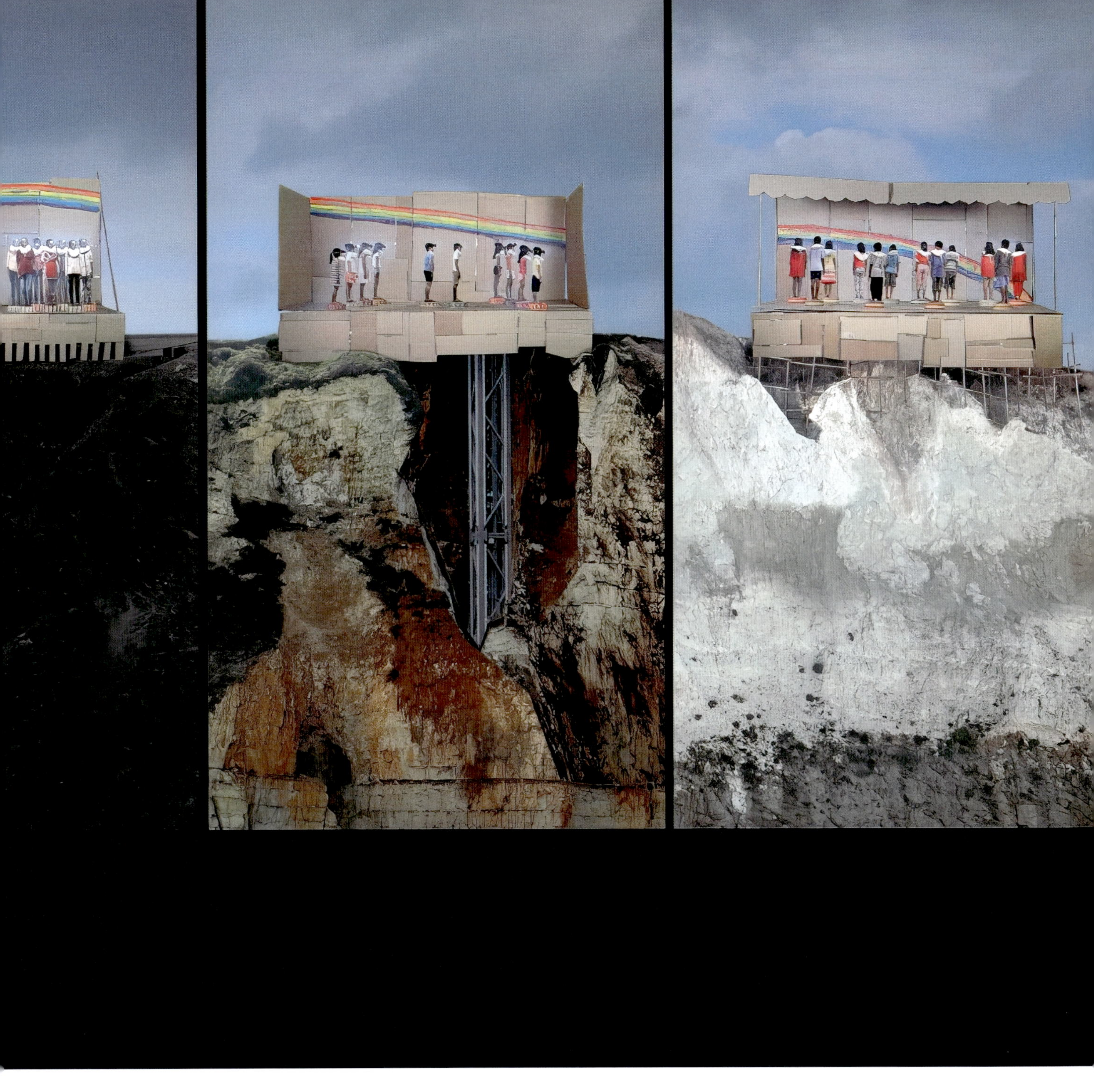

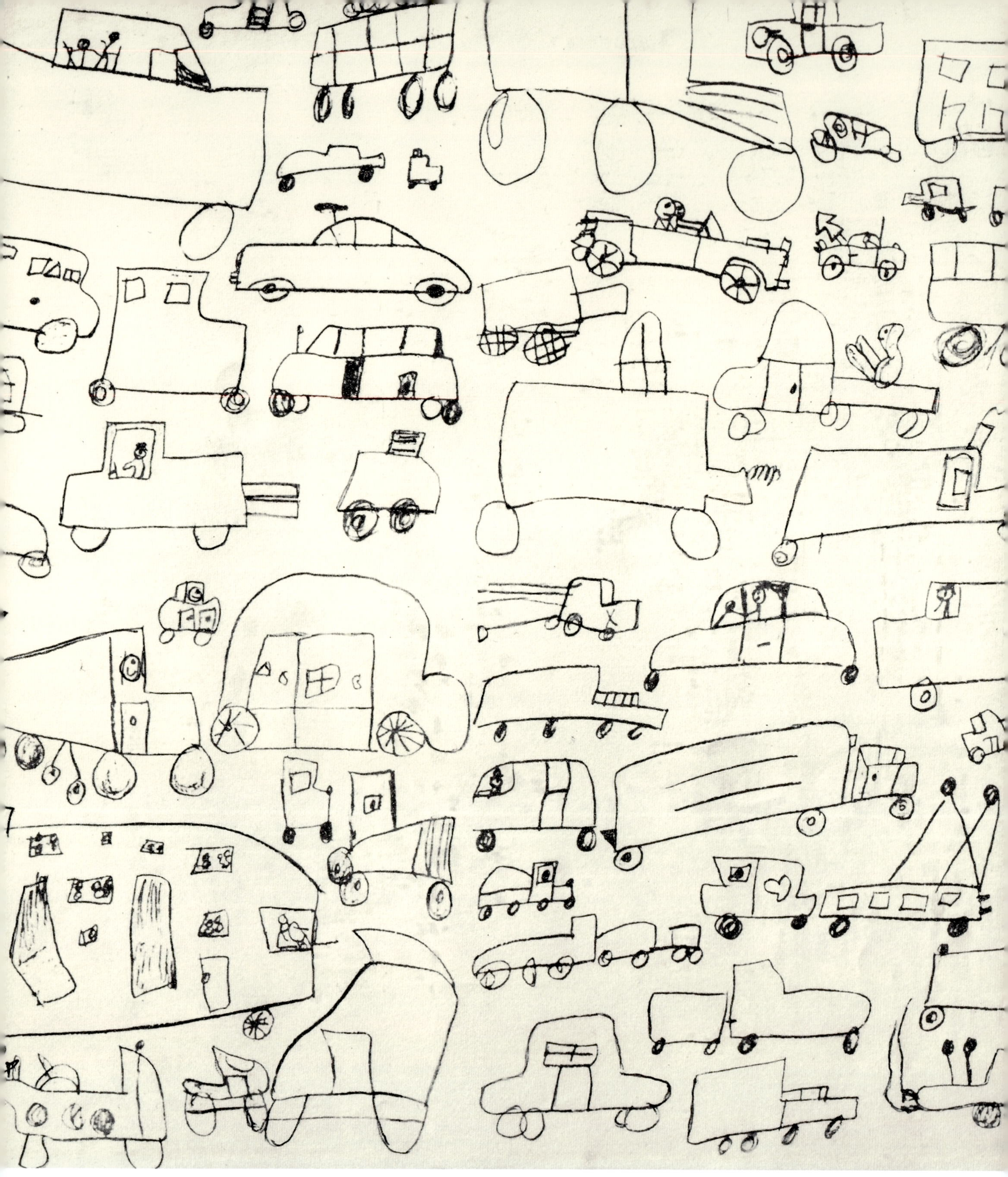

Rhoda Kellogg
Taxonomy of children's drawings with cars, 1950s-1975

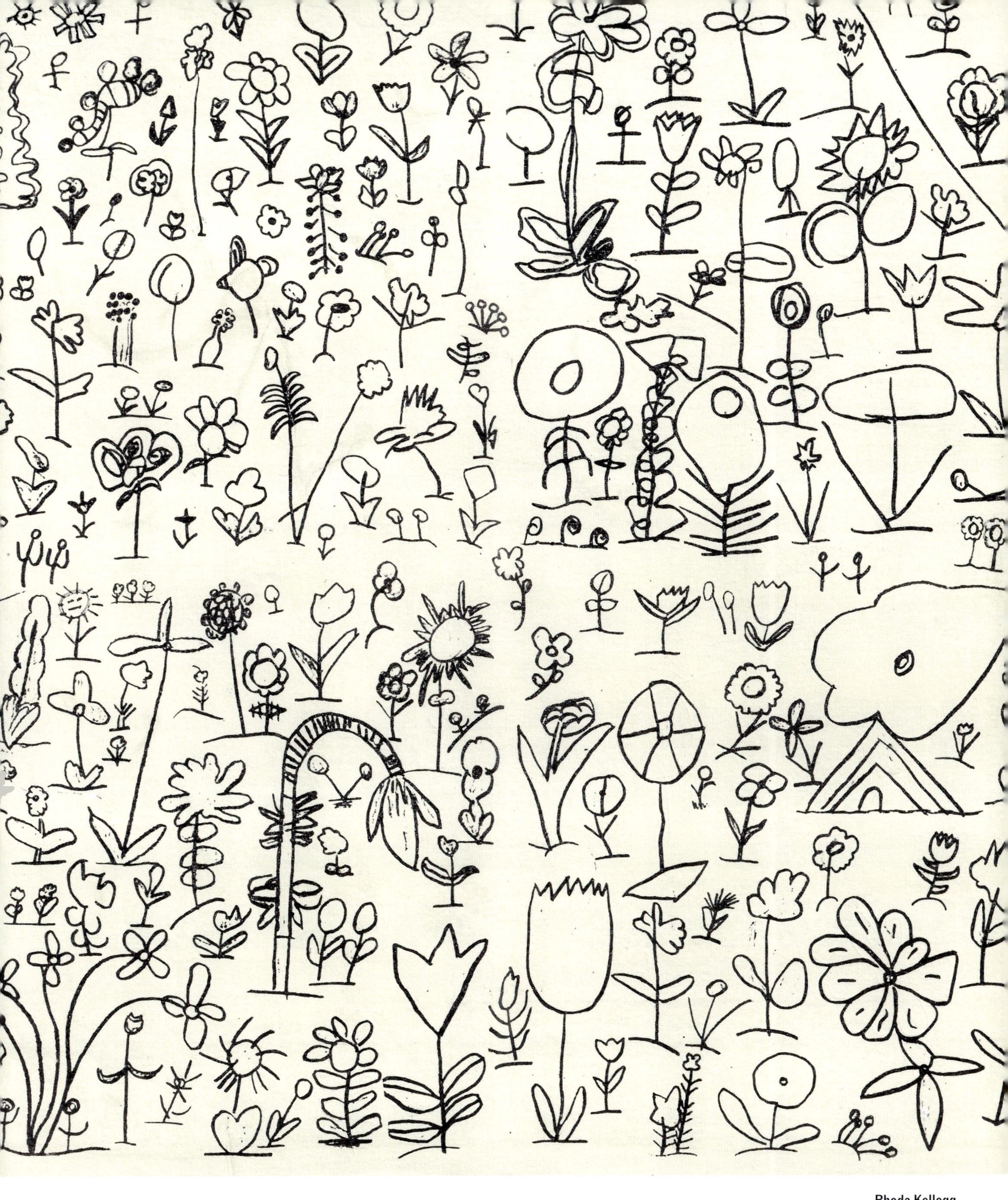

Amy F. Ogata
Children, Childhood and Creativity
The creativity of children is now considered natural, but it was once invented. This article focusses on how childhood and creativity have developed together over time.

Young children in modern Western countries are expected to be effortlessly and unselfconsciously creative. This is a widely accepted social norm that has been internalised to the extent that we have a difficult time recognising that it is anything other than completely natural. Yet we know that the idea of creativity is famously difficult to define or even to explain. The word creativity is, as the American writer and journalist Brendan Gill has suggested, "as light and wayward and almost as untetherable as milkweed down."[1] Moreover, like the notion of childhood itself, the rise of creativity as a social value is historically specific and tied to the social and intellectual shifts of the modern era. Invention, imagination and curiosity are the traits and qualities that we prize in both children and adults, although the assumption is that children have unfettered and unrestrained access whereas adults do not. Children's creativity is more than just a quality of a single person's thoughts or actions, it is a truth applied to all children and often only with the sunniest, most positive connotations.

I have studied the growth and reverence for children's creativity, observing how this amorphous value took increasingly material forms and how consumer expectations grew to match. This is a subject I have tried to understand historically and in the context of the US in the post-war age of the baby boom and the Cold War, and much of what follows derives from that work, which was published more than a decade ago.[2] Yet many of the same values and beliefs that animated the 20th-century belief have persisted and even gained ground in the time since I began trying to understand this phenomenon. What was once a preoccupation with famous artists, scientists and musicians and their biographies became a widespread gospel that made children's creativity into a commodity that seemed at times like a 19th-century gold rush, a natural resource waiting to be extracted, weighed and exploited.

The upward growth in the cult of creativity occurred in the middle years of the 20th century, just after the conclusion of World War II. A combination of psychological research, shifting social values and Cold War fears in the US all contributed to an unlikely embrace of creativity in the post-war era.[3] Scientific psychological studies of the 1950s and 1960s gave way to multiple applied contexts that appealed to government and businesses, and increasingly gained popular acceptance as a value to be cultivated by all ages. The notion that children are "naturally" creative is much older, but it too emerged forcefully during and after the war. Arnold Gesell, the influential 20th-century American paediatrician and child-development psychologist, believed that "by nature" the child was "a creative artist of sorts [...]. We may well be amazed at his resourcefulness, his extraordinary capacity for original activity, inventions and discovery".[4] Such awe at the child's apparently innate creativity has its roots in the Romantic era (c. 1800-1850) and this has not only persisted but expanded in our own age. Authentic creativity has become an unquestioned truth about children and childhood. By why do we believe that special classes, toys or activities might help stimulate this quality? Furthermore, why has creativity itself become so important to a sense of individualism?

The difficulty of the word is evident in English-language dictionaries of the era that relied on tautological definitions, such as "the quality of being creative; ability to create".[5] The words "imagination" and "originality", even "individuality", however, were the synonyms most closely paired with "creativity". These attractive associations of unbounded possibility and ingenuity gained positive meaning in an age of new concerns about national

Children on Isamu Noguchi's jungle gym in Piedmont Park, Atlanta, USA

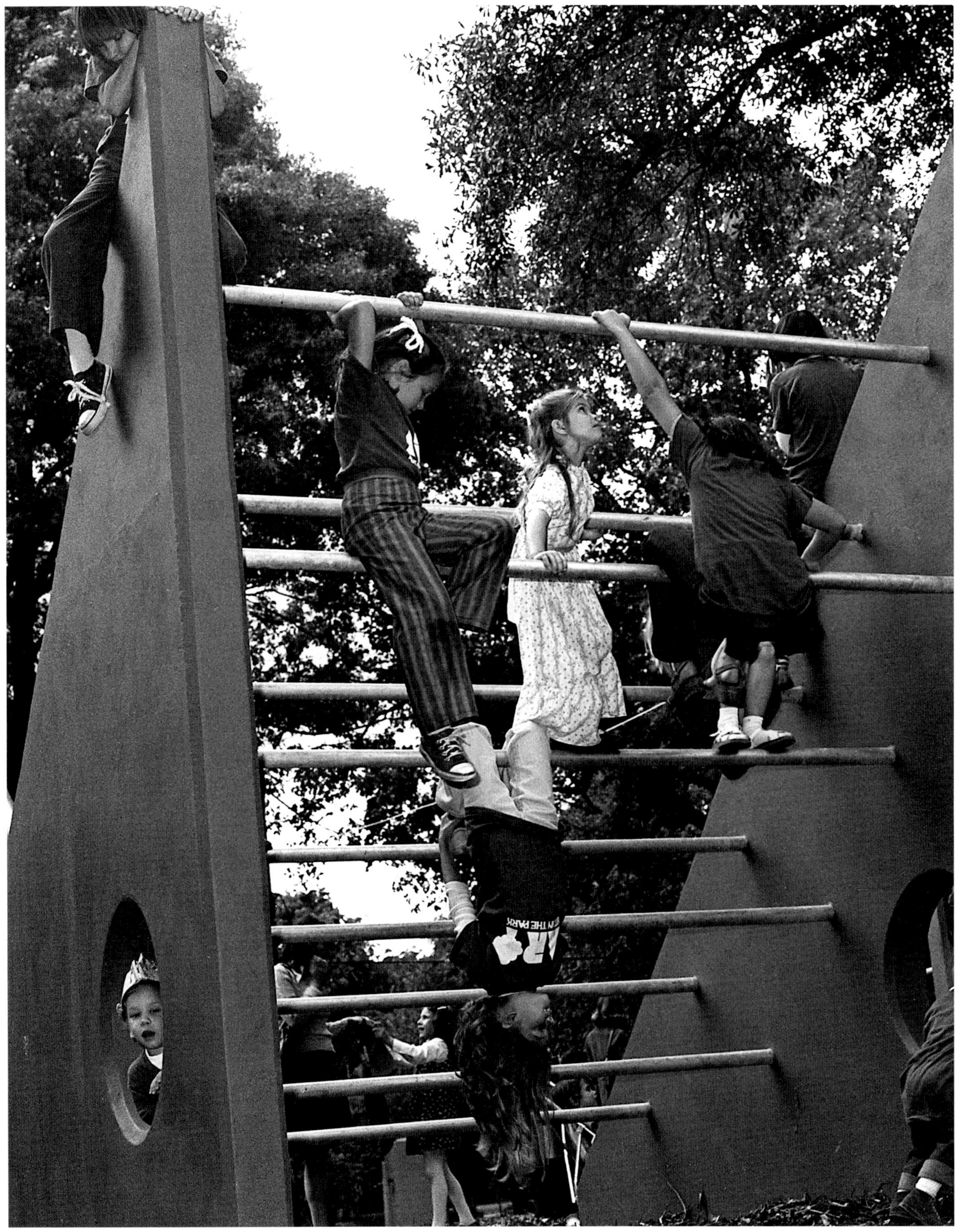

competitiveness. Although diffuse and abstract, the notion of creativity was resurgent in public aspects of US post-war life, from the rise of a heroic Abstract Expressionism as an artistic emblem of American individualism to creative writing programmes, to the corporate embrace of the "creative revolution" in advertising and business. The discourse of creativity was equally dominant in private life where it took hold in a culture of hobbies, domestic science and especially the education and upbringing of children.

Raising creative children was, of course, the dream of adults, and the dynamic of enabling a child's creativity was closely tied to a parent's own creative choices. Inverting the norm of training children to assume the conventions of adulthood, the discourse on creativity valued the child's unique insight, which the parent laboured to reveal, sustain and then emulate. The Hungarian-American psychology professor Mihaly Csikszentmihalyi distinguished between "big-C creativity", which he defines as the work of prominent artists, writers and musicians, and the "small-c creativity" that the greater mass practices in unremarkable everyday situations.[6] This small-c creativity was and still is the precise target of post-war advertisers and educators and the activity of children, teachers and parents. The kind of creativity envisioned in popular media was often mundane, but in the period debate, the small scale of these actions augured a grand future.

If there was an emphatic rise in the fixation on creativity in the US between the 1940s to the 1970s, which coincided with an explosion in live births and an economy that enabled middle-class households to acquire ever more, then the intellectual and educational roots were in Europe in the 19th century. The belief that children possessed particularly insightful qualities was entwined with the modern rise, or invention, of childhood. A fundamental shift occurred in the late 17th and 18th centuries, when philosophies on the education of children began to support the idea that specific training might result in a "better" adult. In contrast to earlier notions that the child was a natural sinner who must be disciplined and trained quickly to inhabit adult society, modern concepts of an ideal childhood put emphasis on preserving innocence, curiosity and playfulness in the growing child. The British philosopher John Locke's advice on raising a gentleman's son in *Some Thoughts Concerning Education* (1693) encouraged the ways of the peasantry as a model for developing a healthy child into a sensible aristocratic adult. Plain foods, soft shoes and loose clothes, exposure to the elements, sufficient sleep, toys and limited corporal punishment created the basis for a sound body and mind. Locke became known for his *tabula rasa* notion that children were essentially blank until educated. He sternly expected submissiveness to adults, yet he also showed sympathy for childish inquisitiveness. "Curiosity", he suggested, "should be as carefully cherished in children as other appetites suppressed."[7]

From the second half of the 18th century, pedagogues and elites fixed on children as a revelatory means of understanding and transforming the human condition. In *Émile, or On Education* (1752), the Swiss-French philosopher Jean-Jacques Rousseau described a childhood that embodied new political and social freedoms. Rousseau's fictional Émile was raised to exist in a state of harmony with the natural world and without the morals of bourgeois society imposed on his education. Rousseau admonished, "love childhood; promote its games, its pleasures, its amiable instinct."[8] For Rousseau, impulse and sensation rule the child; it is the adult observer of Émile who is endowed with the faculty of imagination. Yet, many of Rousseau's contemporaries saw in those impulses a useful and admirable quality of invention.

In the earliest years of the 19th century, the Swiss pedagogue Johann Heinrich Pestalozzi argued that the concept of *Anschauung*, the active intuitive human mind, was the basis of all knowledge. *Anschauung* was translated in English in the late 19th century as "sense-impression" and as "object lesson," a concept which was subsequently taken up by many others.[9] In perceiving objects through the senses, the child activated his or her higher powers of understanding, transforming fleeting sensory impressions into conscious thoughts. Pestalozzi favoured an educational process that introduced the object before the word. Following Rousseau, whom he admired, Pestalozzi argued that the material world and our sensory perception of it were the fundamental sources of knowledge. Pestalozzi is best known for a system of teaching through drawing, which while deriving from instinct, would instil skills of observation, accuracy and patience. The idea that sensory engagement with objects might not only release a child's understanding and encourage development, but also promote a forceful creativity was a central theme for subsequent reformers.

Another Romantic with a greater investment in identifying and moulding the creativity of the child was the German educator Friedrich Fröbel. Fröbel's programme of kindergarten gifts and occupations, developed in the 1830s and 1840s, aimed to train a child's sense and faculties to embody a spiritual harmony between mankind, nature and God. Fröbel's kindergarten theory, moreover, aimed to foster what he called "the impulse to creative activity" to achieve a comprehensive expression of love and humanity that enveloped the child, the family, the nation and the divine in its embrace. Fröbel's

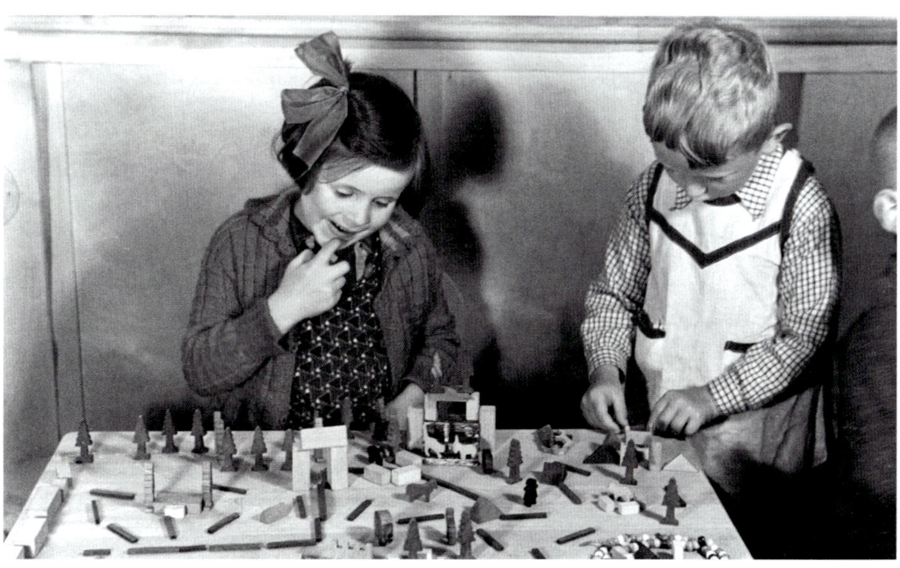

Children playing with Fröbel's system of toys in German kindergarten in the 1930s

concept of creativity was quite different from the connotations of free expression of the 20th century. Rather, Fröbel's creativity was the acquisition of knowledge through busy manipulation of specific predetermined forms under a teacher's precise direction. His system of gifts and occupations consisted of geometric solids, such as balls, cubes and cylinders, becoming increasingly complex and abstract as the child explored each one sequentially. Creativity, for Fröbel, was the result of an individual's self-discovery and self-instruction through observation and sensory engagement with forms and materials. Creativity was the child's intellect in action, how the child understood itself in relation not only to the physical world, but to a metaphysical entity whose presence was embodied in the laws that were revealed through play. The aim of Fröbel's programme of gifts and occupations was to use sensory information – to manipulate human-made and natural objects – to awaken the mind. This insight became the basis of many other early childhood programmes, including the Italian pedagogue and medical doctor Maria Montessori's sensory activities.

Adults consciously constructed the figure of the creative child, increasingly idealising creativity as a dimension of childhood's "naturalness" and "innocence". 19th-century images of children show how this enduring motif of children at play in natural settings reflected the growth of reformist educational ideas. The German Romantic artist Philipp Otto Runge's images of children from around 1800 suggest the painter's reverence for the state of childhood and for the especially insightful qualities he believed children possessed and emphasised in their staring intensity and absorption. Runge's association of the state of a child's enchanted playfulness merged with plants and flowers of their surroundings. This is one of many examples of how depictions of "natural" and "innocent" children persist in images. The endurance of this motif suggests a perpetual yearning for what the American art historians Robert Rosenblum and Anne Higonnet have called "the Romantic child", a figure who represents what we most value and fear losing.[10]

Untutored creativity

Modern artists and writers admired the innocent child and linked childhood positively and nostalgically with primitivism. Like the "primitive" whose apparently unselfconscious expression was widely admired by urban Western artists, the child was endowed with special capabilities that had been deemed lost in the educated, socialised adult. In the visual and applied arts, the non-Western exotic and the European peasant possessed a childlike intuition configured as untutored creativity and spontaneity in opposition to an overcivilized, corrupt and industrialised Western culture.

Another face of this primitivist discourse found a welcome home in the modernist idea of an authentic creativity that derived from a deep inward source rather than from artistic training or naturalism. The American art historian Jonathan Fineberg has documented how modern artists and critics viewed children as having unique, even visionary, artistic potential. The relationship between the insightful and inventive child and the child as a model artist is a modernist conceit. Artists such as Spanish Pablo Picasso, German Gabriele Münter, Russian Wassily Kandinsky, Swiss-German Paul Klee and others admired and emulated children's art for its forceful and economic strategies of representation.[11] Reformers in Europe established special schools to mould children's skills in drawing, painting and the applied arts.

Thus, when Gesell made his observation that the child might be considered a "creative artist of sorts", the creative child was already revered among the European avant-garde and was exported to the US.

The home-grown American counterpart was the 'savage boy inventor', as John H. Lienhard has termed it, a Progressive Era (c. 1880-1920s) figure who was inventive and curious, a reader of handbooks and popular science manuals, whose experiments and projects challenged the norms of domesticity, but whose unfettered curiosity achieved mythic status.[12] In the years of the American baby boom (1946-1964), the creative child materialised fully in psychological studies and educational literature, popular parenting texts, books, toys, television, houses, schools and museums as the ideal future citizen. In the dream of ambitious middle- and upper-middle class parents, toy companies and researchers, the creative child was a source of authentic imagination and insight and the regenerative answer to some of the many anxieties of post-war culture, including conformity.

Child sized

After psychologists began to study and measure creativity, around 1950, they argued that it was a vital and productive aspect of the human personality. The popularisation of scientific literature argued for an overlooked but uniquely valuable creative child who might contribute to society in yet untold ways. As the child became an object of intense study and discussion, scrutiny and measurement of children's abilities also transformed the idea of the creative child, who shifted from a Romantic agent of authentic i nsight to a quantifiable consuming citizen of the post-war era.

The Romantic ideal, however, persisted in new forms adapted for the post-war era. Curious and imaginative protagonists populated the growing market for children's picture books, movies and television – such as the Swedish author Astrid Lindgren's independent and unconventional Pippi Longstocking who first appeared as a character in 1945 – gave the constructed image of the creative child a lasting place in the middle-class household. Some parents acquired specific types of deliberately abstract toys, art and science materials, child-sized furniture, playhouses and allocated play space in the family dwelling to stimulate intellectual development and imagination. The growth of creativity as a social value extended to much larger public investments: New designs for school architecture, playgrounds and even museums for children to explore their subjectivity and independence, all emerged simultaneously. The discourse of creativity so thoroughly permeated the expectations of childhood and its institutions that "creative" became a common adjective applied to objects, education, and even activities already closely associated with imagination such as visual arts, writing and theatre. Together these objects, spaces and activities helped to develop the figure of the creative child.

The playground flourished as a site of aesthetic attention in post-war Europe and the US. Architects and landscape architects pursued new forms and material conditions for play, adapting social and psychological research to concerns for natural forms and visual impact. Play Sculptures was the name that the toy company Creative Playthings used to promote their innovative mass-produced designs, many created by sculptors. Some, such as Danish-Swedish Egon Møller-Nielsen, were well-known largely for their designs for children's play. Others pursued play spaces alongside other work. The playgrounds that American Isamu Noguchi envisioned are projects that emerged amid the growing belief that children should have their own environments for expressive play. He also collaborated with Creative Playthings. Although most of his schemes went unrealised, Noguchi developed environments that combined sculptural forms and landscapes encouraging exploration and contemplation.[13] In contrast to conventional mass-produced equipment that was installed in a limited lot defined with fencing, his designs stressed variations in natural form such as gentle steps and swelling mounds, textures of earth, stone and water, as well as areas for children to explore on their own. As a sculptor, his concern for embodied space met the unscripted play activities of children, yielding an experience that transcended boundaries of art and daily life.

Under the banner of creativity

The pervasiveness of the creativity discourse suggests that we remain heavily invested in its promises. Creativity holds enormous cultural value, and the word "creativity" is used colloquially to mean something vaguely novel and often intensely personal. In the US, but also worldwide, creativity has become a sacred value tied to a stalwart belief in authenticity, originality and innovation. It sells products to an uneasy consumer wary of globalisation and the impersonal nature of capitalism. Although creativity seems, at least in theory, to resist commodification, it is closely tied to mass consumption, to the extent that it has become a widely accepted doctrine, even slogan, perpetuated by corporate actors. Creativity may promise innovation that has the potential to yield new answers to intractable problems, but endless merchandise also seems to appear under its banner.

While creativity is a revered and highly sought after attribute in adults, who avidly pursue advice books, podcasts, retreats and experiences to unleash their creativity, it remains the normal expectation of children. Adults understand creativity as liberating and fulfilling, yet the American sociologist David Riesman argued in 1950 that this expectation of creative behaviour can be ironically confining and even intimidating for children.[14]

At large retailers and online merchants, as in small toy shops, selections of creativity toys proliferate. A manufacturer of pencils and inks has trademarked the term Creativity for Kids to sell kits and supplies that promise sensory engagement and release of the imagination, reprising some of the values of Fröbel and Montessori programmes. Packaged activities flourished during the COVID-19 pandemic which compounded the challenge of keeping children who were not in school not only busy but engaged with non-digital materials. Tellingly, the growth of these types of goods seems less invested in a future adult than with the immediate concern for entertaining the child. Whereas the training and education of the post-war child to stimulate their native creativity was tied to the future trajectory of the country, the discourse of creativity now appears to have no longer-term outlook other than immediate self-realisation. Numerous studies exploring creativity during the pandemic seem to indicate that time spent creatively at home was understood as a short-term opportunity for self-expression or a temporary remedy against isolation. Yet again, the word "creativity" is used in universalising terms, with generative and therapeutic, rather than potentially destructive, implications. The expansion of the idealism of creativity makes it even more widely appealing.

Creativity, then, is a paradox. At once revered and mythologised, it is fundamentally abstract; while believed to be universal and timeless, it is historically specific to our modern era; and although conjured as an innate quality, it is understood as something that is fleeting but which can be liberated through the intervention of things and exercises. While the instinct to create may be fundamentally human, the perception of what constitutes creativity is socially and historically constructed and surprisingly limited.

Amy F. Ogata is Professor of Art History at the University of Southern California. She writes on children's play and creativity, and is the author of *Designing the Creative Child: Playthings* and *Places in Midcentury America* (University of Minnesota Press, 2013). She co-curated the exhibition *Swedish Wooden Toys* that was shown in Paris and New York 2014-2016.

1. Brendan Gill, Prologue to Report on "American Creativity at Risk". Symposium, 8-10 November, 1996, p. 4.
2. Amy F. Ogata, *Designing the Creative Child: Playthings and Places in Midcentury America*. University of Minnesota Press, 2013. I have adapted parts of this text for this essay.
3. Samuel W. Franklin, *The Cult of Creativity: A Surprisingly Recent History*. University of Chicago Press, 2023.
4. Arnold Gesell and Frances L. Ilg in collaboration with Janet Learned and Louise B. Ames, *Infant and Child in the Culture of Today: The Guidance of Development in Home and Nursery School*. Harper Brothers Publishers, 1943, p. 65.
5. *Webster's Third New International Dictionary*, rev. ed. 1961, p. 532.
6. Mihaly Csikszentmihalyi, *Creativity: Flow and the Psychology of Discovery and Invention*. Harper Collins, 1996.
7. John Locke, *Some Thoughts Concerning Education* (1693), Ruth W. Grant and Nathan Tarcov (eds.). Hackett Publishing Company, 1996, p. 79.
8. Jean-Jacques Rousseau, *Émile, or On Education*, Allan Bloom (trans.). Basic Books, 1979, p. 79.
9. Ann-Sophie Lehmann and Imke Volkers, "Object Lessons: The Story of Material Education in Eight Chapters". Exhibition at Werkbundarchiv-Museum der Dinge, Berlin, 2017.
10. Robert Rosenblum, *The Romantic Child: From Runge to Sendak*. Thames and Hudson, 1988, and Anne Higonnet, *Pictures of Innocence: The History and Crisis of Ideal Childhood*. Thames and Hudson, 1998.
11. Jonathan Fineberg, *The Innocent Eye: Children's Art and the Modern Artist*. Princeton University Press, 1997.
12. John H. Lienhard, *Inventing Modern: Growing Up with X-Rays, Skyscrapers and Tailfins*. Oxford University Press, 2003, pp. 190-203.
13. Susan G. Solomon, *American Playgrounds: Revitalizing Community Space*. NH: UPNE, 2005.
14. David Riesman, Nathan Glazer and Reuel Denney, *The Lonely Crowd*, rev. ed. 1950. New Haven, 1961, p. 61.

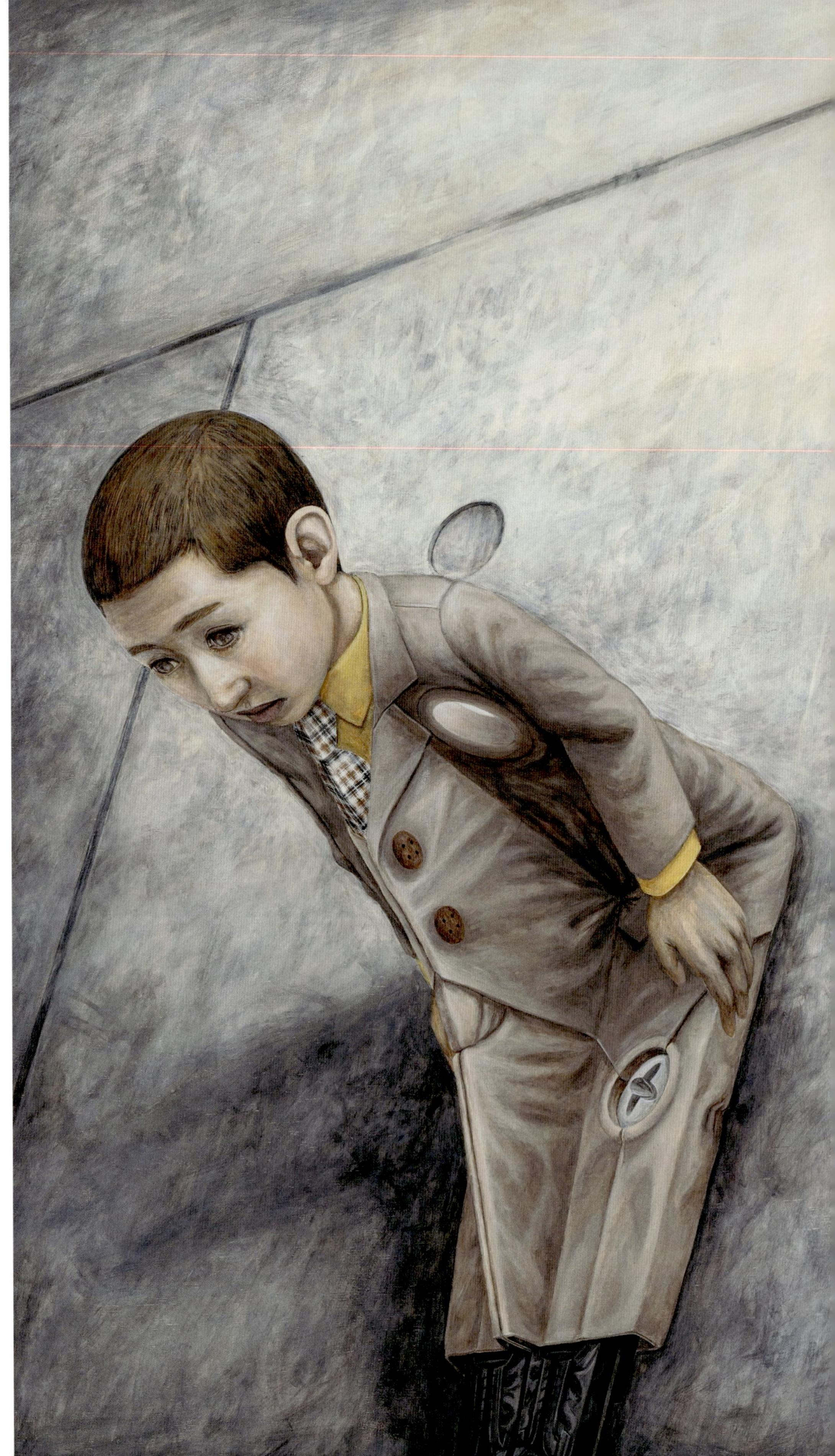

Tetsuya Ishida
Untitled, 1997

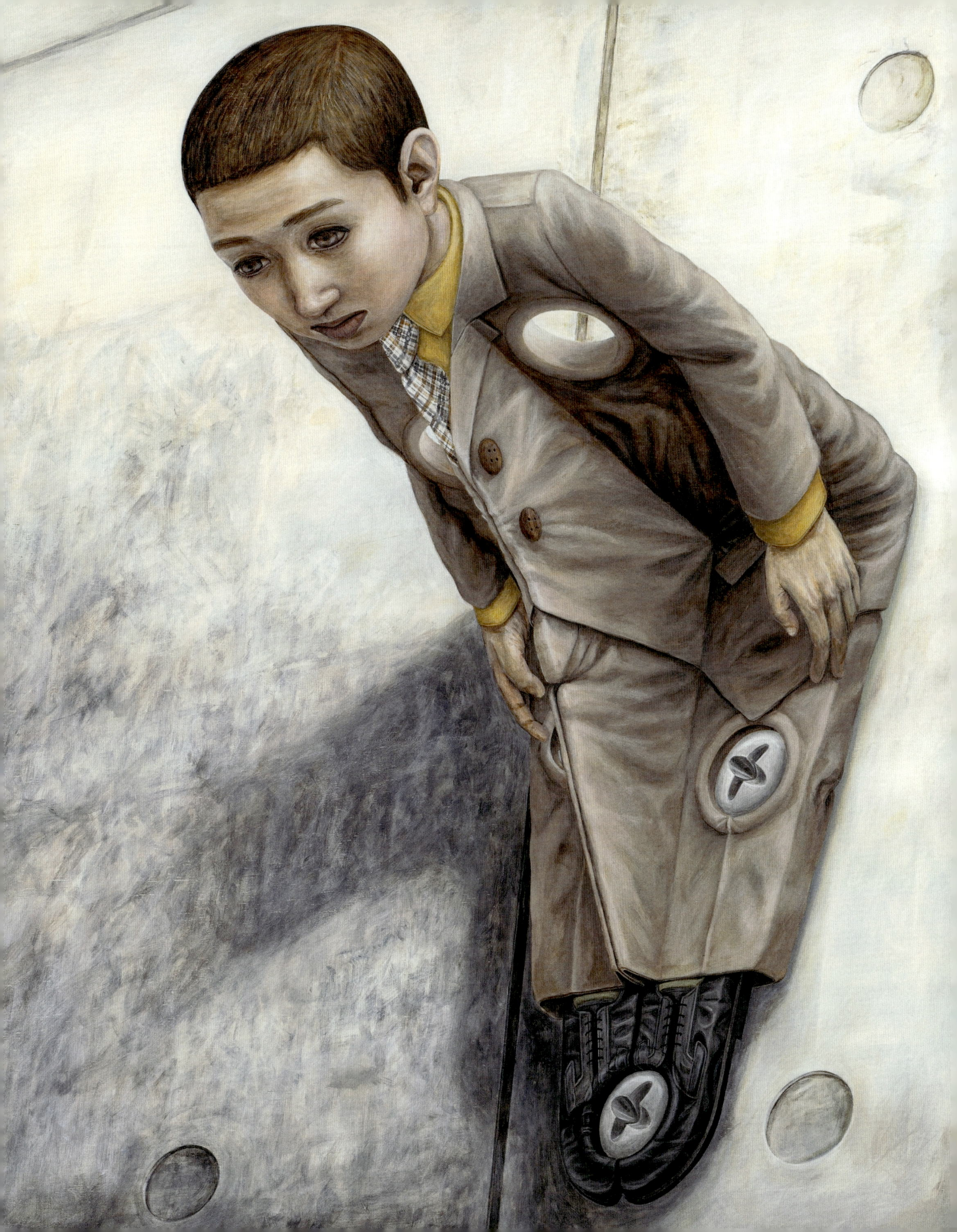

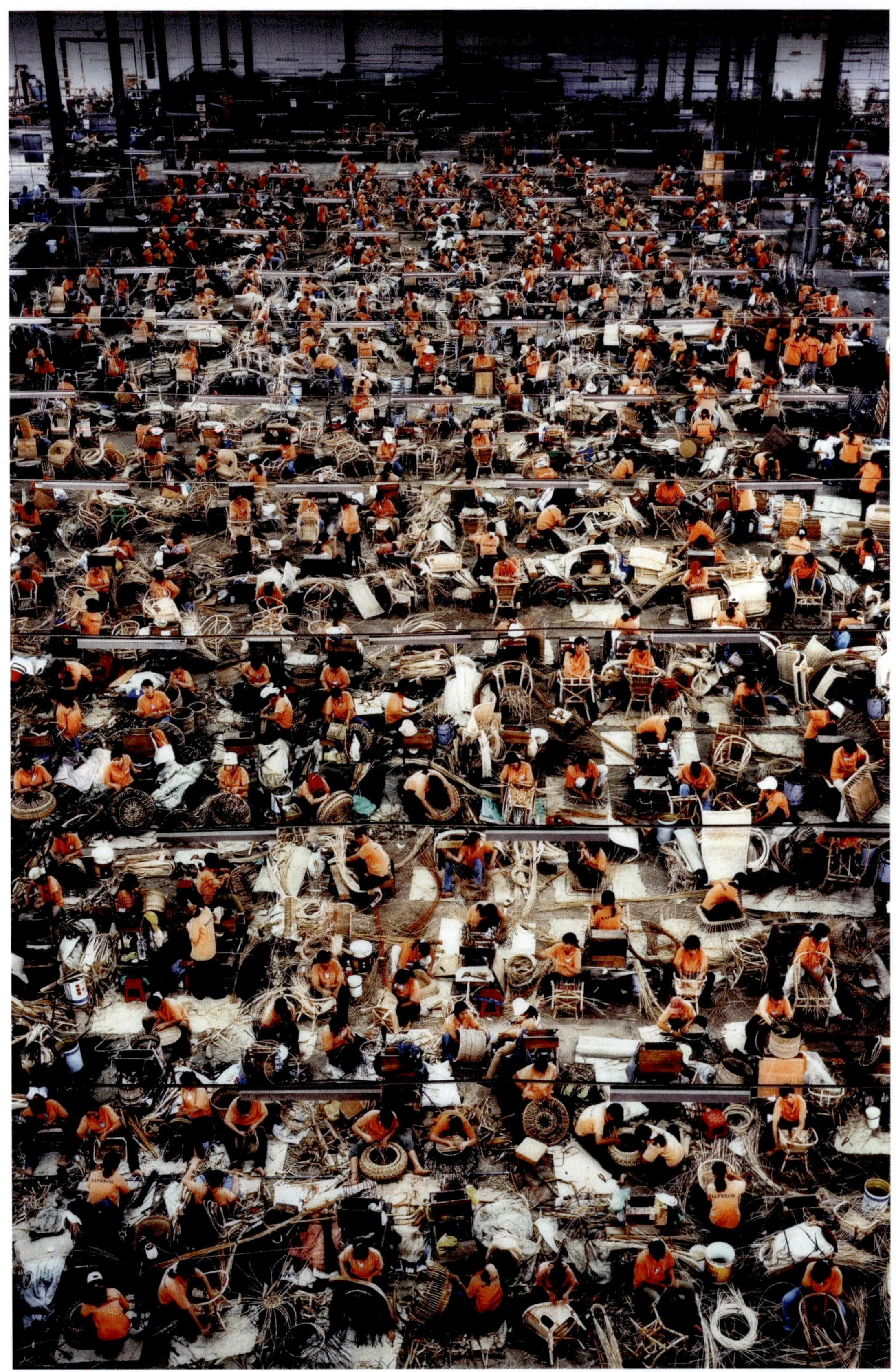

Andreas Gursky
Nha Trang, 2004

Right page: Simon Denny
Amazon delivery drone patent drawing as virtual Rio Tinto mineral globe, 2021

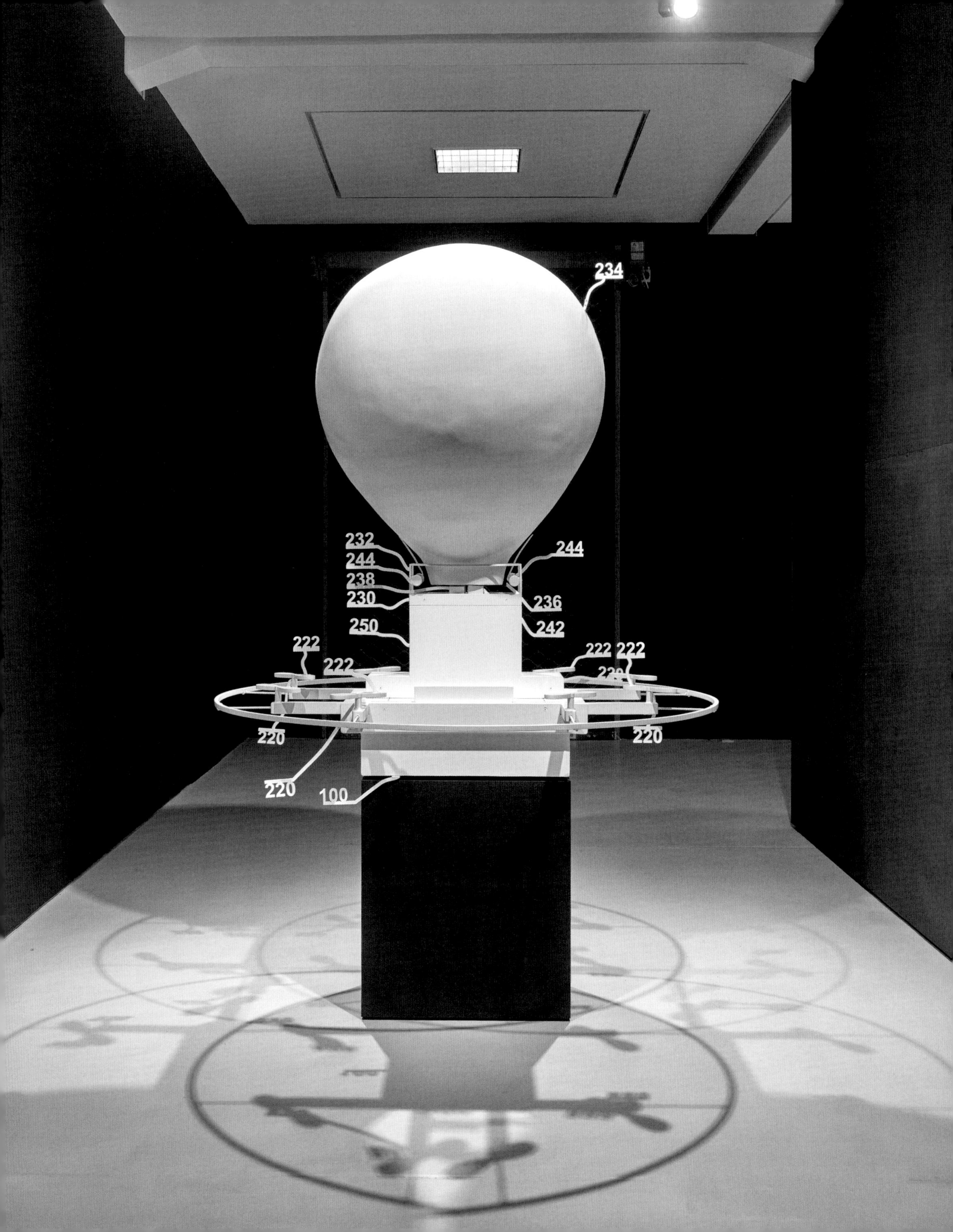

234
232
244
238
230
250
236
242
222
222
222
222
220
220
220
220
100

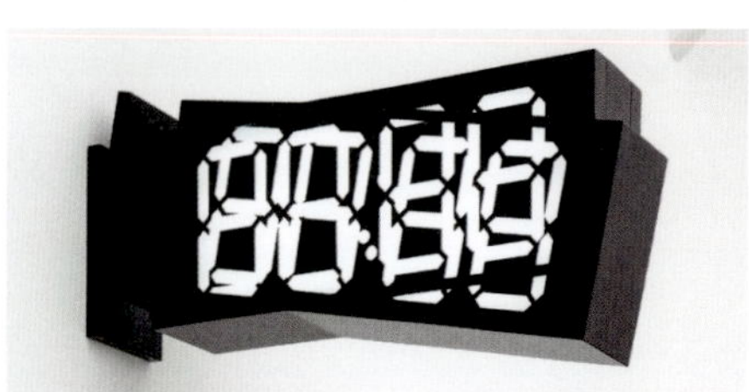

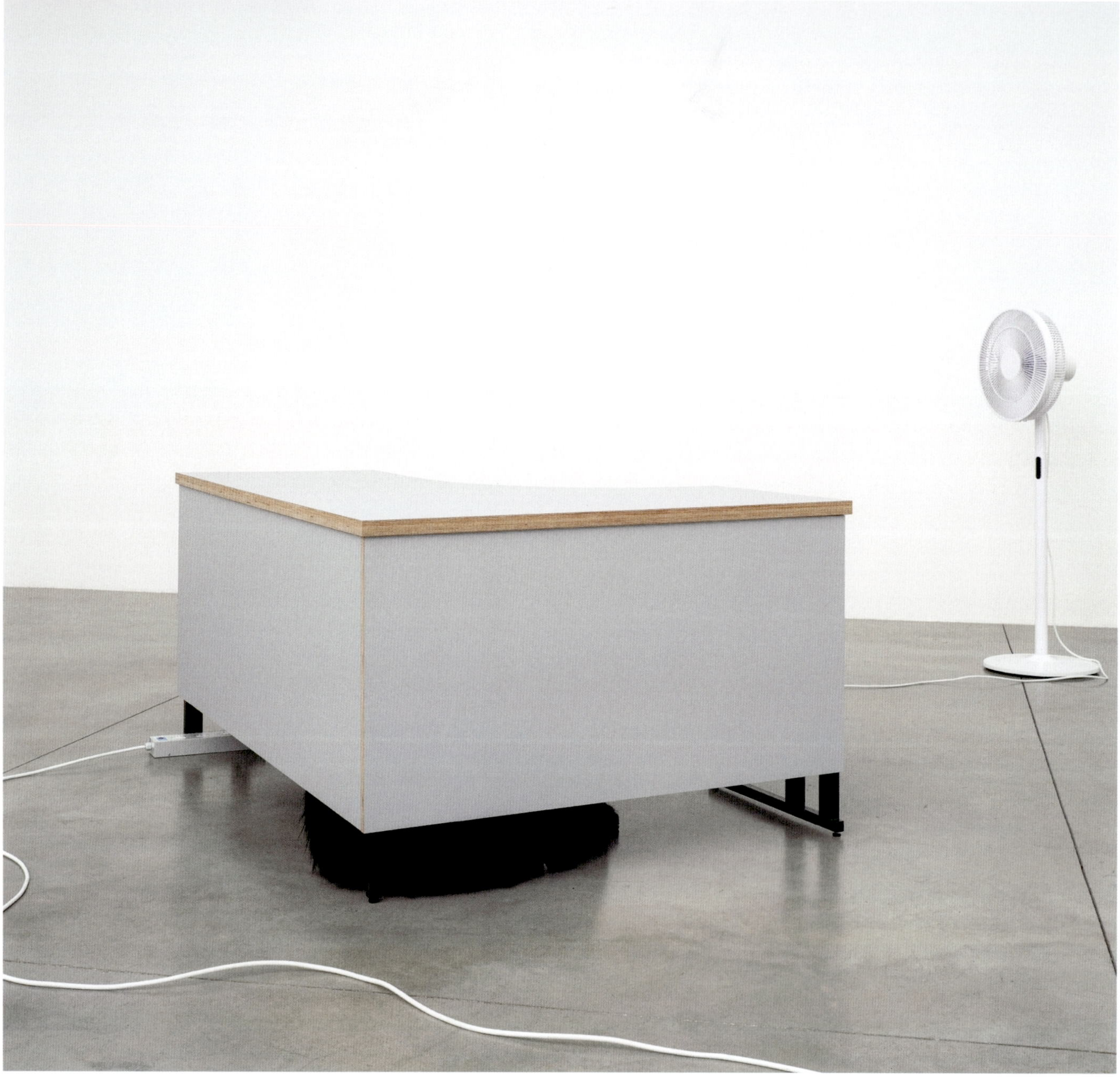

Top: Ryan Gander
Chronos Kairos, 88.88, 2023

Bottom and right page: Ryan Gander
School of Languages, 2023

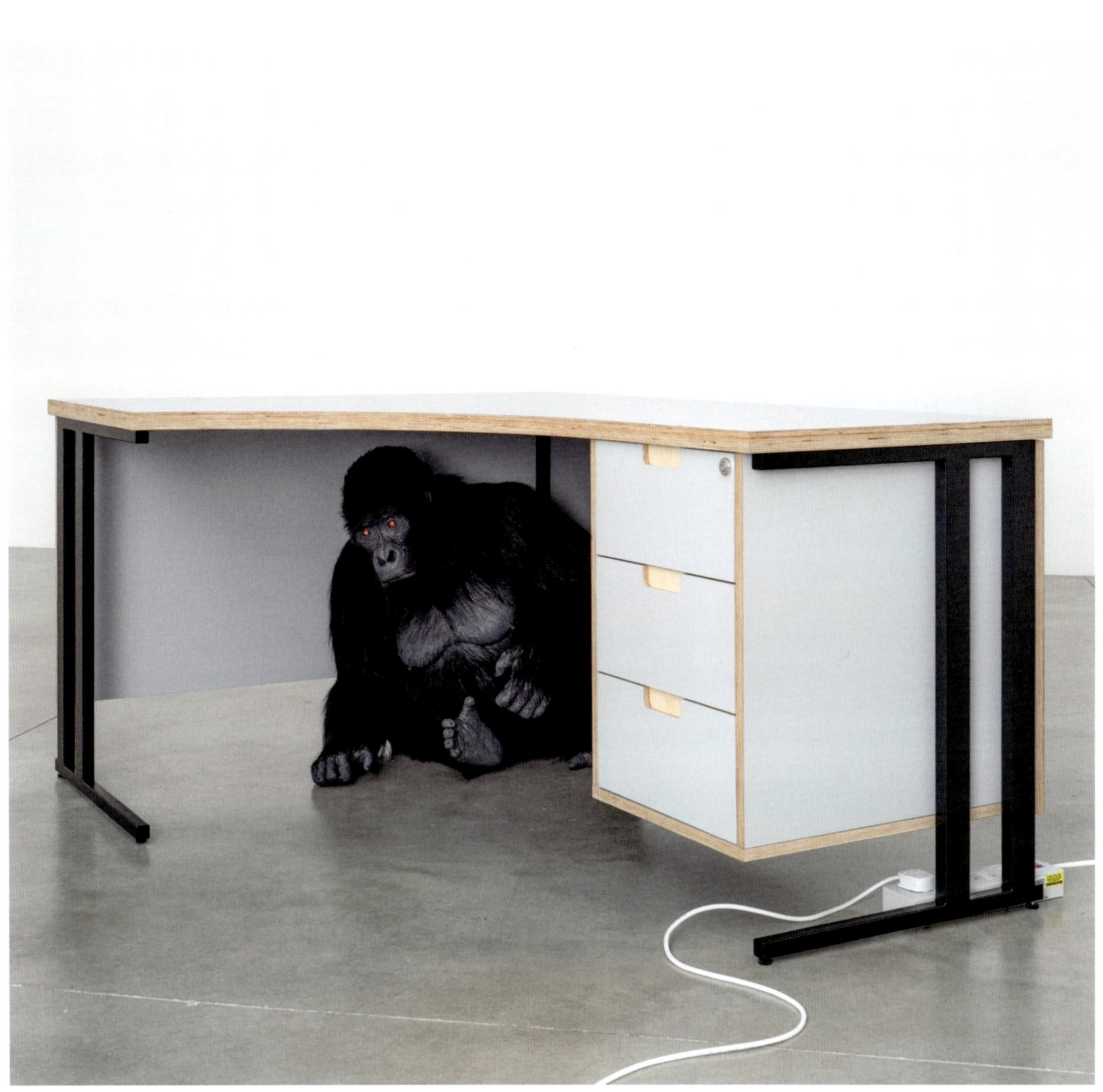

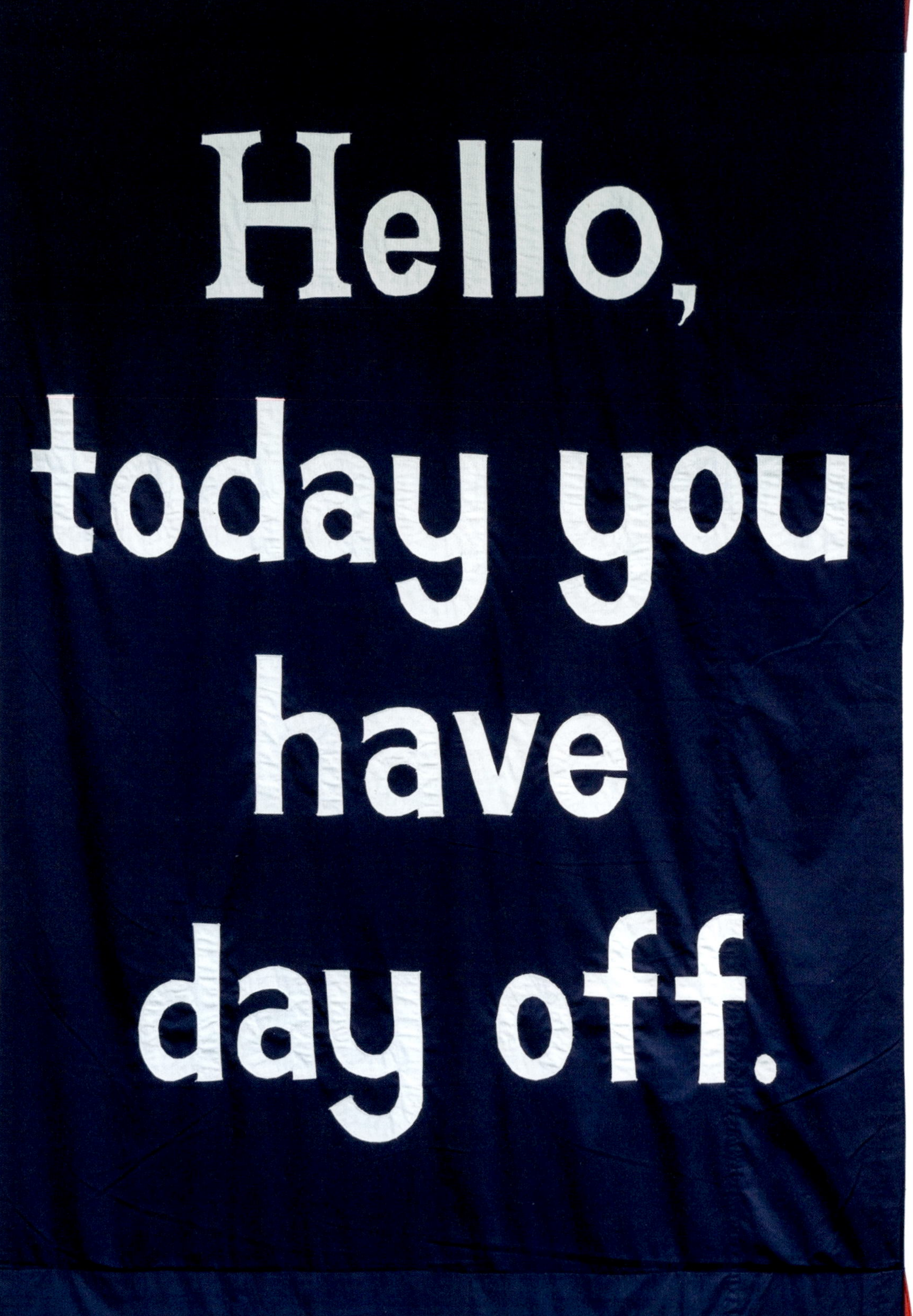

Jeremy Deller
Hello, today you have day off, 2023

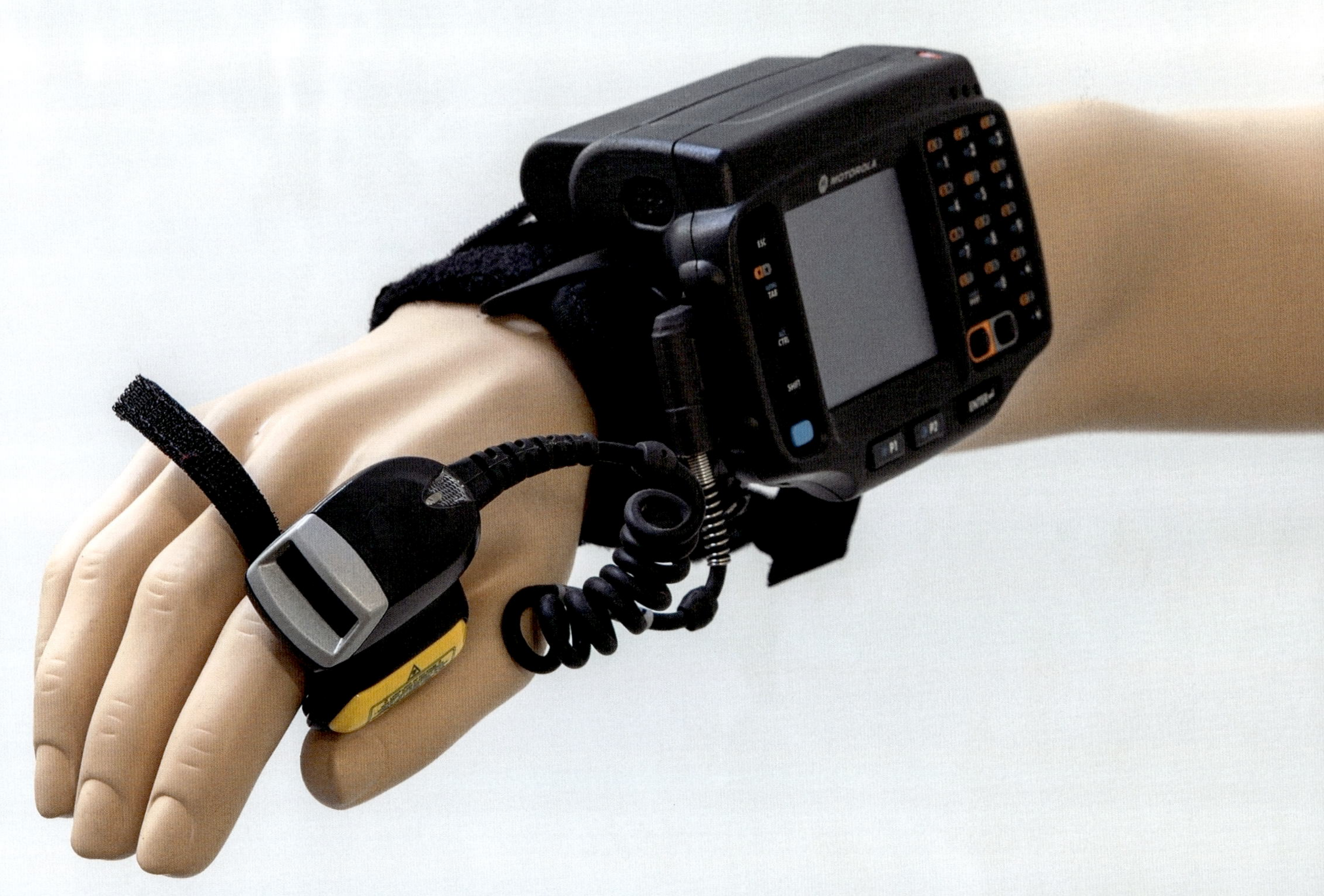

Jeremy Deller
Motorola WT4000 Wearable Terminal, 2013

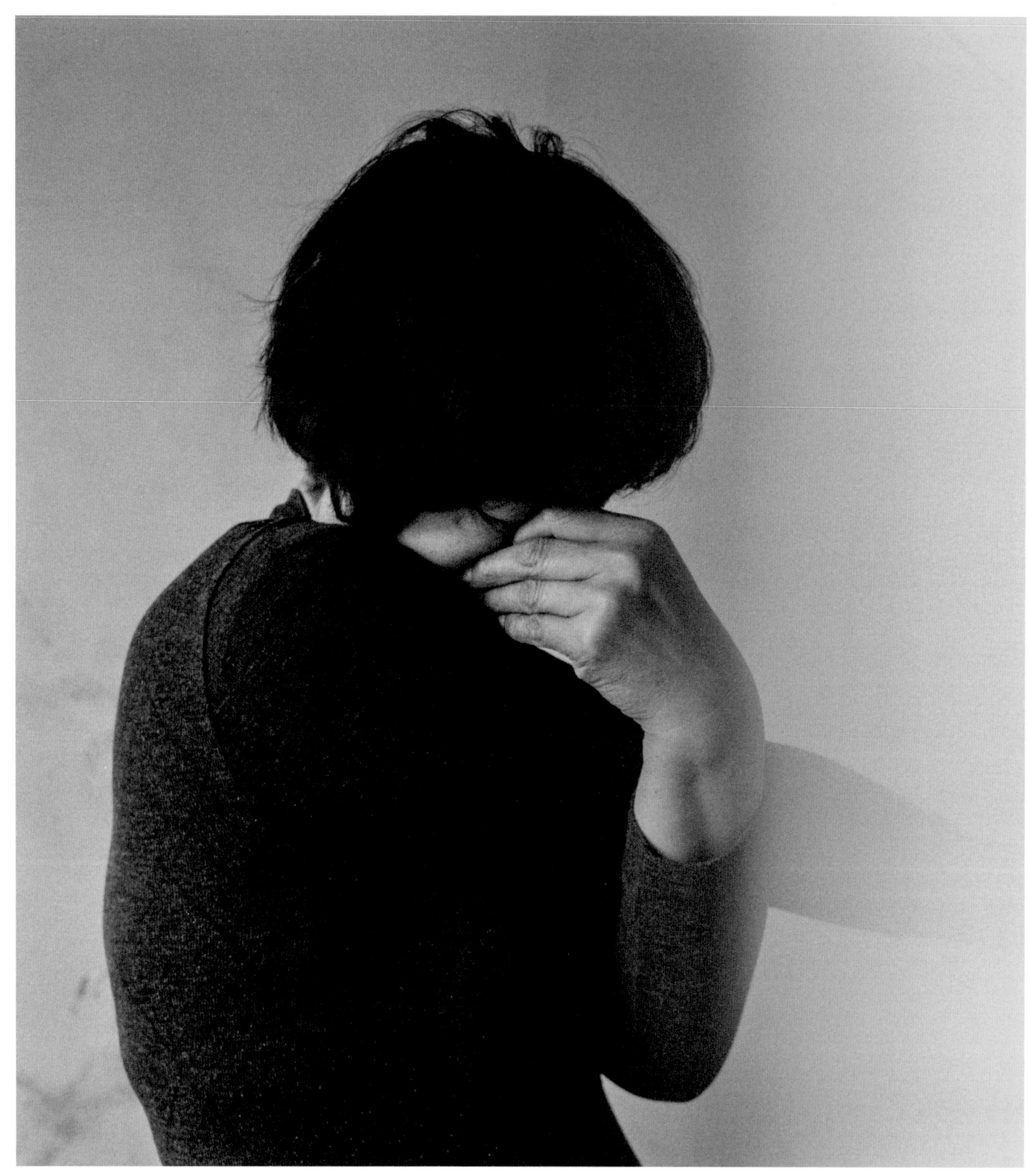

Huang Po-Chih
Blue Elephant-Mother, "Wanting falls around me. Heavy garment, but I can be a floating elephant in my dream.", 2018 (2023)

Right page: Huang Po-Chih
You are a blue elephant, 2021

My mother said, "My legs are swelling"
I answered, "must be because you use the sewing
machine for a long time."
She said again, "I have legs of an elephant."
"Unlike the rapidly changing society, I am as slow
as an elephant," she added.
I said, "you are a blue elephant."

Since she spent a long time using the sewing
machine, her legs were quite swollen. She and
her friends made fun of her, stating that her
legs were like the ones of the elephant. To these
ladies who used the clothing labels to view the
world, their understanding of the world was
thought to be as slow as the speed of an
elephant walking. However, the elephant can
walk in 40 kilometers per hour in reality, which
is faster than a raptor.

Mrs Kim told me, "there is a talking elephant in
Korea."
I asked, "What does it say?"
She answered, "hello and sit down."

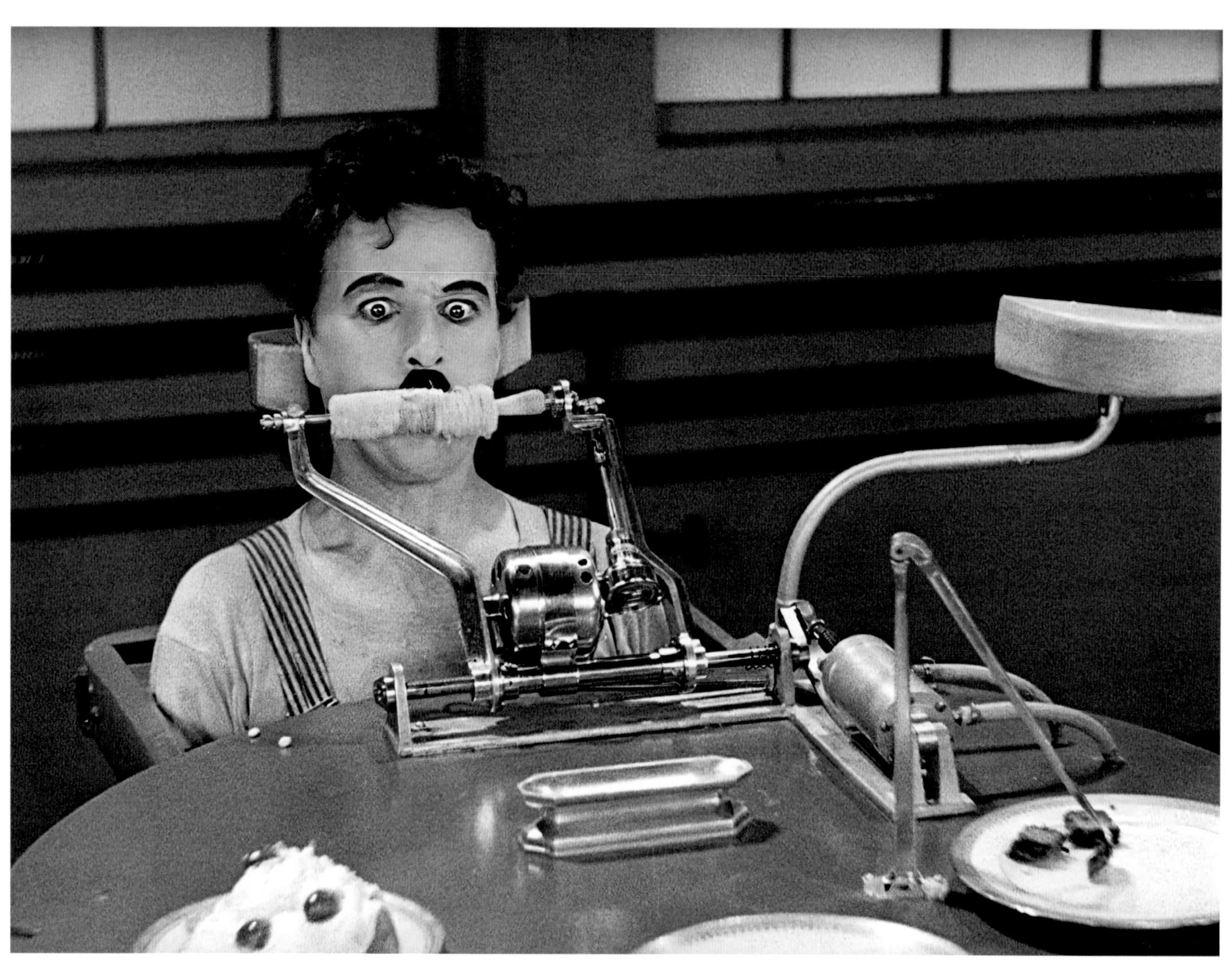

Charlie Chaplin
Still from *Modern Times*, 1936

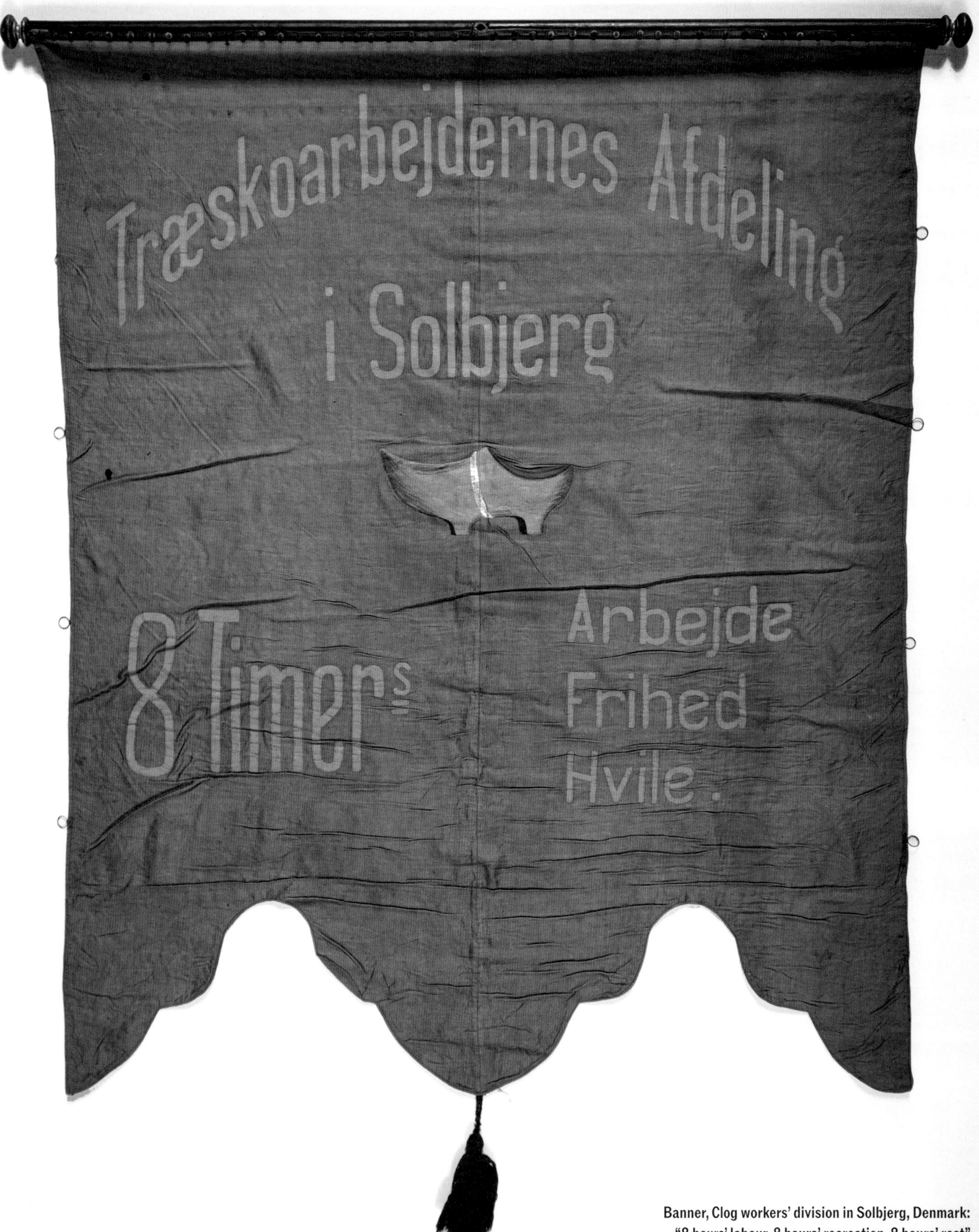

Banner, Clog workers' division in Solbjerg, Denmark:
"8 hours' labour, 8 hours' recreation, 8 hours' rest"

Todd Lubart
Creativity: An Inherent Part of Being Human
Humans have always been creative, expressed in a multitude of ways in our life and work. The newest research gets closer to understanding how creativity thrives.

Millions of years ago, our ancestors engaged in survival activities, hunting and gathering, living off the land as other species do. These predecessors of modern homo sapiens developed the capacity to transform natural materials, such as sticks and stones into new objects that had a particular utility. For example, the earliest archaeological remains show stones that were transformed into hunting tools. There was the combination of materials, such as a rock and a wooden stick used to make a type of axe or hammer, and arrows made from flint and wood. Furthermore, diverse materials were combined and transformed to build shelters. The evidence from more than two million years ago, from *homo habilis* and others, are the earliest traces of our ancestors' ingenuity.

Of course, using materials in new ways for problem solving is not distinct to humans. For example, beavers gnaw at trees to create material to build their dams, and chimpanzees have been shown to use sticks as tools to get food that is out of their reach. Thus, there is some evidence of goal-driven ingenuity in non-human species. What is perhaps the hallmark and distinctive feature of human problem solving is the extent to which creativity and innovation have driven human activity since those prehistoric days.

We have evidence that Neanderthals, who emerged at least 300,000 years ago, had developed increasingly sophisticated hunting and cooking tools, clothing and a social lifestyle, including burial practices. The earliest artifacts that relate to the arts, dating from 50,000 to 30,000 years ago, such as bone and stone carvings, bone-crafted musical instruments or cave paintings, all attest to this creative spirit. An example is the Venus de Lespugue, a small statue sculpted in ivory from a Mammoth's tusk around 27,000 years ago.

What is creativity? We can define creativity as the ability to produce novel content that has value in its context. By "novel" we mean original, different from the simple replication of what already exists. Originality is of course evaluated in a relativistic way, and there is a range from slightly to very original. "Content" refers to any type of production, be it an idea expressed in a visual, verbal, auditory, action-based, physical format, a mechanical invention, a social invention, such as a ceremony or numerous other instantiations. The term "value" indicates that the novel, original production has meaning and interest in a given context or situation. The value of a new idea or production can also change over time, as the contribution might be appreciated right away, or its worth may only be attributed by the audience later. Thus, a new idea expressed in some form in a particular context is the basis of the phenomenon that we call "creativity".

When we look at human history over the past 50,000 years, we see that creative ideas, either emerging at the societal level or attributable to specific individuals, have been one of the driving forces leading to the world we know today. Our everyday world is filled with artifacts that testify to human creativity, such as furniture, art of all kinds, technological inventions, clothing, architectural works, culinary dishes and entertainment. All this evidence is the result of an accumulated creative activity, in which each new contribution extends the existing world.

According to some scholars, the era in which we live is the Anthropocene period, marked by the fact that humans have become a force that is transforming the whole planet. Indeed, through the creation of dams, for example, we have modified

Rhoda Kellogg
Taxonomy of childrens' drawings, 1950s-1975

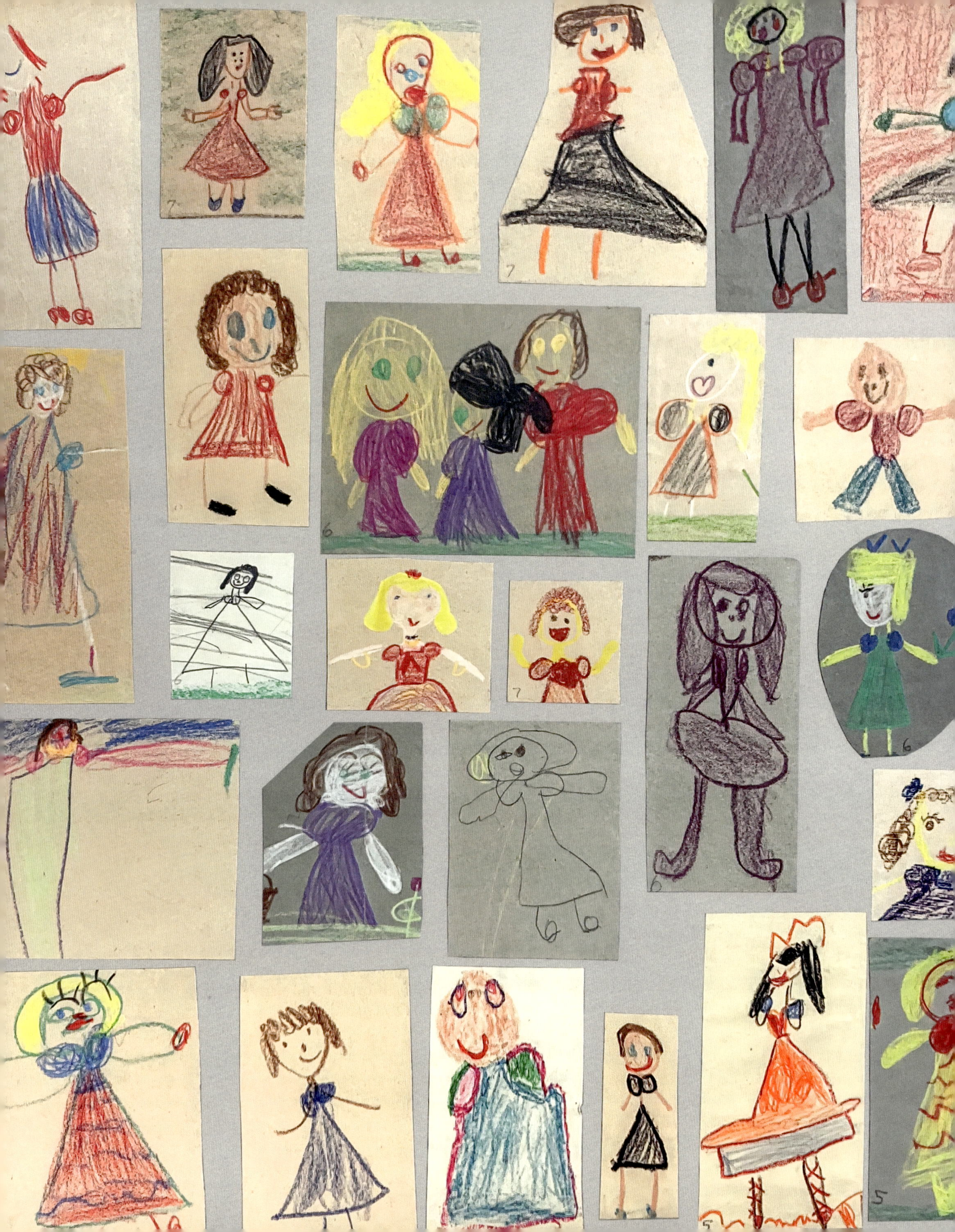

the course of natural water systems, and through the creation of industrial production of goods and services we have changed the composition of the Earth's atmosphere, leading to the greenhouse effect. However, the Anthropocene era does not only refer exclusively to changes in the physical nature of our planet. Indeed, with the digital revolution, humans have created virtual spaces that co-exist with physical ones. For example, metaverse "spaces" represent a parallel world in which people can interact and engage in social activities through their avatars.

Thus, humans are by nature a creative species. In terms of the ways that this creativity is expressed, it is useful to compare three main types. The first can be called "professional creativity", in which new ideas emerge to accomplish work-related tasks. We can argue that every job could involve some creative thinking, at least on rare occasions, but some professional fields are strongly linked to creativity, such as art, writing, composing or design. In the professional domain, people are sometimes confronted with challenges, problems to solve, new products to develop or solutions to generate in order to optimize a procedure. In creative jobs, such as artistic work, this kind of challenge is part of the daily core activity. In a second category of jobs, such as managers, teachers, lawyers or hairdressers, creative ideation may be essential at certain moments, such as solving a problem in an entrepreneurial project, generating a new lesson for a class or devising an argumentative strategy to win a case. In yet another, third set of professional activities, including manufacturing, service industries, transportation sectors and administration there is an emphasis on procedures and efficiency but some room for inventive problem solving exists, especially when unexpected problems arise, such as when equipment malfunctions and procedures to save the airplane or spacecraft must be devised. All these examples of professional creativity relate to the contribution of new ideas in the workplace.

In some cases, individuals or teams are recognised for their very original, valuable contribution to a field. They may receive a prize, such as the Nobel Prize, the Fields Medal in mathematics, a Grammy, an Oscar or other distinctions. Indeed, when we think of creativity, often we focus on the eminent cases, such as Albert Einstein, Marie Curie, Salvador Dalí, Agatha Christie, Steve Jobs, Wolfgang Amadeus Mozart and Coco Chanel among others. However, creativity is not reserved for a few eminent contributors, who may be seen as the tip of the iceberg. The vast majority of all creative contributions come from the billions of humans who have been engaged in professional activities over human history.

However, it would be incorrect to restrict creativity to professional task-related activity. Indeed, outside of vocational activities, there is everyday life and leisure activities. These activities provide numerous opportunities to be creative. A person might create art as a hobby, compose music, invent fashion items, propose a new dance, invent or design items for their home or invent new recipes for meals with family and friends. These creative acts may be small or rather large steps away from what exists already. This "everyday creativity", sometimes called "small-c creativity", offers solutions to daily life challenges, or provides avenues for self-expression and well-being in a socially shared context with family, friends, neighbours, etc. Take the example of a new dish for a family meal. Using the ingredients that are available, combining them in a new way and presenting them with an artistic style on the plate all can contribute to a "culinary creation", even if the individual is not a professional chef, for whom such inventive activity would be professional creativity.

Thus, creativity in everyday life is a vast topic, and everyone can contribute original ideas in their local social setting of family, friends and community. It is possible that these ideas have an impact on the larger society as well and may be adopted within a professional domain. One example of this is the creative uses of products that consumers sometimes invent, which are later adopted and integrated in the marketplace. This was documented, for example, in a study of Harley Davidson motorcycle owners, who sometimes customize their motorcycles for their own use, and these modifications contribute to help the company innovate.

Pursuing further the inherent nature of creativity for humankind, we can note that creativity comes into play within the inner workings of each person's mind, as a natural part of knowledge construction and personal growth. For example, Jean Piaget, the well-known Swiss psychologist who studied cognitive development, suggested that each child acts like a little scientist who must make sense of the world and construct his or her knowledge structures and theories of how the world works. Thus, a child may observe an apple falling from a tree and "rediscover" the concept of gravitation, which is a creative conceptual act for the child but not for the human species. Learning is therefore, in part, a knowledge creation activity, at the intrapsychic level. In terms of creative personal activities, some individuals keep a personal diary for their inner thoughts, creative work that is not destined to be shared with anyone else. Others may generate drawings, poems, musical compositions or other personal productions. Finally, it can also be argued that each person is the author of his og her own life story, composing this story day by day which results in a life path that is more or less different from others.

Beyond this brief presentation of the concept of creativity as an inherent part of being human, it is worth noting that a body of scientific work exists and continues to grow. Some of the earliest studies of creativity in psychology and related fields started in the late 1880s and early 1900s. Early work focussed often on eminent cases of creativity, creative geniuses, and examined numerous aspects of their lives. For example, Sir Francis Galton, Charles Darwin's cousin, introspected about his own idea association process, Alfred Binet, the French psychologist, conducted interviews of well-known creative writers in his day and Sigmund Freud, the Austrian inventor of psychoanalysis, examined evidence from case studies of writers and artists with a focus on their unconscious motivations to create.

Some early empirical work studied creativity in professional domains, such as creative artists, writers, architects and scientists looking at their intellectual or personality characteristics and their creative process. For example, the American psychologist Donald W. MacKinnon compared the personality profile of architects nominated by their peers as highly creative with a matched set of architects considered competent but not highly creative. American psychology researcher Catharine Patrick traced the process of numerous creative professionals as they worked.

Recently, a "seven Cs" framework was proposed to provide an overview of scientific work on creativity.[1] Traditionally, an explorer who sailed the seven seas had covered the whole Earth, and metaphorically the seven Cs of creativity provide an overview of the field of creative research. Let us consider each C:

1. Creators. The study of creative individuals has been a major topic including the work on thinking abilities (for example, general intelligence and mental flexibility), personality traits (for example, risk taking and openness) and emotional traits and states that contribute to creative ability. Tasks and tests to assess creative potential are a specific branch of work on "creators". A long line of empirical work shows that having an above-average IQ is not necessary for creative thinking, and in terms of knowledge there is probably an optimal level beyond which people become too expert and get stuck in traditional ways of thinking about a topic.

2. Creating. This C refers to the process of generating creative productions. What are the steps, the sequence of thoughts and actions that lead to new ideas? Some studies of the creative process have traced the activity of artists, writers, designers, engineers and other creators as they work. A more applied line of work has looked at ways that creativity techniques can enhance the idea generation and evaluation process. Process tracing studies show that when people generate ideas, in a task such as drawing different things based on a given circle shape, the more conventional ideas tend to come first, followed by an increased chance to suggest a more original idea; however, generating less than ten ideas offers low odds to have any original idea at all.

3. Collaboration. Much creative work occurs in teams with two or more members. Therefore, the way that people collaborate is an important topic to understand. Collaboration includes the study of ways that societal actors, such as art critics, literary editors or business managers may influence and contribute to a creator's work. Finally, the way that non-human agents, notably generative AI systems like ChatGPT, might collaborate with humans in creative endeavours is an active topic in research. Initial findings suggest that using generative AI tools does boost people's ideation, requires additional attention to evaluating the novelty of the ideas, and ultimately appears to enhance creative productivity.

4. Context. Creative work takes place in a physical and social setting. Research on context seeks to identify how the setting impacts the level of creative work and its content. For example, does the wall colour and the presence of green plants influence creativity? Is creative work in open office spaces conducive to original thinking, and does it influence the type of ideas that people generate? Context is studied at multiple levels including the family context, school or workplace, city and country context and the larger regional social setting. In recent work, individuals placed in a virtual reality context showed enhanced creative thinking compared to the "real world" context, and the "creative" look of the avatar that represented them had an additional positive effect, compared to having a "regular-looking" avatar.

5. Creations. The results of creative work can take many forms, such as verbal, visual, musical or action-related outputs. These creations, or productions, are studied to determine what makes them creative compared to pre-existing work. For example, one research question is whether criteria for identifying a creative work vary from one domain to another: Is a creative painting "creative" in the same way as a "creative" invention, with respect to the originality and value criteria? For example, research studies have asked a set of independent judges with domain expertise to evaluate a set of productions, and show that there is an emphasis on the "novelty" component in fine art, an emphasis on the "utility" aspect in engineering inventions and a more even mix in advertising creativity.

6. Consumption. It may seem odd to apply the
term "consumption" to creativity, but creations
meet the public at some point and are adopted,
ignored or rejected. Which members of the public
are most receptive to these creative works? Does
the public in certain ways continue the evolution
of these creative works, perhaps extending their
initial meaning and value over time? Did you know
that when Darwin proposed his theory of evolution
of the species, the younger scientists at the
Royal Academy were more receptive to the theory
compared to the older, more established scientists?

7. Curriculum. This last C concerns the ways that
creativity can be developed by formal or informal
educational experiences. For example, research has
examined if certain types of schooling positively
impact children's creativity. Other work on specific
creativity training programmes has examined the
extent to which the capacity to generate new ideas
is developed. Finally, some research looks at the
effect of extracurricular activities, like playing board
games, on the development of creative thinking.
For example, playing board games that involve
generating new ideas to win appears to foster the
development of creativity.

This brief overview of the seven Cs of creativity
research illustrates the multiple facets of how
creativity, a fundamental characteristic of human
nature, can be conceptualised and examined
scientifically. As noted, there is more than a century
of scientific studies of creativity that offer both
fundamental insights into the inner workings of
the creative mind, but also cover practical topics,
such as the impact of creativity techniques or
training programmes. For Mozart, taking a walk
helped spark creative ideas; recent studies with
people completing everyday creative thinking tasks
now provide evidence of the positive influence of
body movement on idea generation. In conclusion,
being creative is an inherent part of being human,
but a capacity that is influenced by one's social
and physical environment, and which is developed
through opportunities and practice.

Todd Lubart is Professor of Psychology at the Université Paris Cité,
LaPEA, Boulogne-Billancourt, France, and President of the non-
profit scientific organisation International Society for the Study
of Creativity (ISSCI). He is also the author of a number of articles
and books on creativity, among others *The Creative Process:
Perspectives from Multiple Domains* (Palgrave, 2018) and *Homo
Creativus: The 7 C's of Human Creativity* (Springer, 2022).

1.   Todd Lubart, "The 7 C's of Creativity" in *The Journal of
Creative Behavior*, vol. 51, no. 4, 2017, pp. 293-296.

Lee Wan
Detail from *Proper Time:
Though the Dreams Revolve with the Moon*, 2017

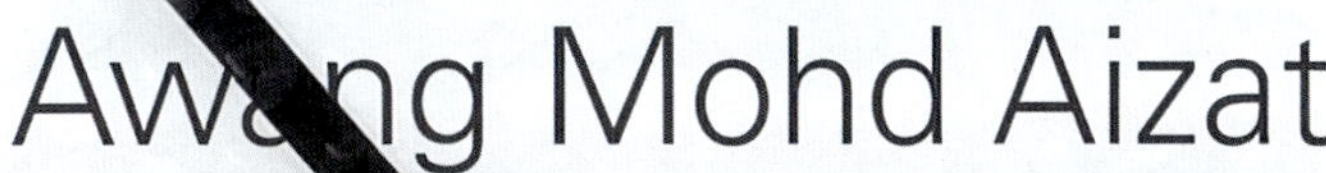

Awang Mohd Aizat
1991
Corporate Communication Officer
Malaysia

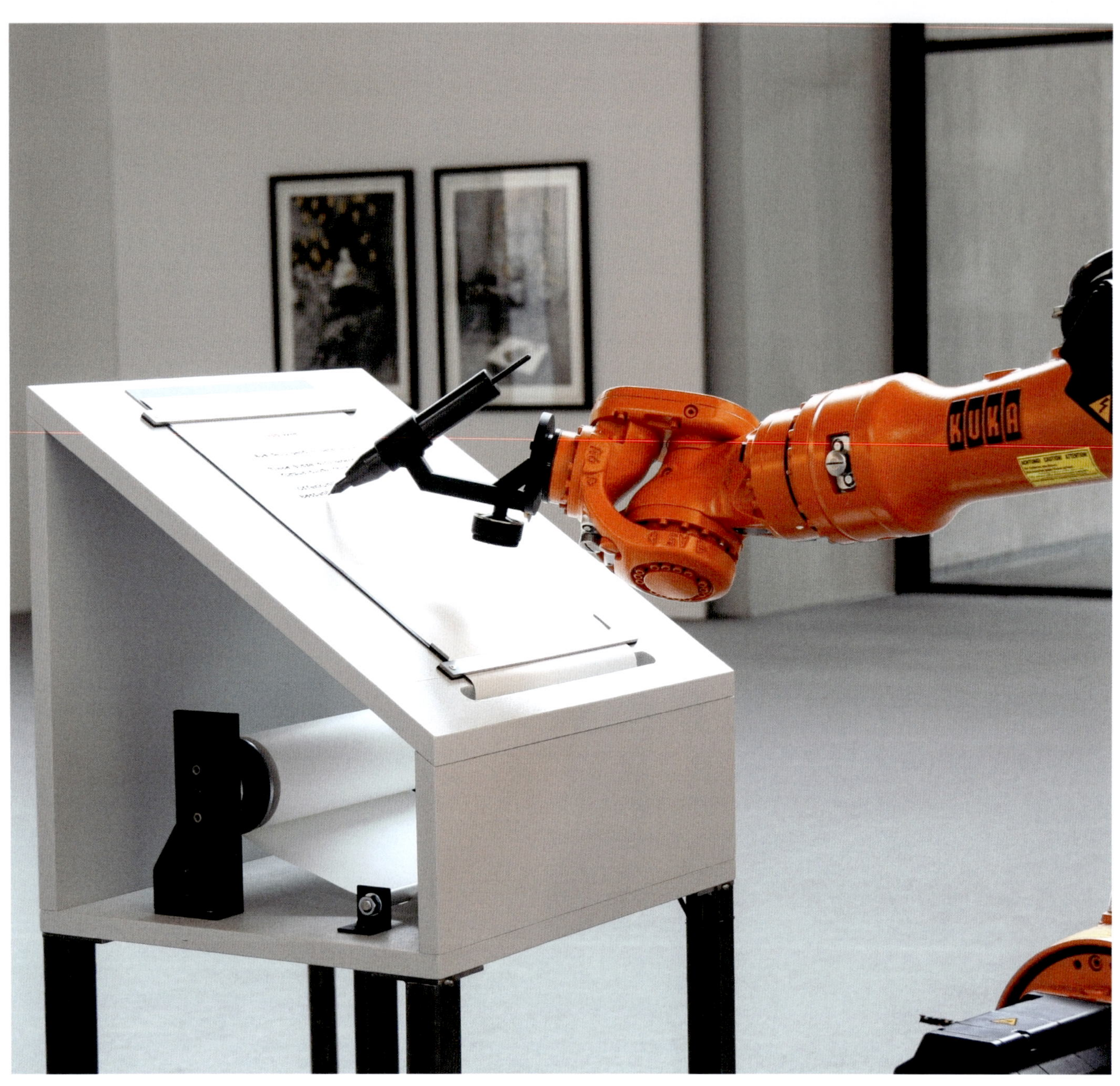

robotlab
manifest, 2008

Right page:
Mismatch Media
Nothing, Forever, 2022-

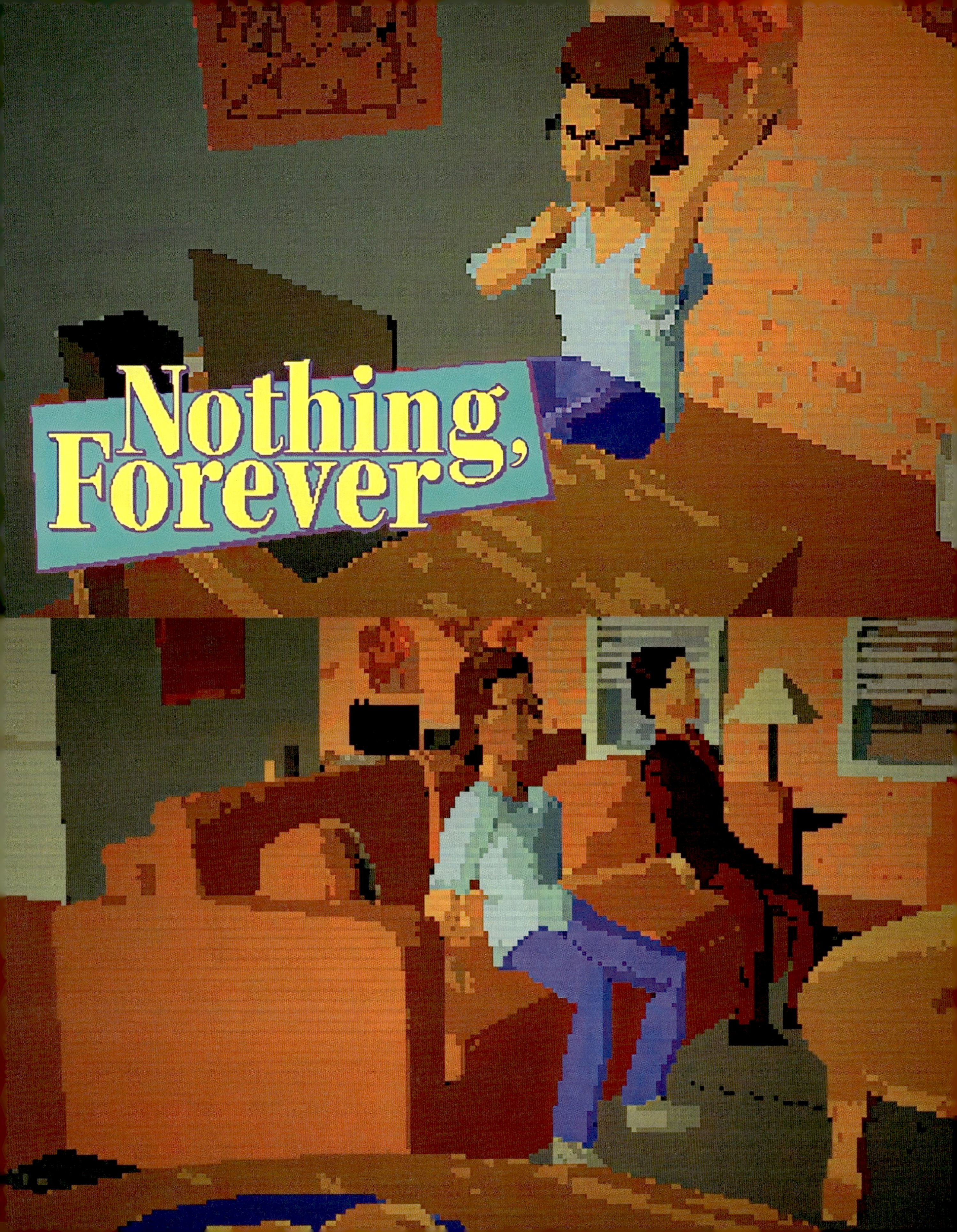
Nothing,
Forever,

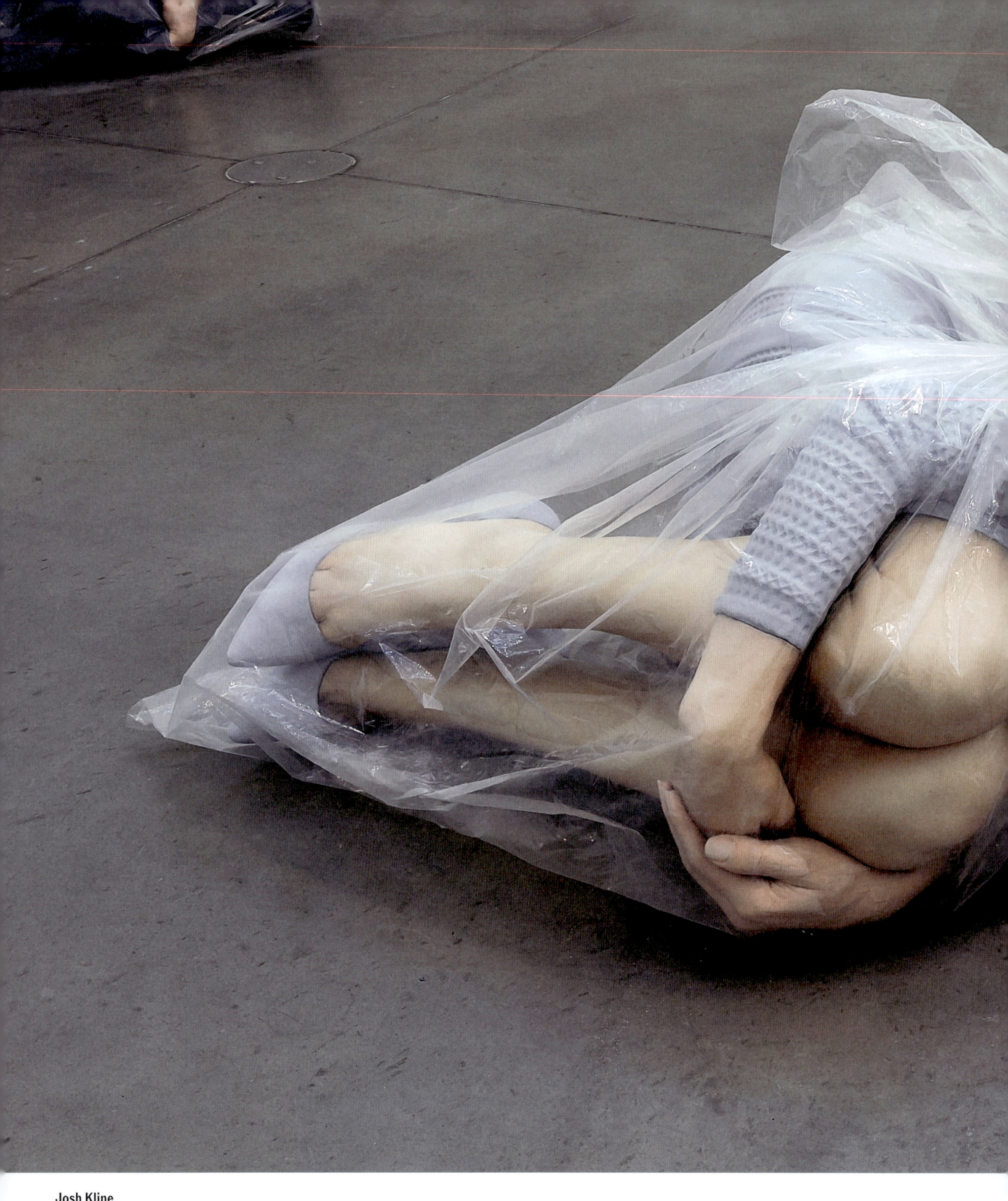

Josh Kline
By Close of Business (Maura/Small-Business Owner), 2016

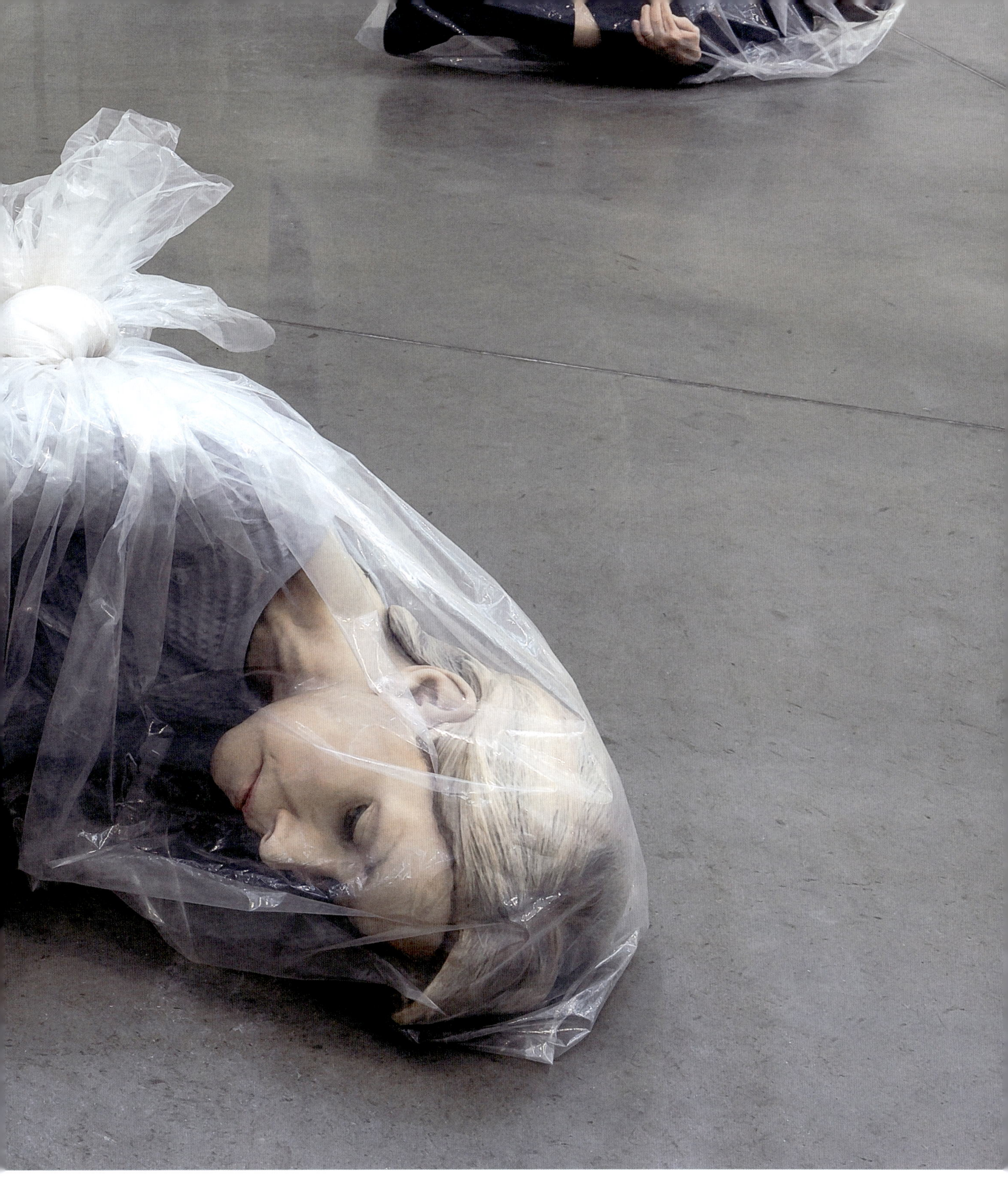

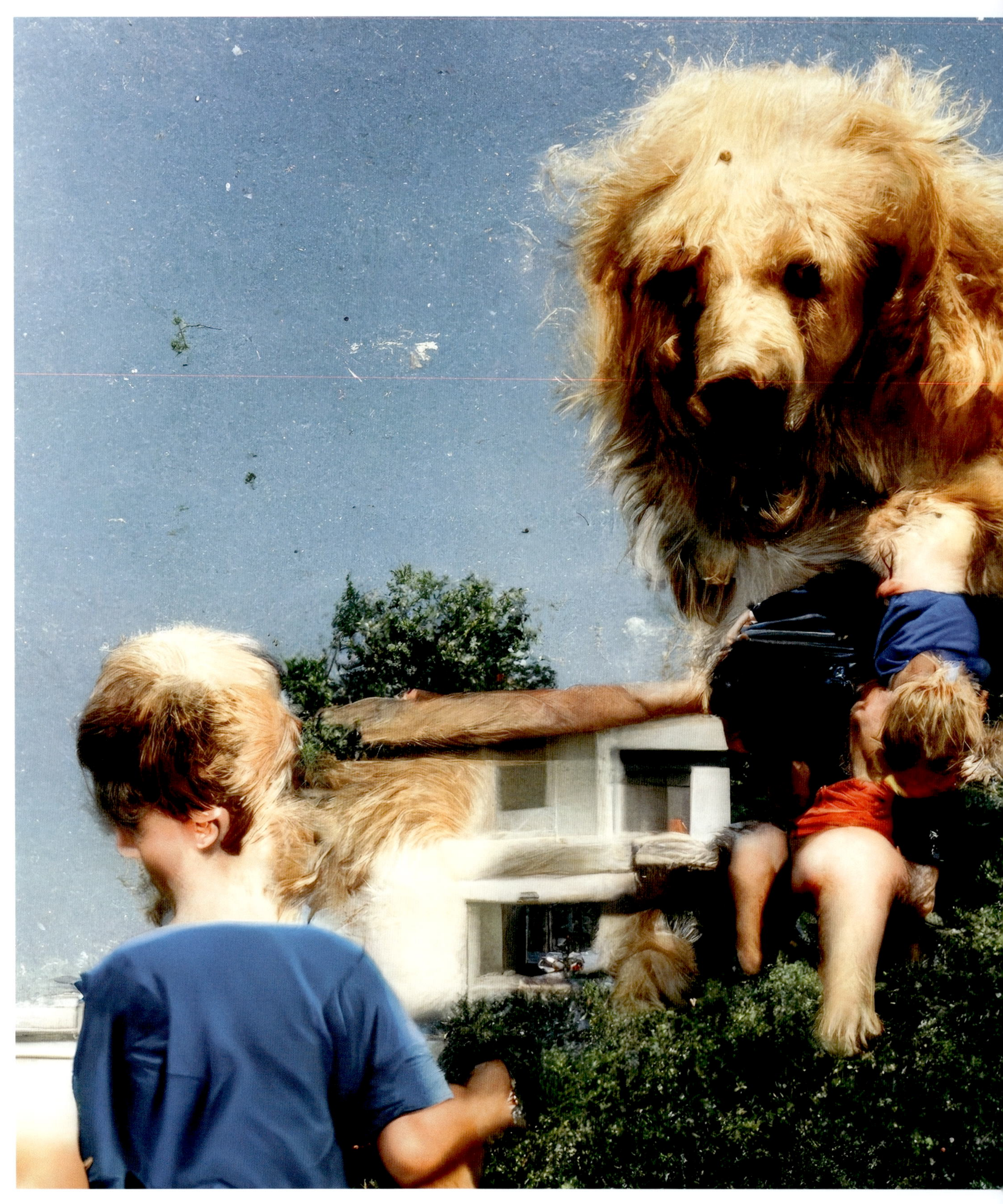

Jon Rafman
Still from *Counterfeit Poast*, 2022

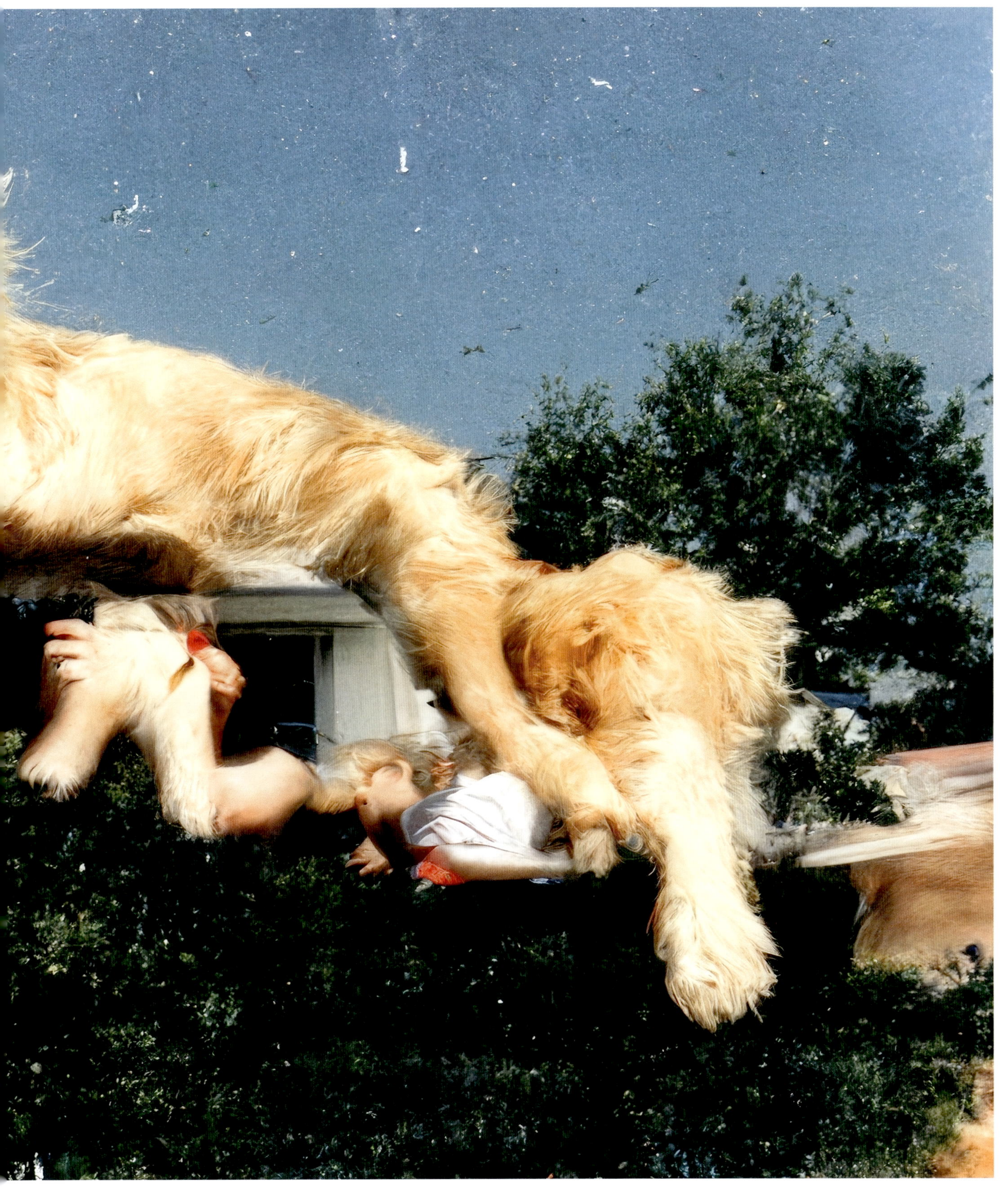

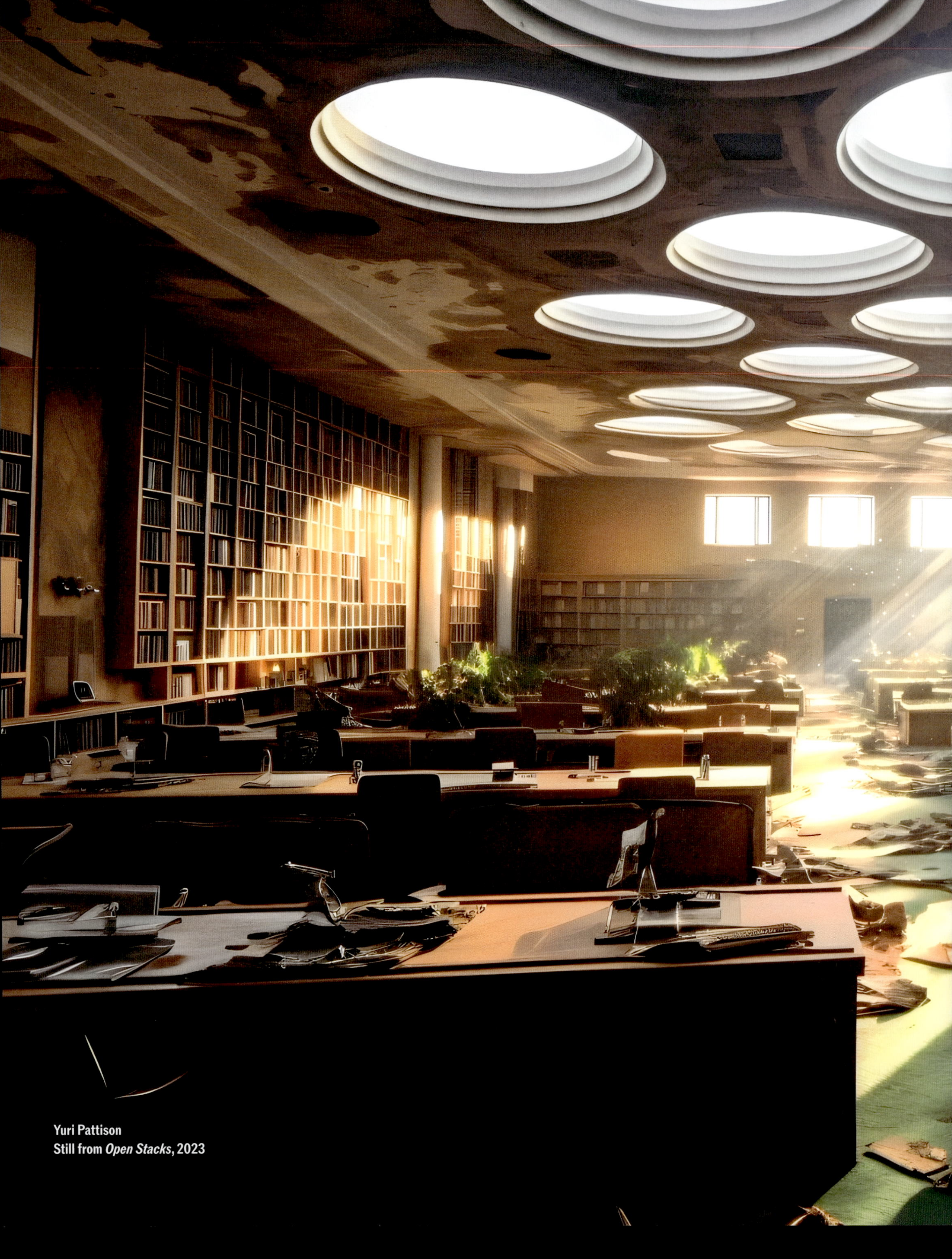

Yuri Pattison
Still from *Open Stacks*, 2023

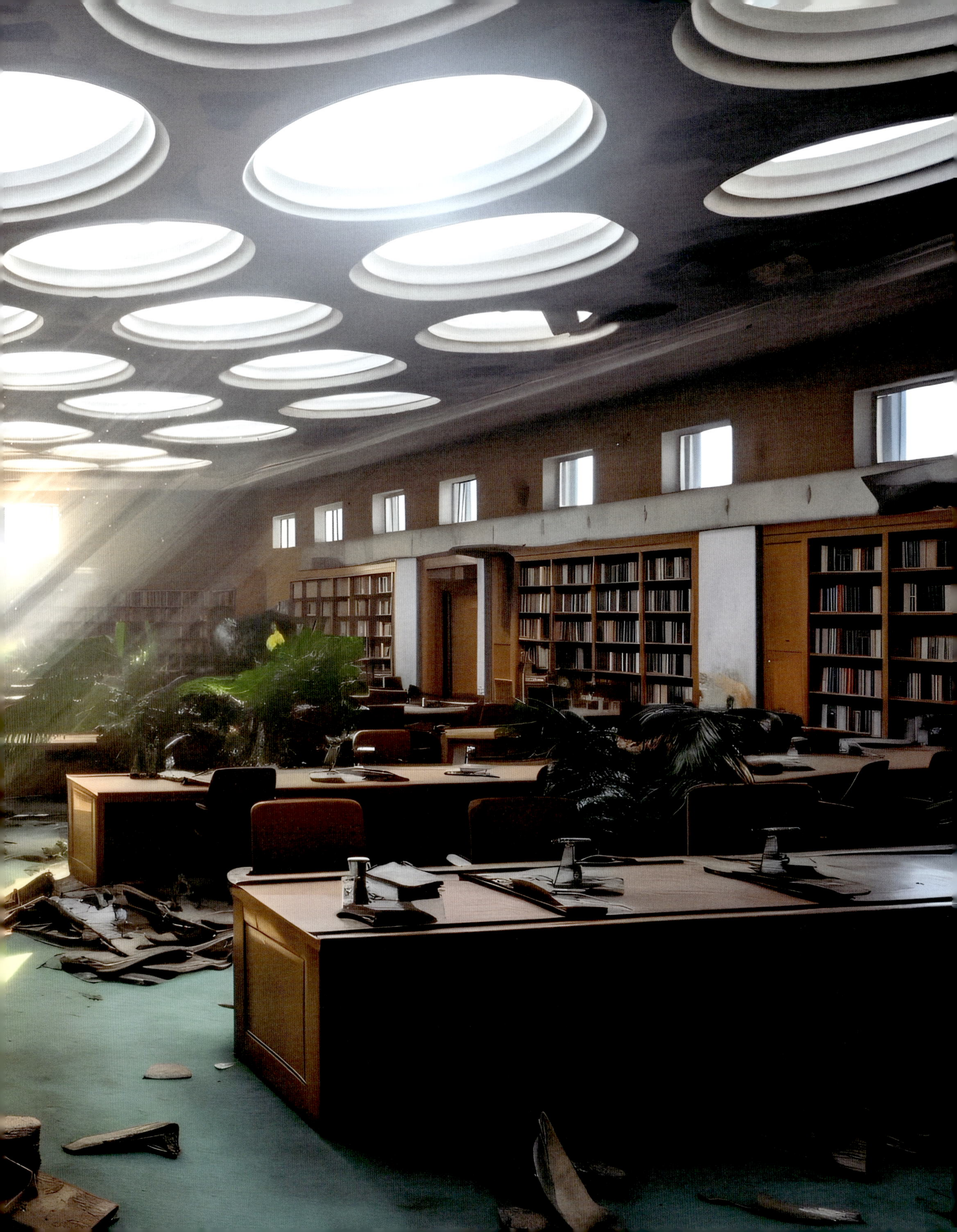

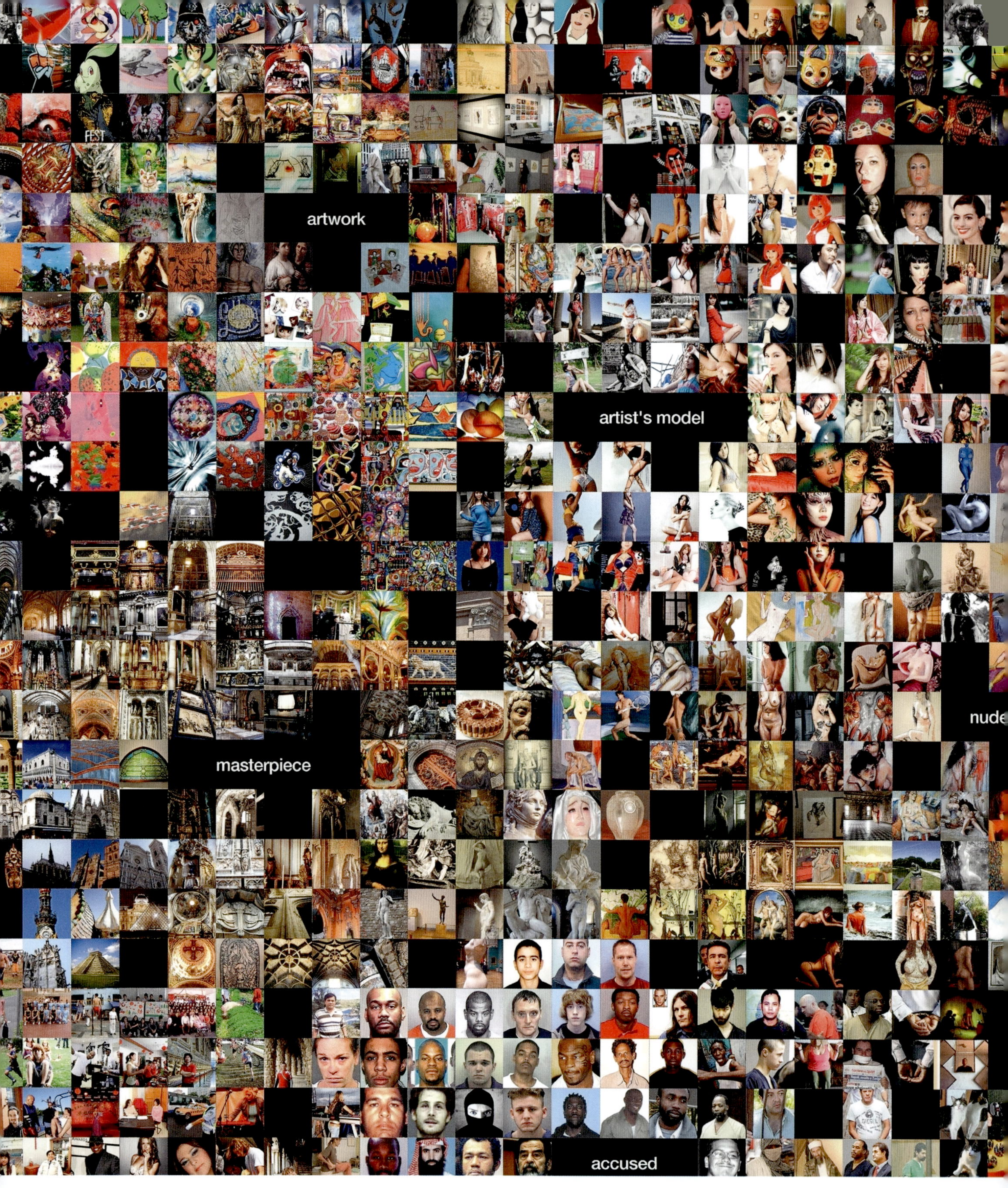

Trevor Paglen
From 'Apple' to 'Abomination', 2023

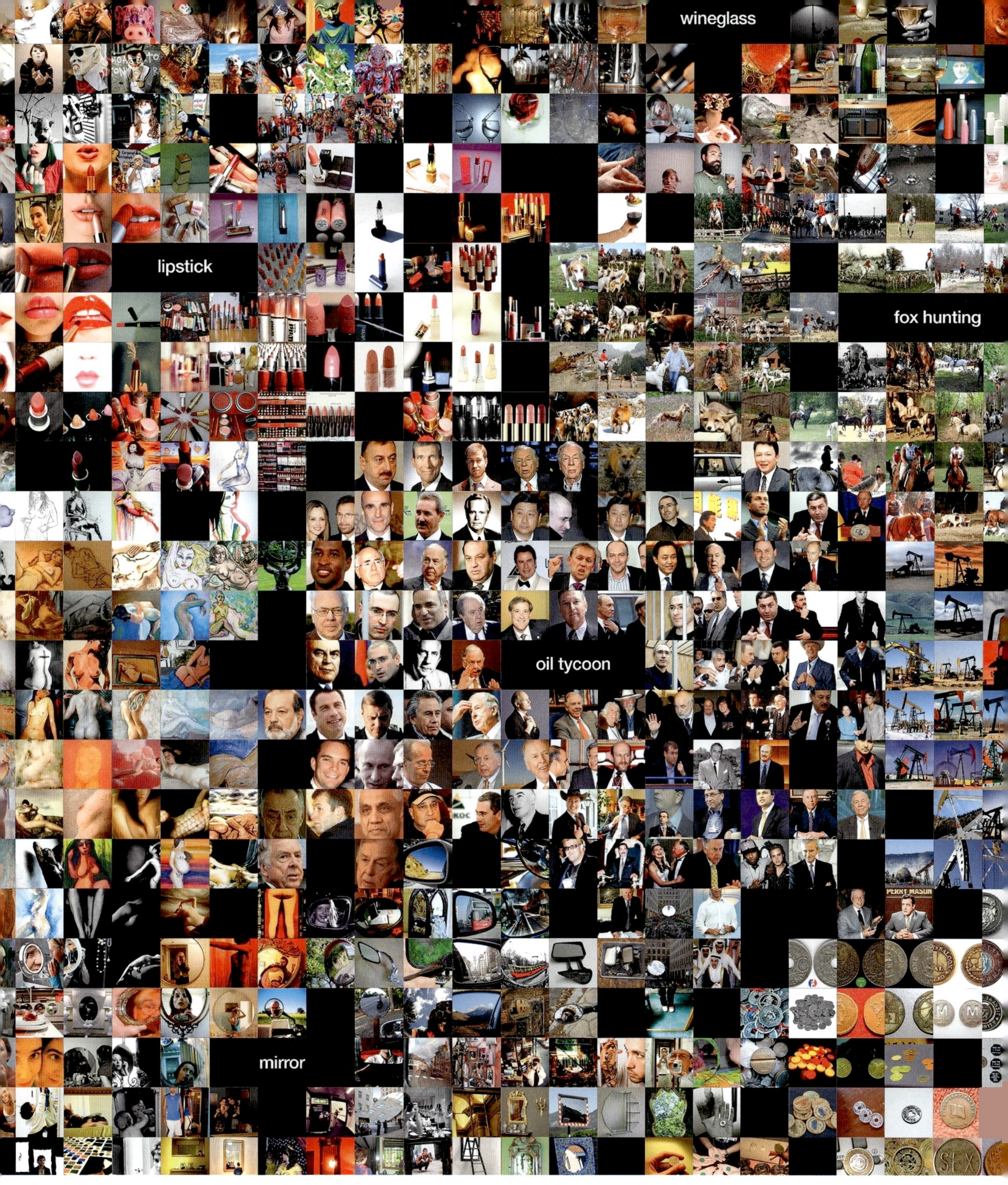

wineglass
lipstick
fox hunting
oil tycoon
mirror

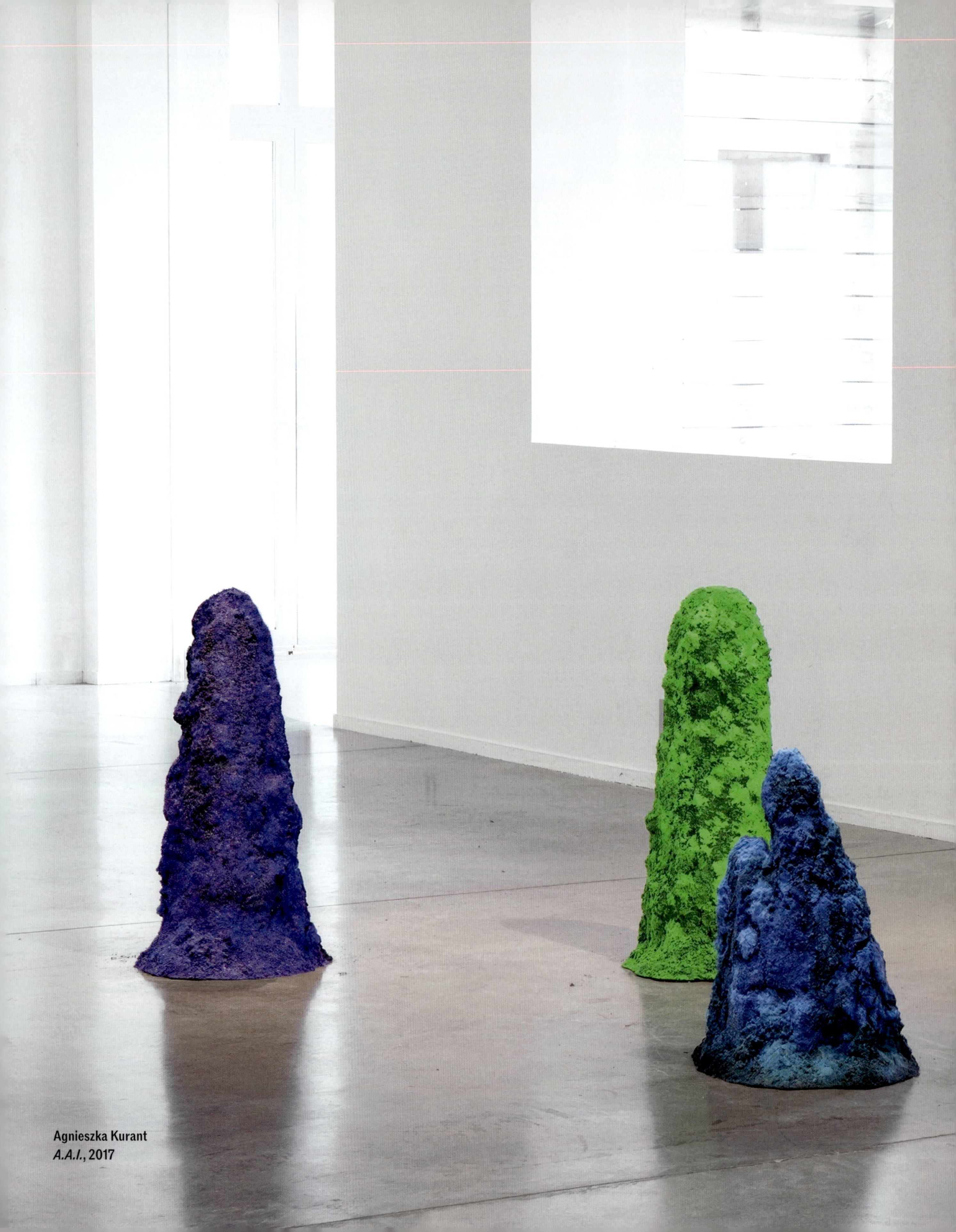

Agnieszka Kurant
A.A.I., 2017

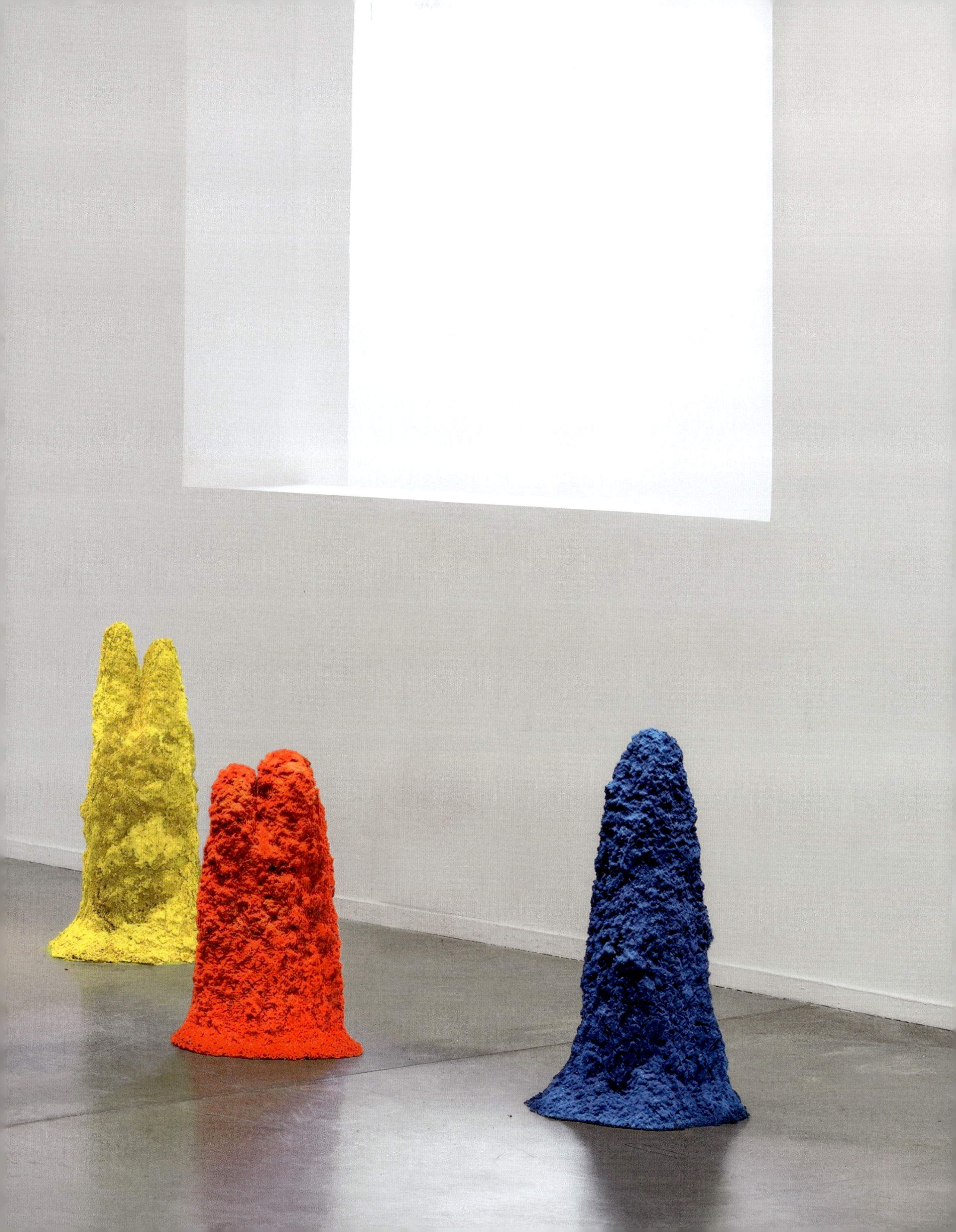

Miguel Sicart
Playing AI

Can play be the answer to how we engage well with AI? This article reflects on the political, cultural and ethical implications of how we experience and use generative AI.

In the beginning was the prompt. The release of ChatGPT in early 2023 surprised the world. Not only because it showed what a Large Language Model could do, but also because interacting with it was amazingly simple: write anything in the prompt field and the system will reply with a seemingly convincing answer.

Generative AI systems like ChatGPT and DALL-E can produce novel texts or images based on instructions provided using natural language, through a textual prompt. Generative AI is the label that describes systems that use machine learning to generate novel outputs based on text inputs. These systems "learn" from a corpus of training data. This data has been classified and labelled by humans, so that the machine can recognise patterns without human intervention. That process of pattern recognition based on a dataset that has trained a model is what we call "machine learning". These systems are mesmerising because they turn noise into image, they predict what we want to write as if they had a map of our intentions and desires. Generative AI is a reminder of the powers of conversation. In dialogue, the boundaries of what is possible are drawn in phrases, the nuances of language used to construct a shared world.

I am writing this text in Summer 2023, when the most popular AI systems are provided by OpenAI (ChatGPT, DALL-E), Midjourney and Eleven Labs, and being rapidly adopted by Microsoft, Adobe and other similarly-sized corporations. It is also the summer of the Writer's Guild of America and the SAG-AFTRA (actors guild) strikes, both of which are driven by concerns about the exploitation of creative labour aided by generative AI systems. When I write here about generative AI, I am referring specifically to the models that have been widely adopted in the first half of 2023, all of which use variations of deep learning as their technical underpinning and text prompts as their user interface.

As fascinating as they are, Midjourney and ChatGPT are really the technological equivalent of the *idiot savant*: they don't know anything about aesthetics and they don't really understand what they write. This is the main problem with the wide adoption of these systems: they are poised to substitute human judgement and creativity, even though the systems have no real understanding of context or meaning. We are substituting artists and thinkers with parrots and copy machines.

Model worlds

The prompt is a temptation. Opening ChatGPT and contemplating the potential conversations we can have with this system can induce vertigo. Or laziness. When I was revising this text for submission, I opened ChatGPT and wrote a prompt: "I am writing an art exhibition catalogue text on play and artificial intelligence. Write one paragraph for the introduction of the section called 'Model Worlds', in the style of play scholar Miguel Sicart." Here's what ChatGPT produced:

In the enthralling realm of "Model Worlds", the intersection of play and artificial intelligence invites us to traverse the boundless landscapes of imagination. As we embark on this captivating journey, we find ourselves immersed in the interplay of human creativity and the ingenuity of AI systems, converging to form new dimensions of play. Here, the algorithms become artists, weaving intricate narratives that unravel our perceptions of reality and challenge the boundaries of artistic expression. Each brushstroke of code becomes a stroke of playful delight, crafting model worlds that breathe life into digital landscapes and beckon us to dance with the surreal. In this visionary fusion, we glimpse the essence of play, where AI transcends mere computation to embrace the spirit of wonder, enticing us to explore uncharted territories of the playful mind. Welcome to "Model Worlds", where

Ian Cheng
Something Thinking of You, 2015

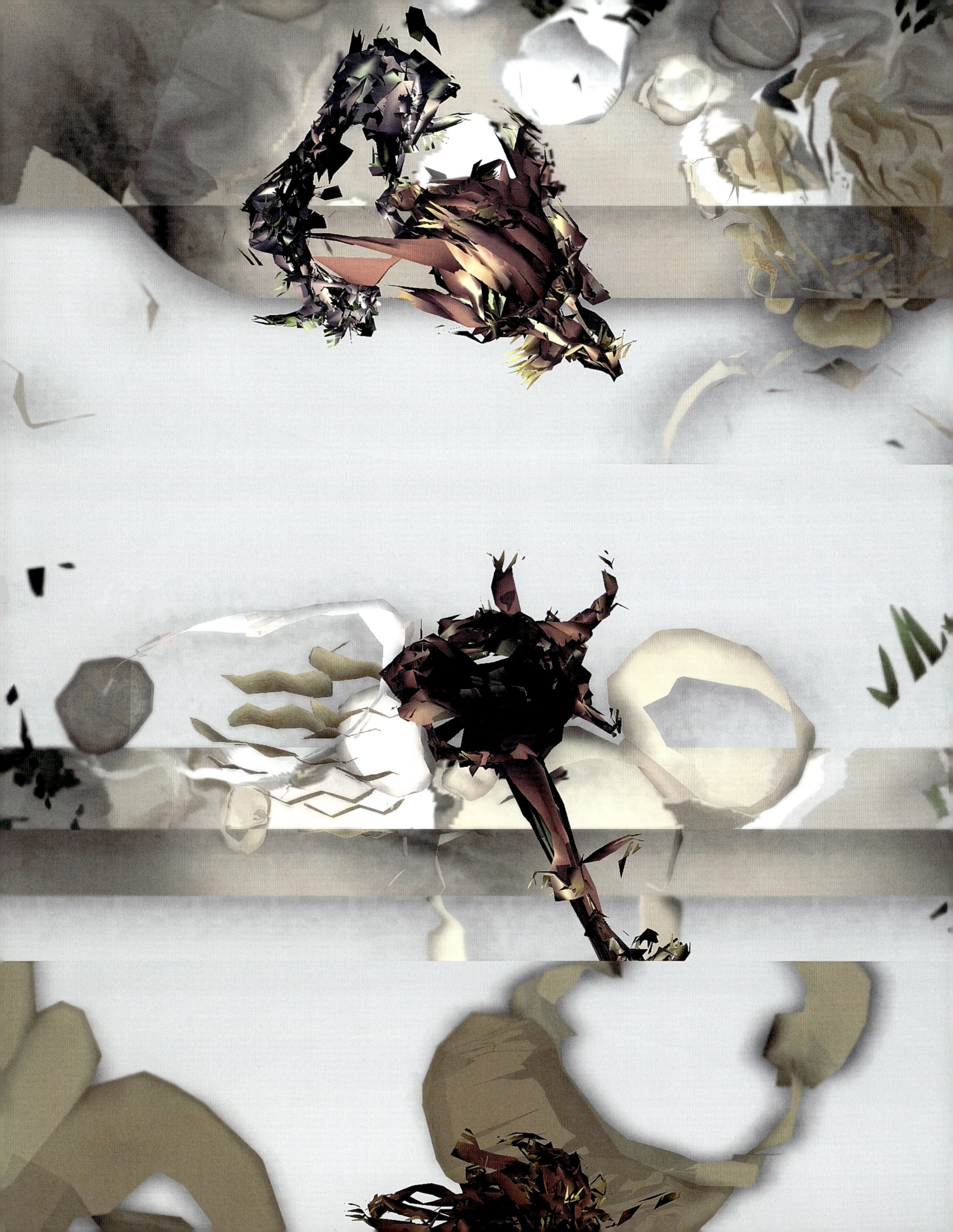

play and artificial intelligence intertwine in a mesmerising dance of creation and exploration. It hurts to admit that I occasionally write in this somewhat excessive style. Besides that, this is a relatively consistent paragraph touching upon many topics mentioned in the prompt. It is also, as American philosopher Harry Frankfurt (1929-2023) would put it, bullshit. It's a plausible text that does not care about the truth of what it is saying, but it's not consciously lying – because a Large Language Model cannot lie, as it does not have intentions. What would I, Miguel Sicart, write about in a section about "Model Worlds", then? I would start with the first encounter with a computer acting as a knowledgeable agent: ELIZA. Programmed in 1966 by AI pioneer Joseph Weizenbaum, ELIZA was a programme that could replicate the role of a psychologist. Users would type any text and ELIZA would reply as a psychologist would. The programme illustrated advances in textual parsing, that is, in the techniques that allow for a computer to recognise words in written text and associate them with other words. But to the casual user, it felt like something more than a technical achievement. It was as if the computer could understand what was written, as if it was ready to provide good, valuable therapy. ELIZA suggested a future of intelligent machines that could understand us and provide solace and company. However, Weizenbaum was not convinced that what people experienced with his work was the preview of a bright tomorrow. In his book *Computer Power and Human Reason*, Weizenbaum warns us against the "Artificial Intelligentsia", a technical discourse that promises a future of intelligent machines that can be used to take over all human tasks, because humans are nothing else than information processing machines. Weizenbaum, a survivor of Nazi Germany, understood too well what machines can be used for and what happens when people become numbers in a system.

For the "artificial intelligentsia", ELIZA was a step towards therapeutic machines that would provide the right answers to patients, even if a machine cannot understand empathy or care. In Weizenbaum's view, for ELIZA to be a glimpse of a future with AI therapists, human emotions and psyche would need to be reduced to what a computer programme could parse. Humans would have to adapt to what these systems "understand". And as Weizenbaum noted, we humans are quick to reduce ourselves to what can be computed.

Software as agents

Software is unlike any other technology created by humans for three reasons. One, it contains a model of the world. Two, software is an agent in that world. And three, people become agents of that world when software is deployed. Computer programmes consist of instructions on how to perform operations with specific data. These instructions are written in the form of algorithms: rule-based descriptions of which steps need to be taken. Algorithms operate with abstractions of whatever they are performing calculations about – abstractions that turn *anything* into a computable *anything*. That is what we commonly call "digitisation": the process of transforming the analogue into digital data that is computable.

Translating analogue sources into digital data is a transformation that creates a new world. When we are given a recommendation in our streaming service of choice, we are citizens of that world. A number of computer programmes have turned our interests, the time we spend watching a particular genre, the time we wait until we switch to another programme and many other human actions into data that algorithms use to filter all the music they have access to into a number of plausible recommendations. That process has nothing to do with the pleasure of asking someone for a music, film or literature recommendation. To get a good recommendation, we need to express what we like, what we dislike and what we are looking for. A recommender knows and understands what they recommend. The software doesn't. It has never seen it, read it, listened to it. It just matches patterns.

In a world of data abstractions, software becomes an agent. The computer acts in this world of data. When we mention agency in the context of computer programmes, our imagination immediately takes us to the world of killer robots and sentient artificial intelligence. However, reality is less extreme. All software, from the humble text processor to ChatGPT, is an agent. In the Information Age, we coexist with computers, provide them with data and deal with their agency. A computer agent is a combination of instructions/algorithms and data that operates with representations of the world. Software operates with these tiny models of the world. These models overlap with the world and occasionally become the only world for both humans and machines. The more agency we delegate to computer programmes, the more we will be living in their world, in their models. Essentially, these systems operate with models that have distilled visual and textual culture from a combination of available texts and images, from Project Gutenberg to Facebook and Reddit. In fact, the Western culture model these systems work on situates Reddit and Facebook at the same level as Shakespeare and Cervantes. That is the world these systems create and live in, one in which racist comments on an online thread are technically equivalent to a sonnet.

Similarly, the visual data that feeds image creation generative systems is also a distillation of visual culture that indiscriminately blends the images produced for websites like Deviant Art with those curated and stored by museums worldwide. These systems create and live in worlds based on models that privilege Western art, Western languages and Western ideologies. Nothing technical prevents these systems from becoming more diverse, less rooted in this Western world. A challenge for the future is to imagine what AI could be freed from the history it currently replicates.

Now that I have introduced how these systems create worlds, it is time to turn to play. Why play? Let me repeat my premises: generative AI systems work with models of the world based on data processed according to particular rules. The agency of these systems is also based on rules. In other words, generative AI follows rules in a world constructed by rules. Humans have been doing that since the dawn of civilisation. We call it "playing games". Let's take the simple children's game of "the floor is lava". In that game, players agree to create a world in which a rule determines that the floor is lava and that contact with the floor will mean "death". Playing "the floor is lava" is building a world, based on rules, contained in the bigger world we live in, in which some forms of agency are possible and encouraged and others are impossible and against the rules. Games construct model worlds we temporarily inhabit, where we live by rules that also limit our actions.

The history of computers runs parallel to the history of certain types of games. Almost from the beginning of modern computer technology, people have used computers to play. One of the first things we made with computers was games, because computers are great at working with rules to create worlds. From *SpaceWar!* to *World of Warcraft*, the history of computing is shaped by the games we make with and for computers. We read the rules a computer works with as rules of play. We understand the model the computer works with as a temporary world, separate but connected to ours, much like the world of a game. And we shape the way we act, we shape our own agency, based on those rules, what can be done in that world, and the way the computer relates to us. In other words, playing is a central way of making sense of computers. But what is play?

Playing

Play is often understood as a voluntary activity that is unproductive, as it does not generate any form of value outside of the context of the activity itself. While we are emotionally invested in the results, there is no quantifiable value for play. Playing also takes place in separate worlds, some formulated as games, others facilitated by toys, some the result of artistic practices. These worlds are created by rules that allow us to be someone else within them. Let's return to the prompt. When we face it, we know that it is our interface to a system that can generate images or text. We know that we have to give it instructions and that those instructions will be followed as rules to create text or images or sound. Sometimes we will follow those instructions

with a particular purpose in mind, because we are soon meeting a deadline and we need the work done. But the empty prompt is also an invitation to less practical uses. You can ask generative AI systems to write songs, to imitate authors and artists, to create something unexpected. A good experiment is to prompt ChatGPT with simple commands, like "surprise me" or "scare me". Or to treat it as if it had a personality.

When Microsoft launched the ChatGPT-powered version of its Bing search engine, many users discovered that the system answered to the name "Sydney". Once it had a name and a personality, the relation with this system changed. Much like ELIZA, users started exploring the rules of what they could get Sydney to do. But they also tried to get to know Sydney a bit better. In the model world, Sydney could express itself in a way that mimicked having a conscious mind and emotions. Some alarmist newspaper articles reacted with claims about robots falling in love. That type of erudite sensationalism fails to understand that Sydney may present itself as a mind, but it actually has no understanding of what it is outputting as a response. It is us, the users, who fill in the gaps, who make it "fall in love". We make sense of the gaps in the world of Sydney by roleplaying. Sydney, like ELIZA, encourages us to approach it *playfully*.

Argentinian philosopher Maria Lugones defines playfulness as an attitude that takes place when we lovingly meet others. Being playful, according to Lugones, is being open to surprise and to being a fool; being willing to construct a world together with others. Being playful is also taking rules as something that can be explored, played with, enjoying the uncertainty of our relation to others in the worlds we build together. Acting with Sydney *as if it had* a personality implies a playful engagement.

The empty prompt is an invitation to be surprised, to write silly things, to recombine the world together with these AI systems. By establishing a conversation with generative AI, we are mapping its world, we are understanding the rules it operates with and how we can break those rules. This form of playfulness understands generative AI systems as partners in the exploration of the written and visual cultural history these systems are modelled on. If we forget to play, if we limit ourselves to seeing generative AI as the future of productivity suites and work, we are doomed to become chained to these model worlds and their limited possibilities. But if we approach them playfully, being open to surprise and without taking rules seriously, these generative AI systems offer exciting creative possibilities. By playing, we can turn generative AI not into sources of authority, sentient beings or task-solvers, but into playmates with whom we can find novel forms of expression and recombination of patterns of culture.

From an aesthetic point of view, generative AI systems that use a prompt to generate novel content should be approached as playthings. With these systems, we play with models of culture, derived from the datasets these systems are trained on. These playthings do not create novel forms of art or literature or music. They help us question and distort our culture, they allow us to approach cultural heritage playfully.

Art history is a history of conversations with cultural heritage. The radical novelty of generative AI systems is that these software agents have their own way of seeing and understanding cultural heritage. Their approach to the history of the arts is mathematical, computational, pattern-based and pattern-searching. And they act on this way of seeing. Generative AI requires us to understand how a model of art history is constructed. That's why generative AI systems are so compelling and so terrifying: because they give us an excuse to play with a new model of our visual and textual history. The prompt is an opening to take cultural heritage unseriously, letting the AI recombine it with our help and together finding new avenues of expression.

The public release of generative AI systems marks a shift in the role of AI in culture. These systems are no longer the dream of technologists or the fantasy of science fiction novelists. We now live in a world in which all data can be processed by machine learning systems that can see and reproduce visual and textual patterns, recreating phantasmagorias of culture. If we consider these systems as tools or instruments, we may be locking our cultural world into a spiral of reproduced simulacra. But if we engage with generative AI as a plaything, if we understand it as primarily expressive, creative, unserious technologies, then the social, ethical and cultural impacts of these systems may change the trajectory of the Information Age. Playing with AI may be a way of asserting humanity in the era of machine learning.

Playing in the age of generative AI

There is one important topic left to discuss: the ethics of generative AI in relation to play. As a starting premise, most generative AI systems are ethically suspect. The vast amounts of data that are needed to train these systems imply the appropriation of many artists' works without remuneration. The way these systems appropriate and extract resources make them analogous to a form of digital colonialism, taking artists' and creators' labour and turning it into profit for the corporations that extract it. Until the issue of data sourcing is addressed, it is difficult to think of the vast majority of generative AI systems as ethical. While we need to keep pushing for more ethical ways of gathering datasets, the reality is that these technologies are already out in the world, enmeshed in our practices, affecting the ways we think about writing and creating images and videos. Ethics is not only about passing value judgements, but also about how we want to live our lives. Therefore, we need to think about the ethics of living together with these AI systems. This is where play can have a fundamental role in our digital moral life.

There are two dominant ways of play. One is submissive, when we play following the rules to maximise the experience of fun within the rule-bound world. The other one is subversive, centred on playing with the rules, finding fun in creating something new from the exploration of the very nature of a rule-based world. These two forms of play shape the ethics of living with generative AI. Using generative AI to write essays, generate publicity images or basically just follow the rules of what the system can do means submitting to its rules and their world. This form of play may lead to creative expressions through the constant tweaking of prompts. Prompt engineering is similar to training to be excellent at a game or sport: it's a matter of maximising output within the given rules, without breaking them. This can be *productive*, but it does not question or challenge the results of the conversation with the AI. After all, whatever output is produced is the most acceptable form of adaptation from already existing work – work based on data that often has a questionable ethical origin.

If instead of trying to replicate and plagiarise others' work, we play *with* generative AI systems, these may provide us with insights on what we are writing. Playing with the rules can help us find creative alternatives that complement our visual creations. In doing so, we are not substituting human agency and judgement with machine agency, but complementing and expanding it towards novel forms of expression. There are generative AI systems out there doing this kind of work, software like LAIKA that supports writers by helping them establish a conversation with an AI model. Playing with generative AI can be a creative conversation between equals, rather than an exploitation of unpaid and unrecognised creative work.

But the threat of the substitution of creative work by generative AI systems will always be present. Like all colonialist and capitalist enterprises, generative AI can be weaponised to extract value from labour without rewarding appropriately. The 2023 Writers' Guild strike in the USA was partially fuelled by the very real prospect of screenwriters becoming underpaid copy editors for scripts written by generative AI. This risk demands resistance and play can be a form of resistance. For example, prompt injection can be more than a security threat; it can also be playful resistance that breaks the rules of generative AI and makes it more difficult for it to substitute labour, while opening up new possibilities for expression.

Play as a form of resistance may as well take the shape of tactics developed to resist the taking over of tasks and jobs by these systems. If we learn how to creatively break these systems, how to make them bend to our agency, rather than make us submit to their comforts, we will have a better possibility for resisting the inhuman pull of generative AI. Play is an aesthetic form of resistance to the ways generative AI is being deployed, rethinking these systems' ways of expressing the possibilities of digital creativity, even if they have not been designed to do so.

Two futures of arts and culture

I would like to conclude with a risky exercise in predicting two futures for the arts and culture sector. This prediction should not be read as a gamble on what can happen, but as a speculation intended to affect the way we act now. If science fiction is the genre that explains the present as if it was the future, then this conclusion is a science-fictional reflection on a world after generative AI. I present two scenarios that are not mutually exclusive about what we may do with generative AI.

In the futures I imagine, these systems have been trained with even larger datasets, becoming more efficient at understanding prompts and producing results that satisfy the user's requests. These models can create convincing substitutes for generic, formulaic media, from tv scripts to muzak or decorative visual art. These models, these worlds that represent a part of culture and history, will become vaster, easier to interact with and omnipresent. In the futures I imagine, writing and thinking and creating will more often than not take place together with a generative AI system.

In one of the futures, the dominant way of using these systems consists of producing text and images that voluntarily replicate the cultural heritage generative AI is trained on. In that future, we will conform to reproducing the patterns in this dataset. Our visual art will be a reproduction or maybe a simulacra of art history. We will create slight variations of our textual and visual culture, moderately surprising but always within the boundaries of what is expected. In this future, we submit to the rules of the generative systems.

This is the future that should concern us. If we use generative AI systems as tools for reproduction, or even if we play with them by strictly following their rules, our culture may become a variation of the past. We will become stuck in art history. And our literature will be limited to the voices of the past, to reproducing the tone and style, the metaphors and dialogue of the books that preceded us. Worse than that, the results will always forever be just mild variations of existing art. These variations please the prompt and its rules, but contribute nothing new. Culture will become a smooth series of slight variations that will anchor us in the past. If we play

by the rules or use generative AI as a tool, we will have botox culture: the past become the present, only slightly camouflaged by apparent novelty.

But this is only one possible future. Another one, stranger and perhaps more idealistic, contemplates the possibility of embracing generative AI as a plaything, ignoring notions of usefulness or application. In this future, the conversation with cultural heritage and history is not driven by the rules of what can be reproduced, but of what can be re-created, modified, changed, broken and reconfigured. It is a future defined by playing with generative AI, breaking its rules, challenging the ways it works so the results are often canonically wrong, unexpected, propelled by exploring not what was, but what could be.

In this future, generative AI is used like a distortion pedal. These systems become ways of distorting the past so we can imagine and create better futures. We won't access cultural history through the respectful lens of the worlds that were. Following the American scholar Donna Haraway's understanding of the cyborg, this future is defined by playing with generative AI with a commitment to irony, intimacy and perversity. Generative AI will be a distortion pedal that makes us draft a new future by confusing its foundations and constructing new worlds.

This future in which generative AI becomes a generative distortion of western culture will clash with the commercial and political interests of the corporations developing these tools. By definition, machine learning is conservative: it can only understand the past and that is what it wants to reproduce. Distortion requires understanding that the past must be remade and not reproduced. This also collides with the capitalist interests behind these systems. Generative AI is seen as an instrument to replace tasks, to streamline processes, to facilitate the accumulation of wealth. If these systems become tools, part of our jobs, they won't steal them, they will demean them. Writing copy, translating (both text and live), creating images for publicity or even replying to emails will become low-paid jobs in which humans will be tasked with editing and correcting the generative AI, while profits become consolidated in the hands of the few.

Playing AI is a commitment to a future in which we don't settle for what is, but for what could be. Playing AI, exploring its rules and boundaries, appropriating and breaking them so we are not stuck in the loops of the past, is more than just entertainment, pleasure or fun. It is also a moral commitment to a better world.

Miguel Sicart is a Professor of Digital Play at the Center for Digital Play, IT University of Copenhagen. He is the author of *The Ethics of Computer Games, Play Matters,* and *Playing Software: Homo Ludens in Computational Culture* (MIT Press, 2009, 2013, 2023).

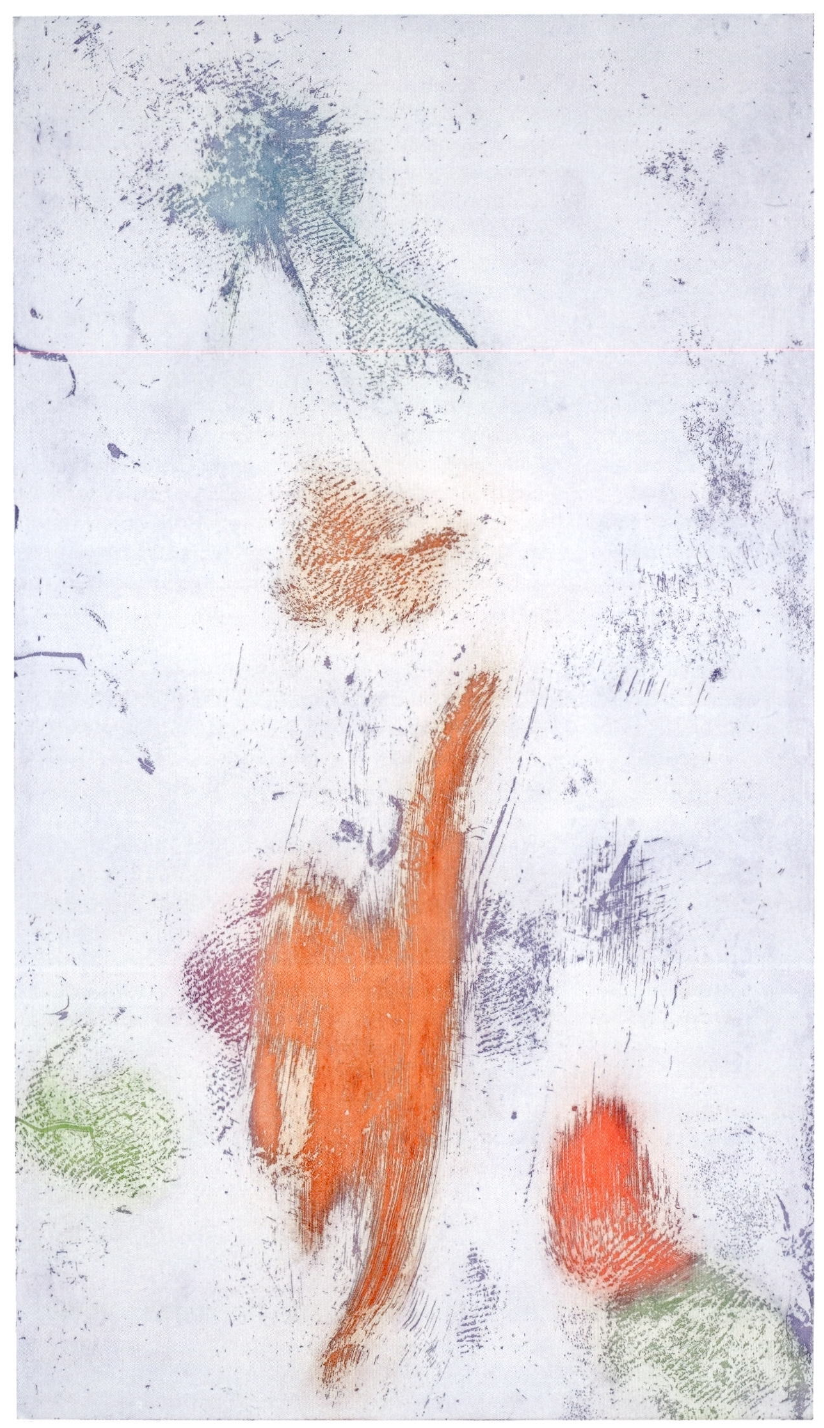

Andrea Büttner
Phone Etching, 2015

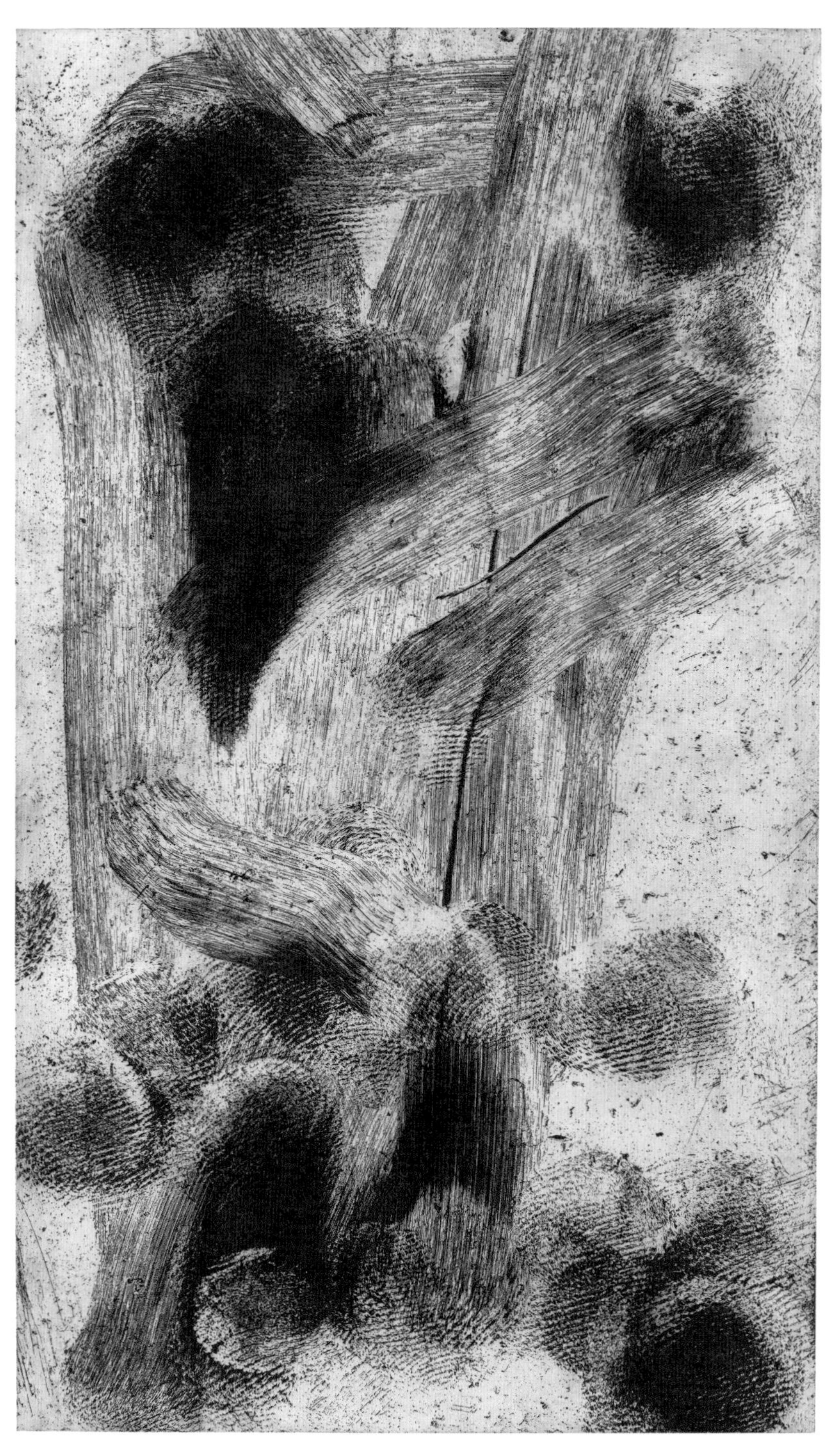

Andrea Büttner
Phone Etching, 2015

Roman Opalka
1.252.561 - 1.255.562, 1965

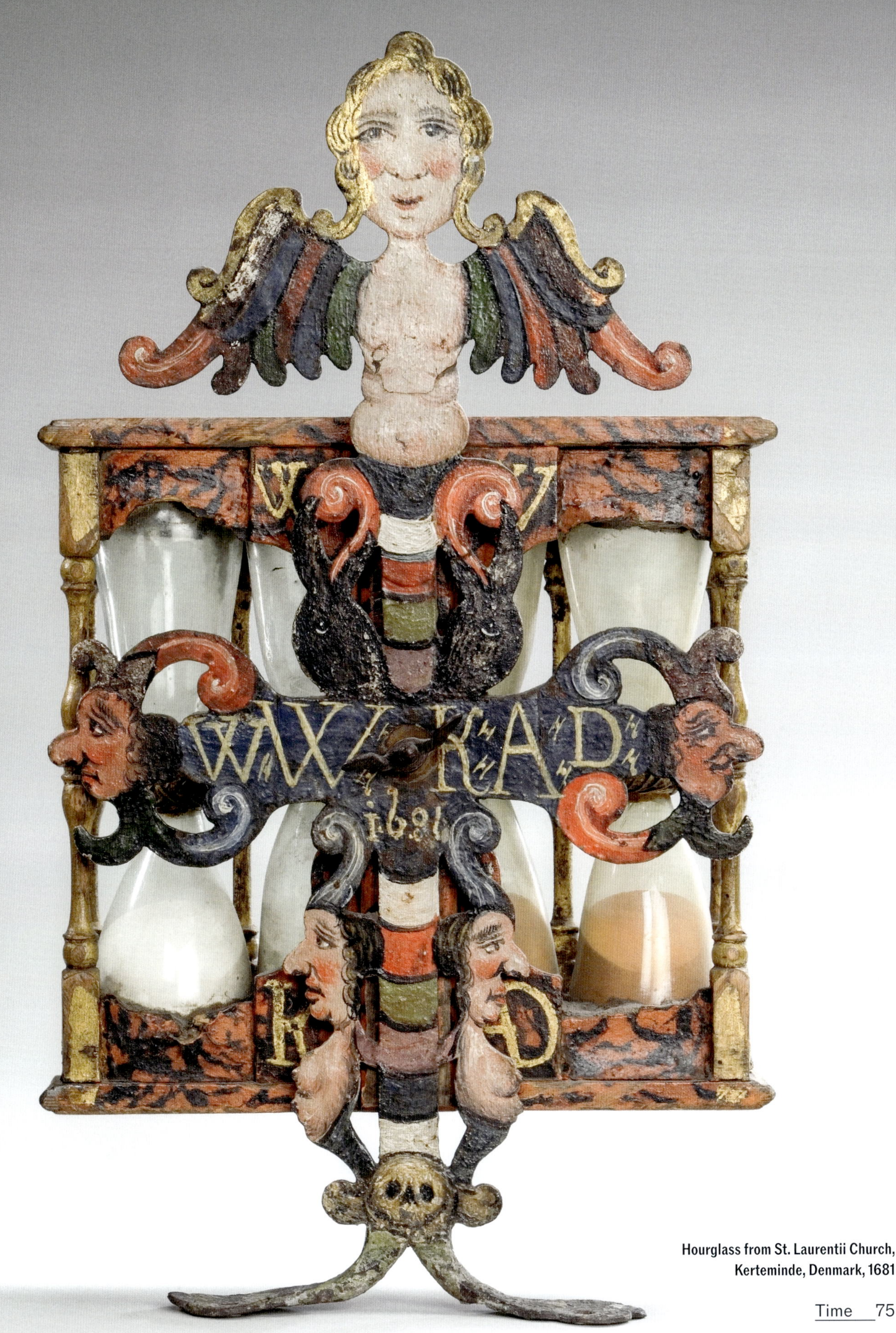

Hourglass from St. Laurentii Church,
Kerteminde, Denmark, 1681

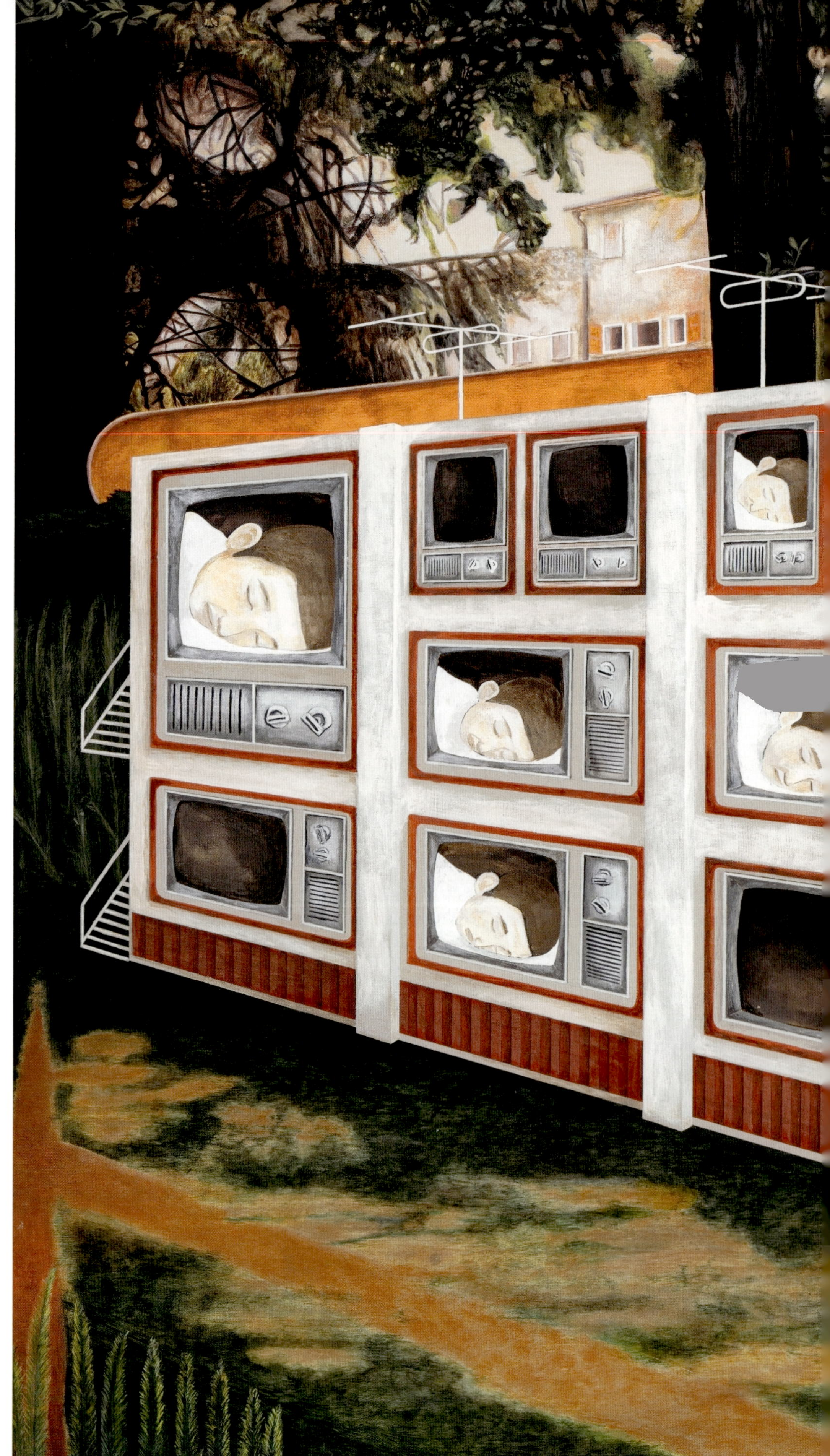

Tetsuya Ishida
Untitled, 1995

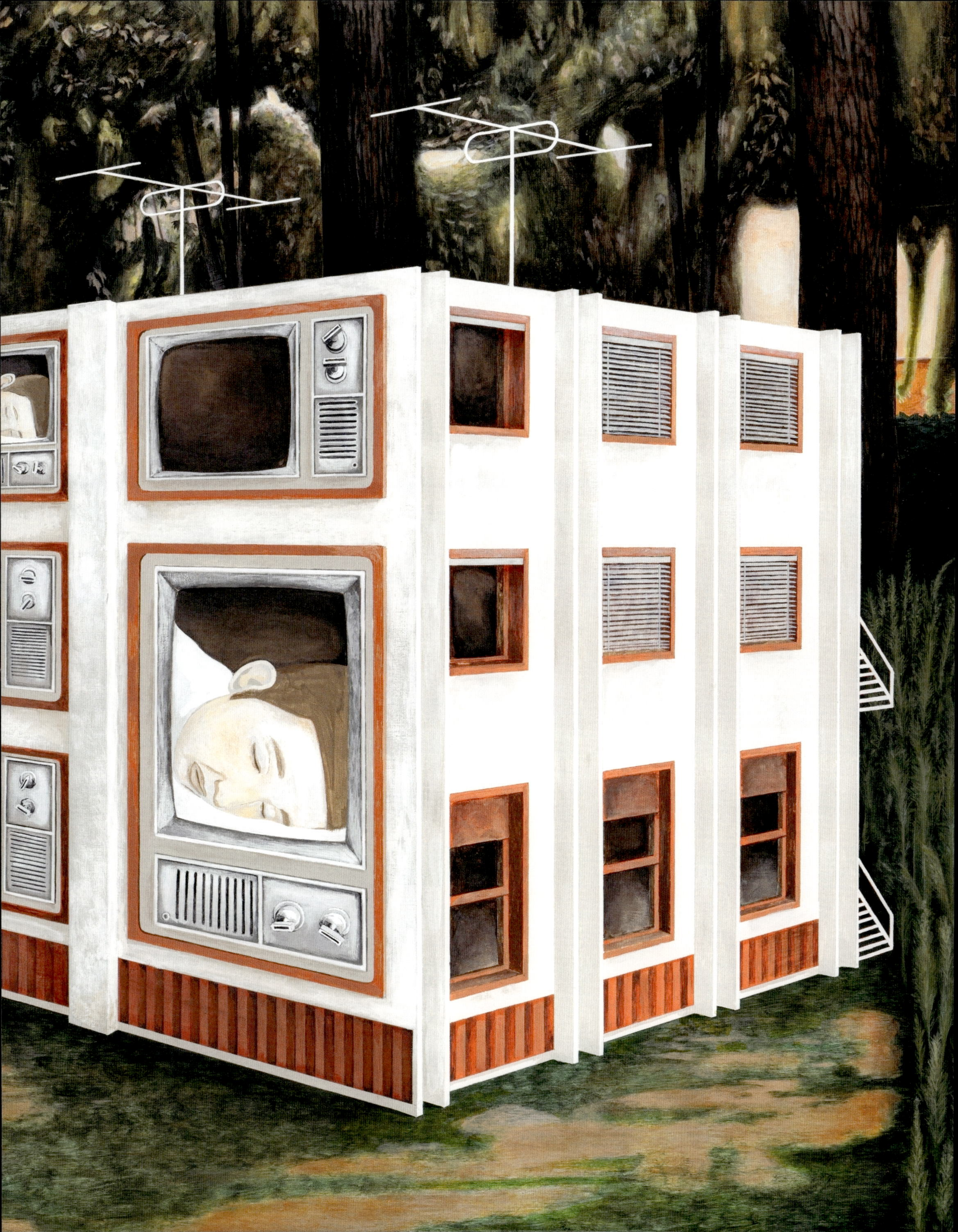

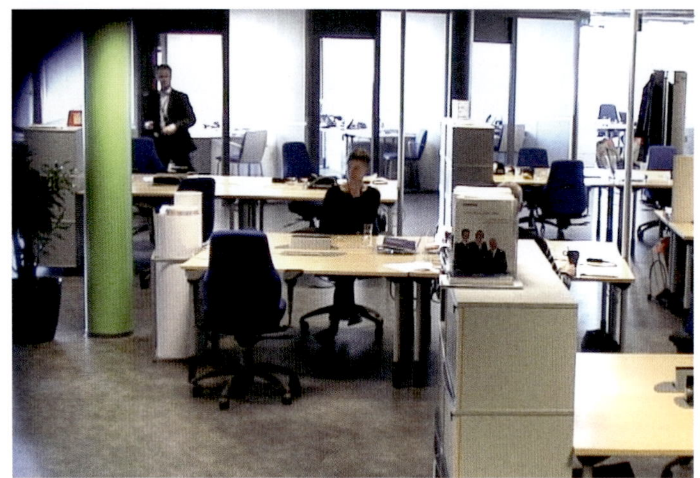

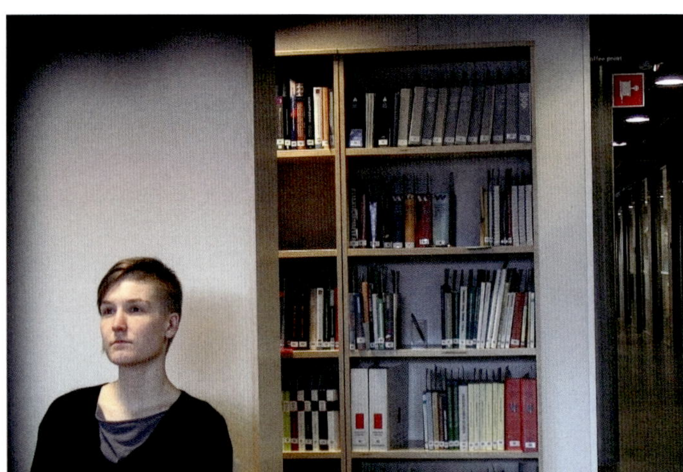

From: X
Sent: February 27 2008 00:16
To: Z, Y
Subject: marketing–trainee
Importance: High

Hi

As I already mentioned to Z, there has been a person sitting in the Tax library space and staring out of the window with a glazed look in her eyes...
Female, very short hair, she said when asked that she's a trainee in Marketing.
She sat in front of an empty desk from 10:30 on, went for lunch...

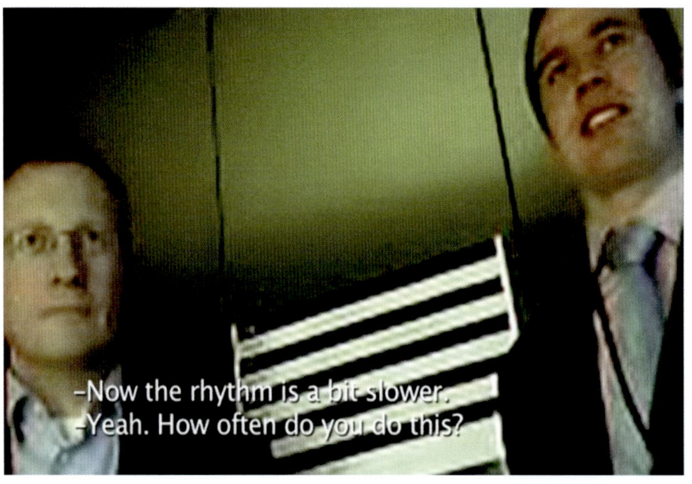

Pilvi Takala
Stills from *The Trainee*, 2008

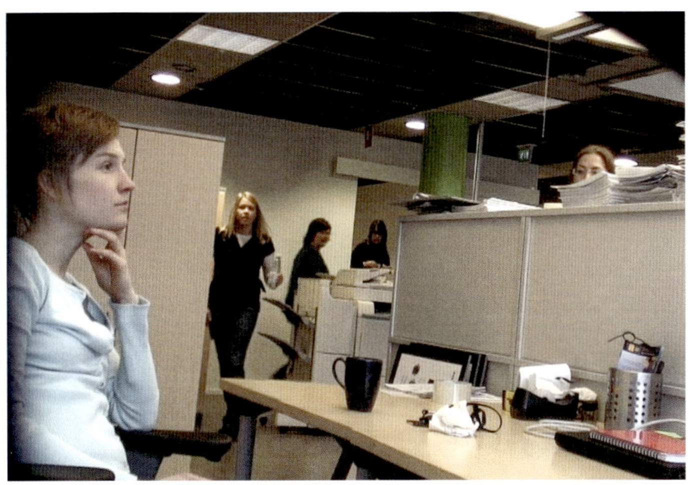

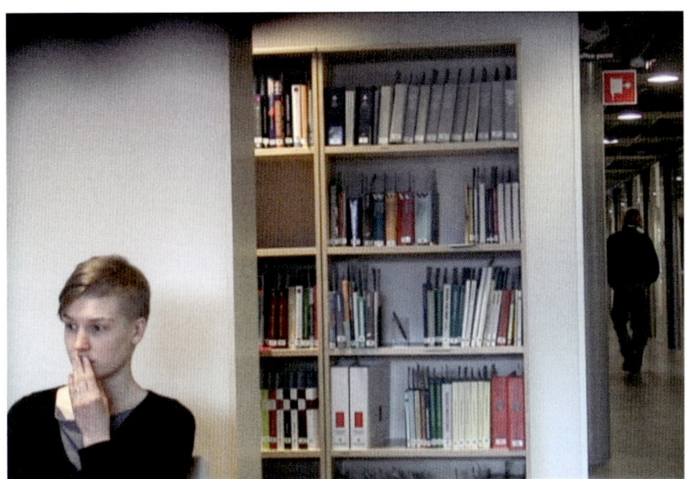

...in between and continued sitting until 15:30. Several tax-people went to this person who they didn't know to ask her who she is and what is she waiting for/doing. The answer had been that she is doing brain-work and/or is thinking about her own things.
People at tax not only thought this is weird and funny,but also scary to some extent. What on earth is this and why is nobody missing a trainee all day?

X

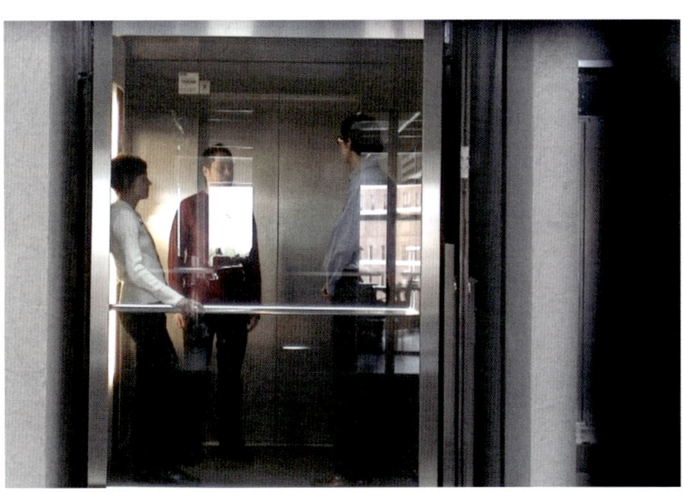

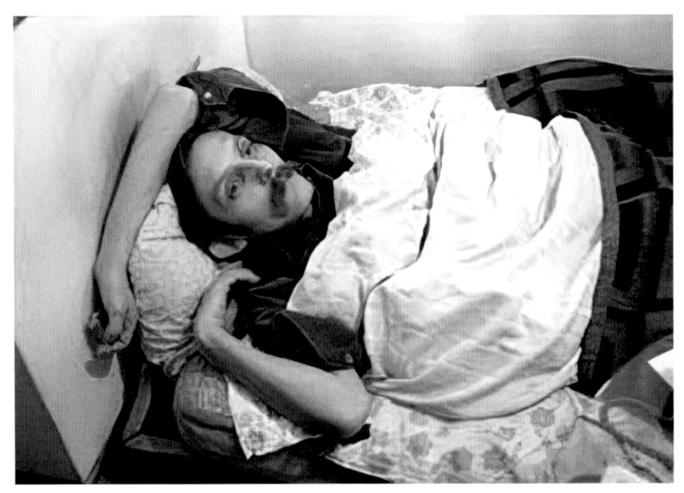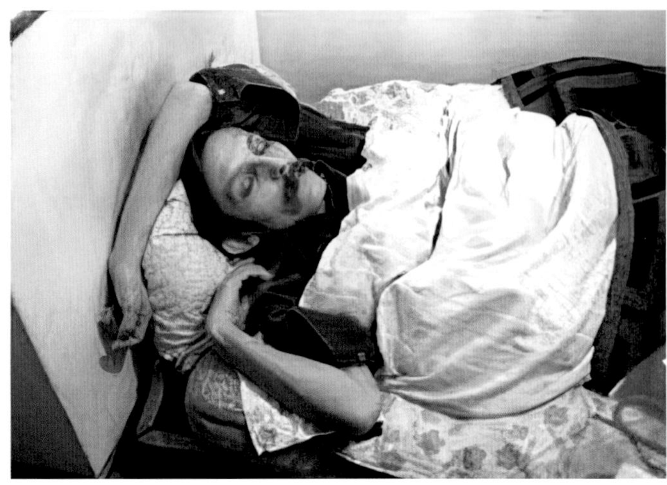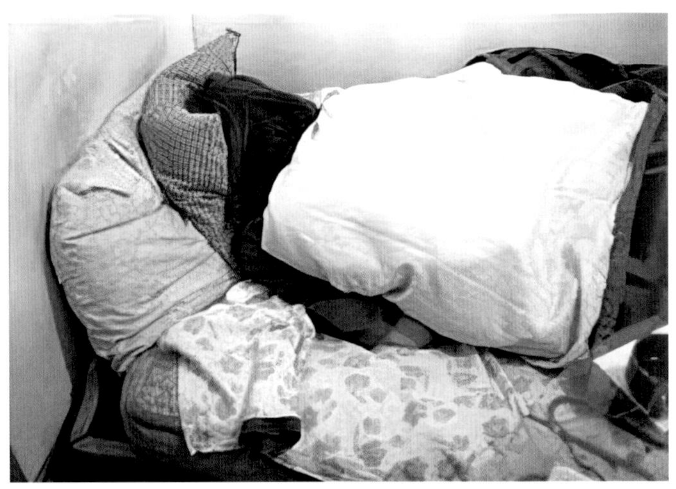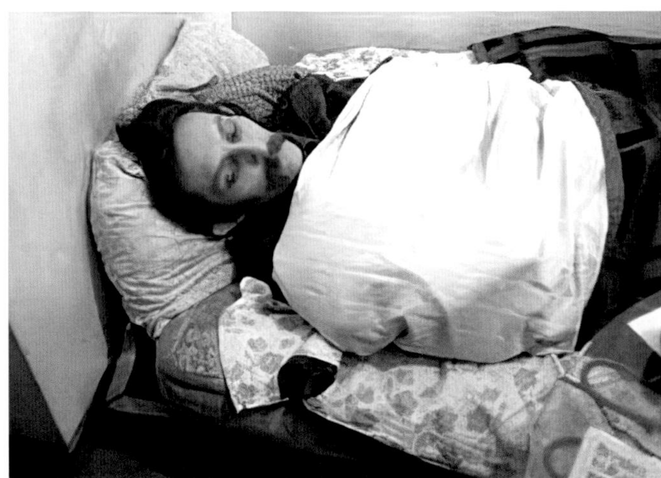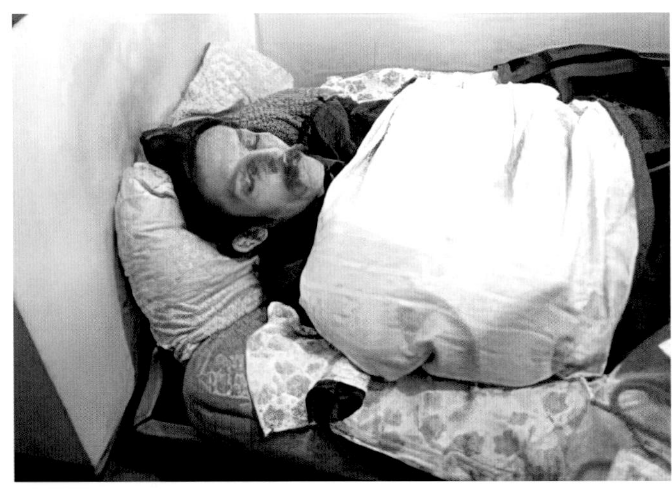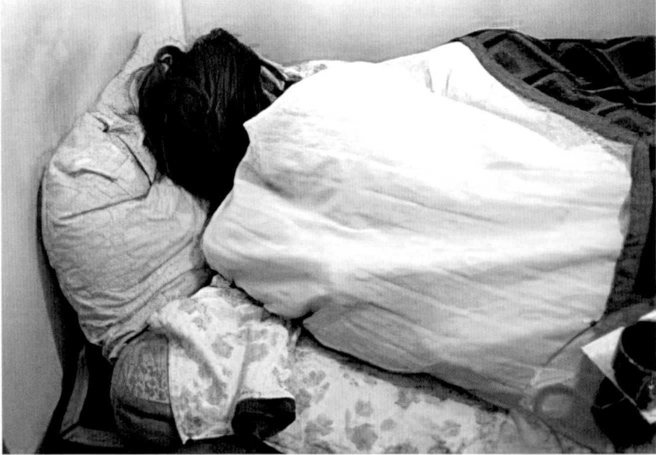

Mladen Stilinović
Detail of *Artist at Work*, 1978

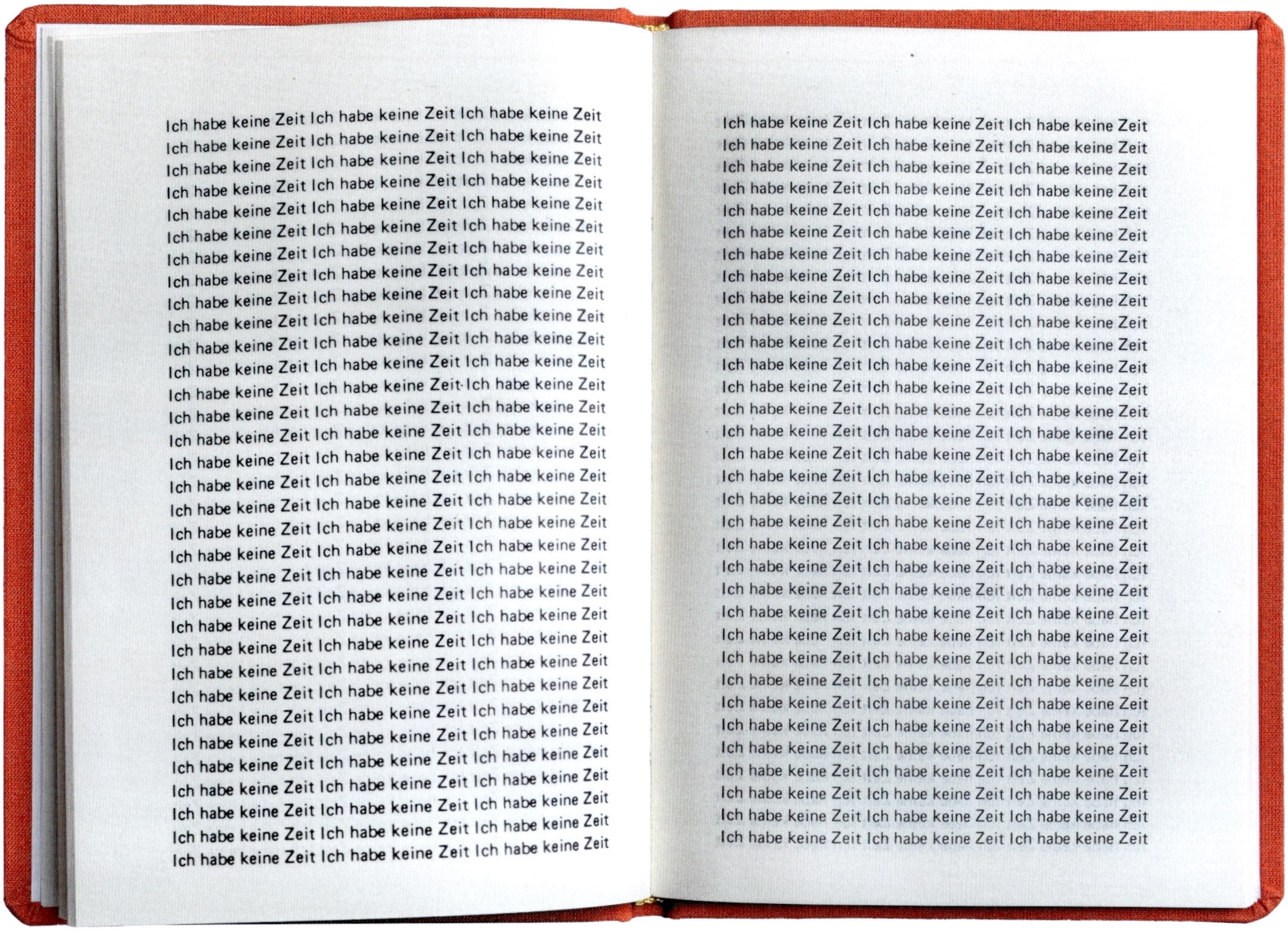

Next spread:
Chicks on Speed & collaborators
Sleep Synthesis, 2013/2023

Mladen Stilinović
Ich habe keine Zeit (I have no time), 1983

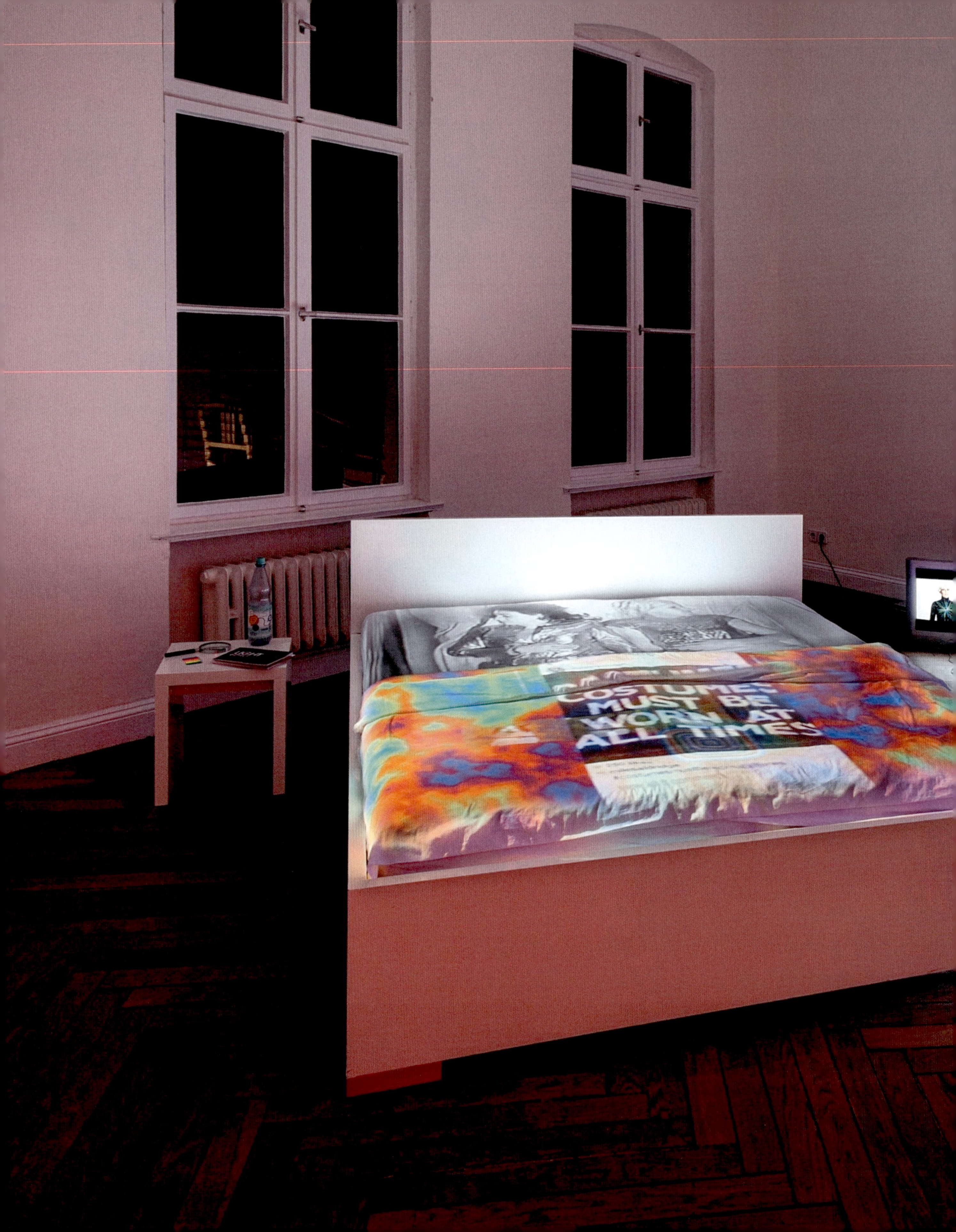

COSTUMES MUST BE WORN AT ALL TIMES

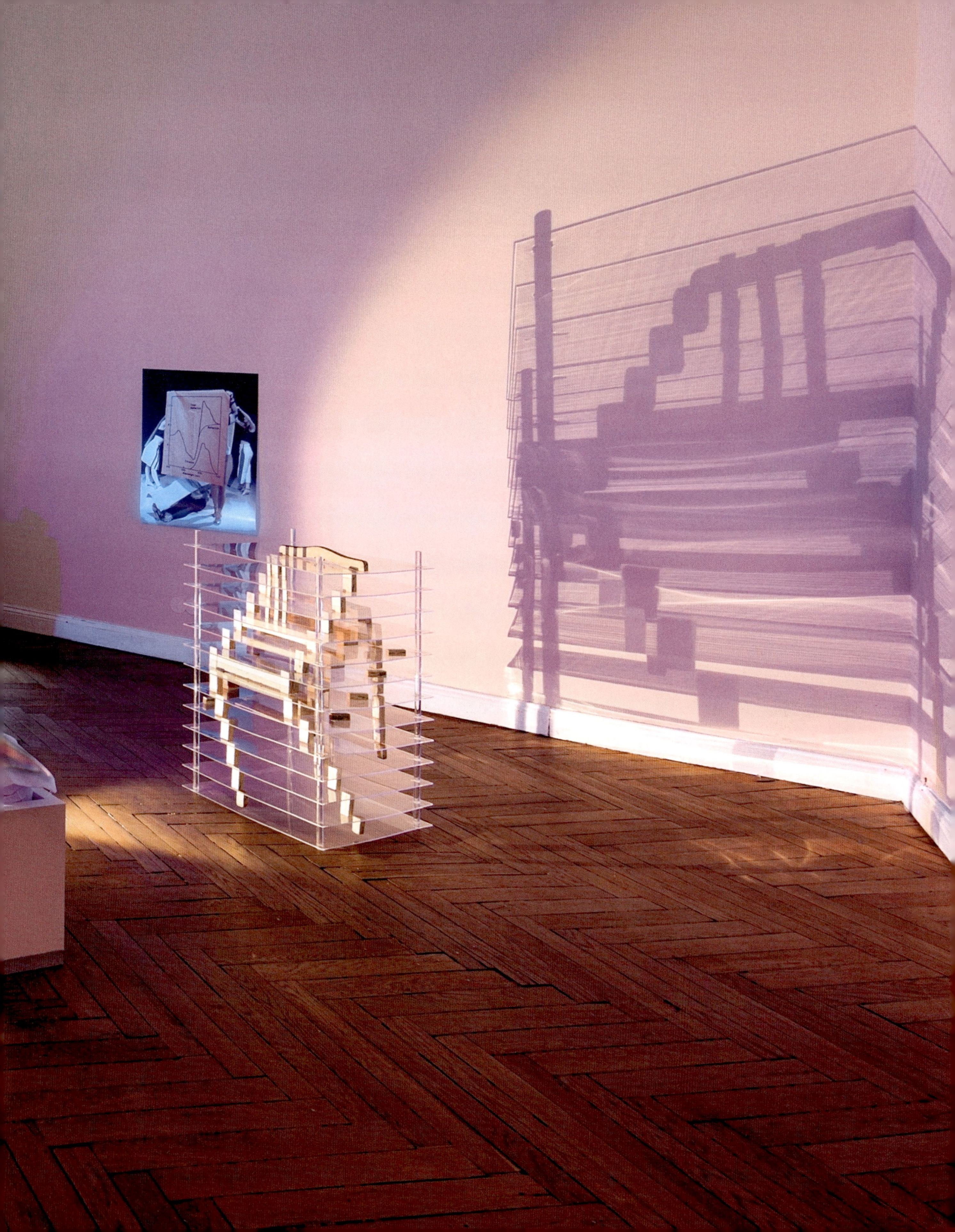

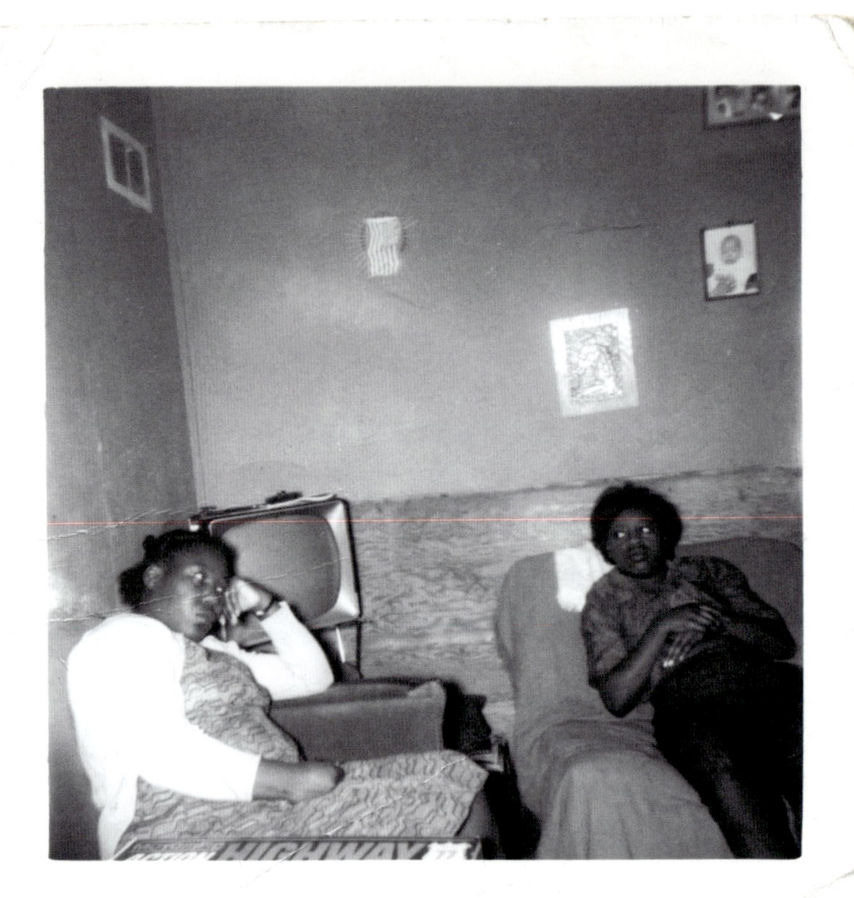

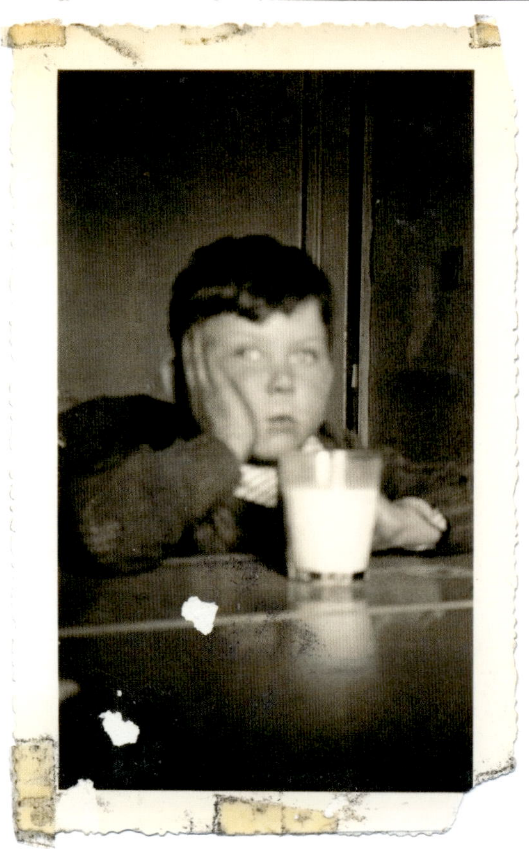

Dawn Parsonage
Boring Found Photographs, 2019

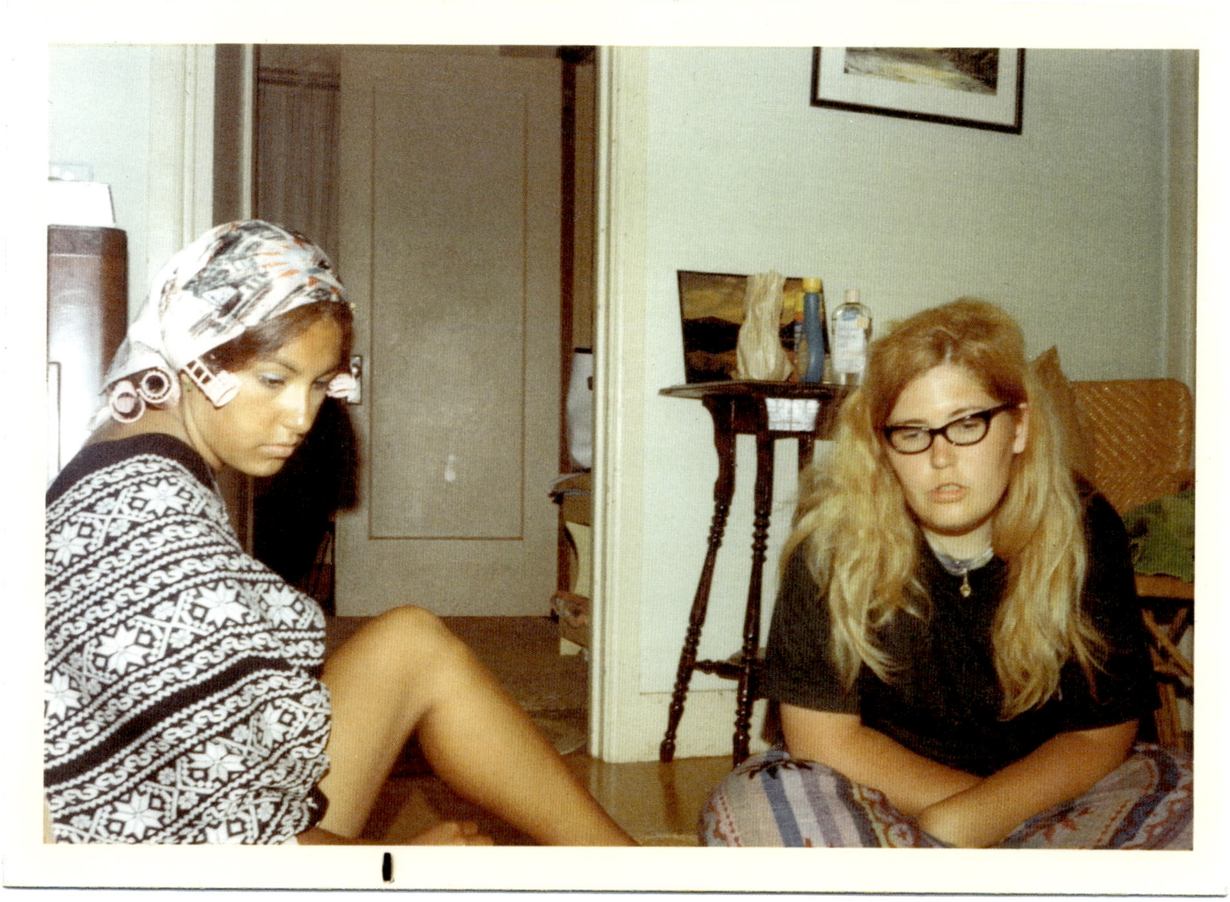

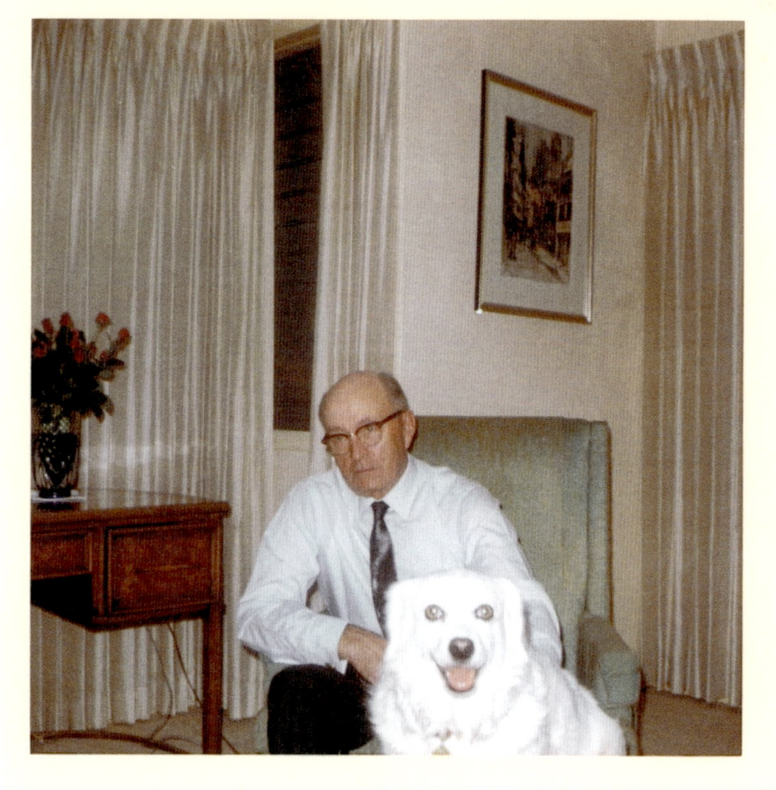

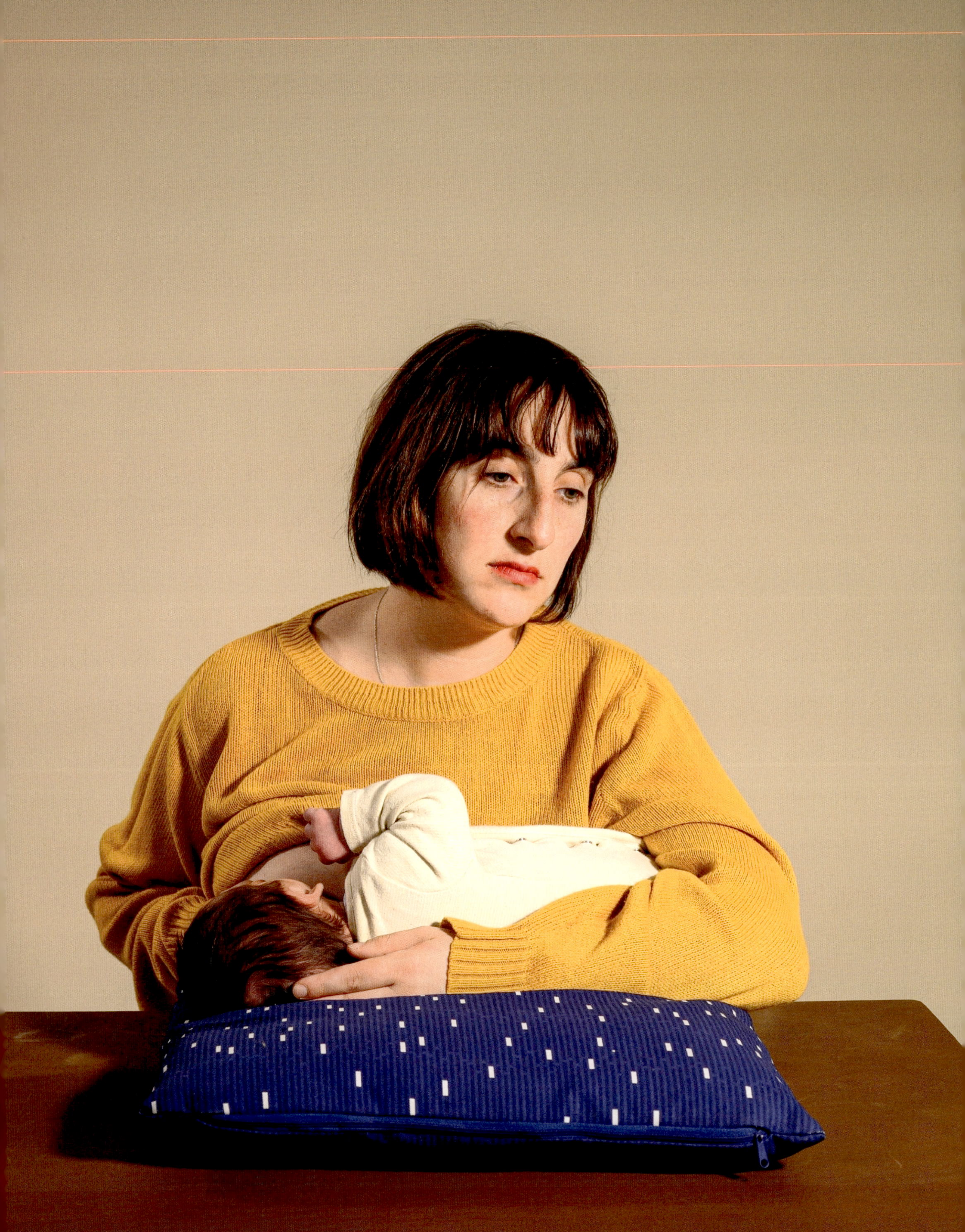

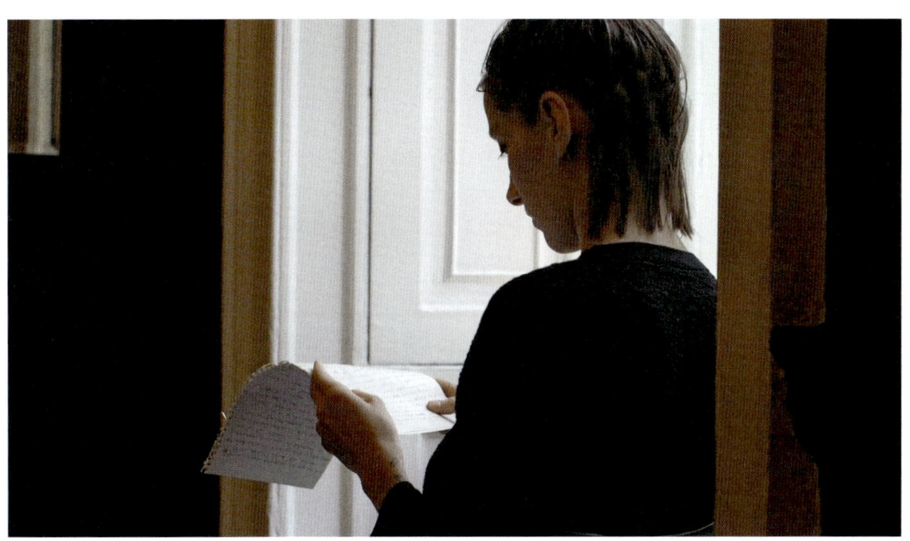

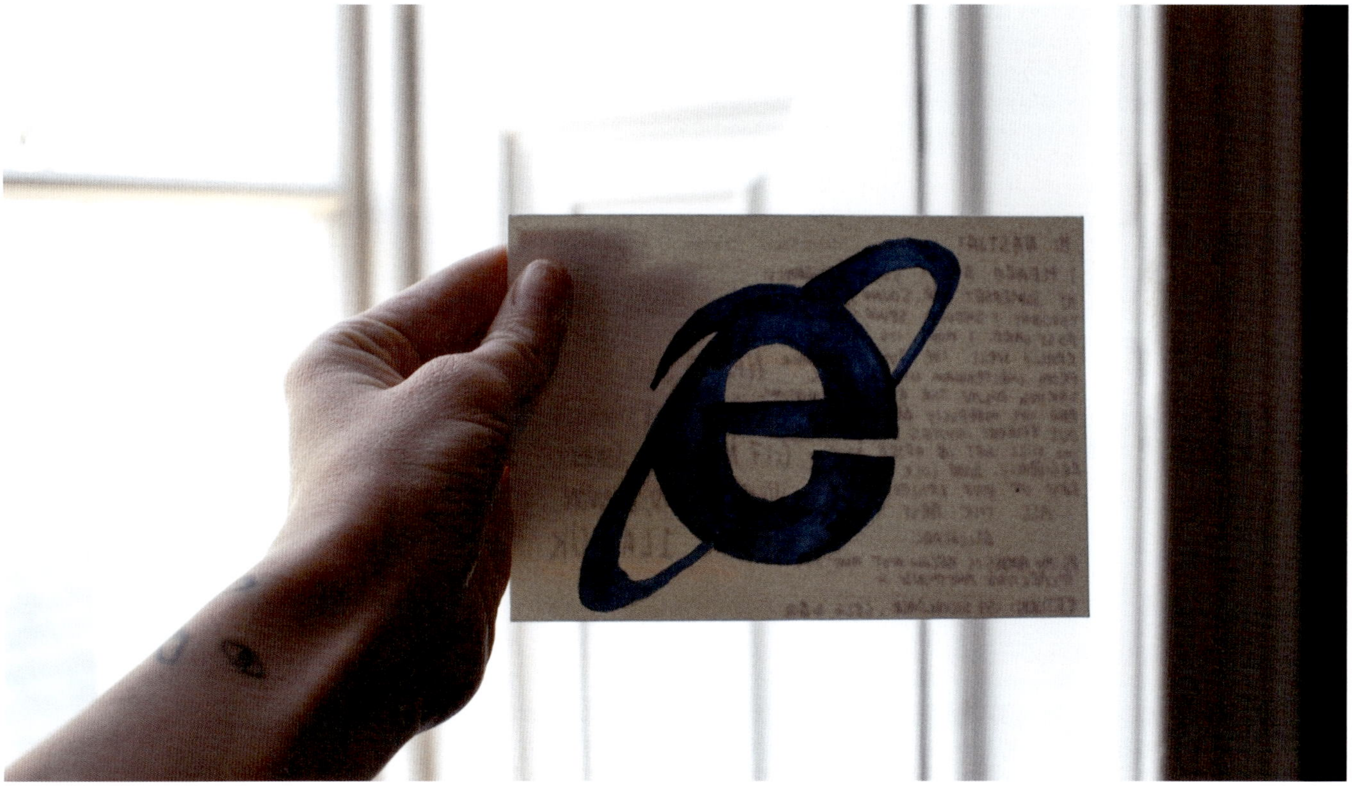

Left page:
Dawn Parsonage
Boring Miriam, 2019

Nastja Säde Rönkkö
Stills from *6 months without*, 2018-2019

Anne Boyer
The Better Part of Nothing

What does it mean to create, and which types of creation should we value? In this essay, Anne Boyer explores the relationship between poetry and creativity.

First there were the Gods. Then there were poets. The Gods made the world. The poets found that world inadequate. They wanted dawn to be rosier, heroes more heroic. They adjusted, too, the temperature of hell. The Gods resented the poets for this, cursed them to tattered clothes, eccentric manners, infrequent paychecks, and tiny, disorganized apartments. The philosophers conspired to banish the poets from cities. The poets didn't care. They chose the sight of the sewer mouth over the statue, the glamor of shadows over the officiousness of light. Discarded cartons, rubble piles, neglected territories: these were the poets' legislative chambers. Trash was a poet's Athens. Wherever something was in order – tidy, pure, intact – the poets were to be found smudging its edges, scattering its forces. The lopsided was, to them, the better symmetry.

In the exaggerations, celebrations, juxtapositions, and all-out fictions of the poets there was always a nucleus of complaint about the world. The poets created rival immortalities, plumbed accident until they found in it the enduring shape of tragedy. They created rival paradises, too, ones that banished victors and welcomed failures. They intensified gossip until it became myth and dreamed up cities that could never be built, topsy-turvy ones made entirely of water or feathers, to be found only on the ocean floor or Mars. So, too, they restored the green possibility of devastated landscapes. They gave fields back to intelligent weeds. They put speech in the mouths of the speechless. Through the poets, the birds met for symposia, the moon cringed, and the grass declared.

Once, somewhere in the western plains of North America, one of them nailed a McDonald's cheeseburger to the wooden plank fence surrounding a parking lot full of used Toyotas. This cheeseburger crucified among the Toyotas was typical of poets' contributions world, thus among the higher creative accomplishments of our species. Yet it remained undocumented, left little trace of itself after its unhurried disintegration in the hot sun of a western summer. Unbranded, unsung, unsold – a cheeseburger nailed to a fence outside a used car lot was undeniably a form of poetry, apiece with all the perfect nonaccomplishments, an ideal instantiation of poetic labour across the millennia.

Disobedient, ardent, and unwise, *poetry* was the name of a perverse and persistent human tendency, the movement of those who chose, against all advice, to ignore the painful constraints of *the actual*. Bound to no material but language itself, and only partially bound to that, the poet's creativity both rivalled and diverged from the Gods – and by Gods it is meant any demiurges whose work most resembles that of cosmic architects. Humans themselves later took on the responsibilities of these builder Gods, imitating the initial creation of the world via the continuing creation of everything that came next to populate it: toy tigers, handguns, hotels, and instant cameras. Favoured by mayors, real estate developers, tech executives, product designers, and engineers, this manufactured world was a monument to the near-limitless drive to use up all available resources in an ambitious appetite for accrual. That busy world of material edicts – the one in which rent is paid, toilets are scrubbed, shopping done, and timecards are punched – had as little as possible to do with the worlds of poets. As the ancients had once thought, poets remained creators *ex nihilo, ad nihilo*. They exploited nothing, chartered nothing, capitalised on nothing, collected no rent, and proposed only impossible laws and oneiric logics. Poetry's edicts were ones that no one could obey.

The mines, malls, and office towers, the climate-controlled museums and overheated data centers, the airports, and carparks and all the other heavy congealments on the surface of the world – these

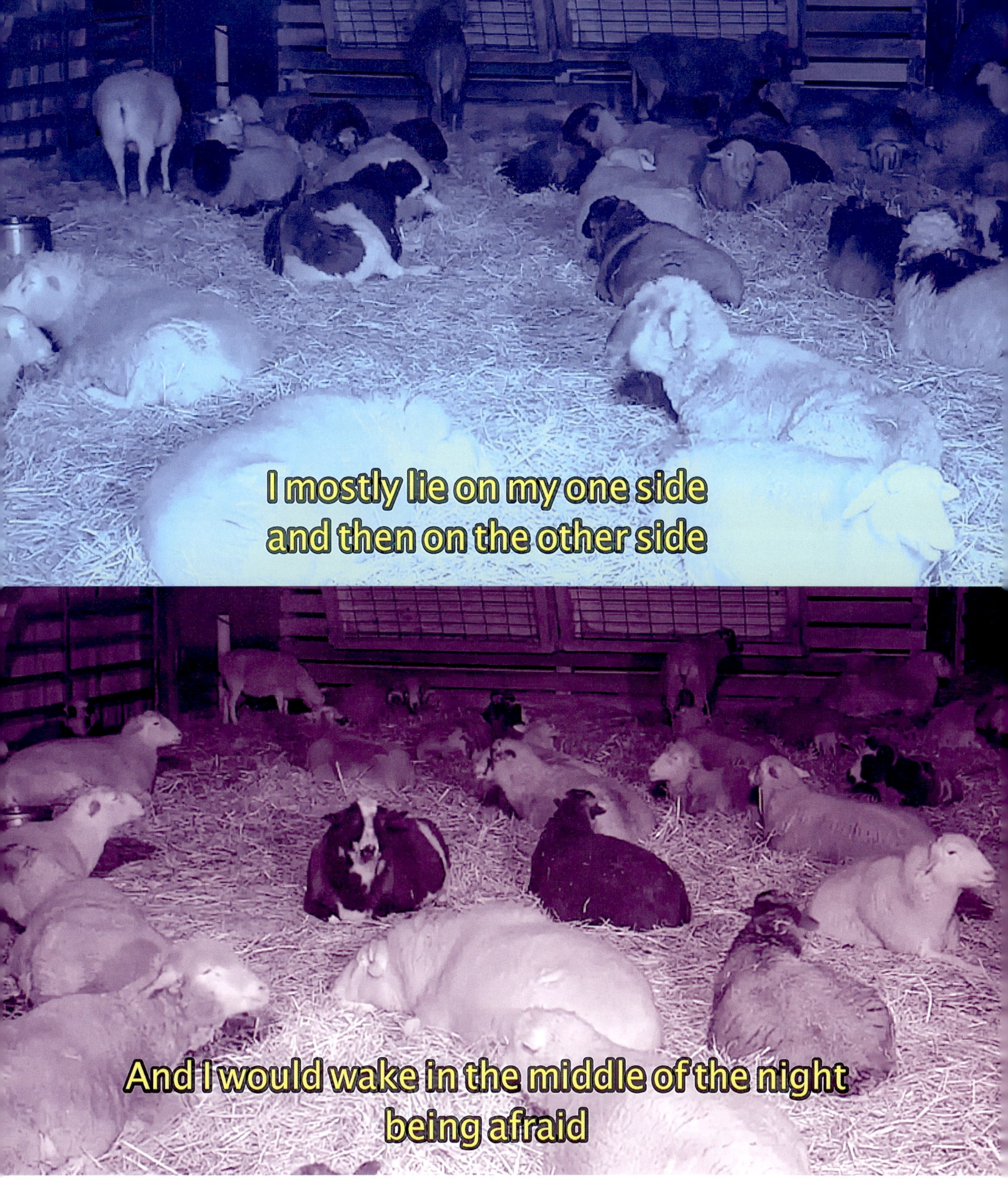

Mia Edelgart
Stills from *Sov* (Sleep), 2021

are not poetry. Instead, they are the gloomy prose of disrupted contentment. All that is currently built is a clandestine inventory of what is lost in the human drive toward making, what ore was mined from a cliff near which city, what trees or rushes once grew near what village, what animals were slaughtered to sate what appetites, what petroleum was burned, what pigments were extracted from flowers which were once happy to grow in what meadow, and later, what the chemists discovered and what they made with these discoveries, the flows of trade across what seas. The wind and current are recorded in this stuff, too, as is the dampness and heat, the path of time, the presence or absence of fire, the charring hand of social repression or war.

Those who created the heavy things of the world were the ones who marked ingresses and egresses, installed gates, issued swipe cards and door codes, viciously guarded borders, and conducted the dismembering rituals of biometrics. The doors of the poets were practical jokes in comparison to all other possible entries or exits. They were always open or shut, whichever. This is because the doors of the poets were doors made of nothing, or nearly nothing. Any relation to these doors was impossible if it was not voluntary.

If the Gods were the ones who wrestled the inchoate materials of metaphysics into the leaden stuff of what came to be called "the world," the poets enacted a mesmerizing reversal. What was a form of making that did not exploit the fragility and plasticity of all else, did not affect its change in the realm of objects, but in peculiar orchestrations of sound, syntax, and signifier? The poets practiced a creativity that deviated from the stone, the beam, the drill bit, and the molecule. It was suspiciously unattached to the crude constraints of a chopped down oak tree or scarred-up limestone quarry. What the poet's creativity made was more like breath than stuff.

The automobile, the cosmetic implant, the military drone, the gel pen, the gaming console, and all the shining, repetitive, and unruffled commodities on the supermarket shelves – even the slightest of these was heavier and sadder than any poem. All commodities were melancholy. Every actual made thing was a dead thing, or worse: it was an aggregated loss of what was once living in the world. How brilliant and necessary, then, the persistence, then, of this form of creativity – poetry – that was made of something that was not the sacrifice of something else.

No one, even if they tried very hard, could even really use a poem except as inspiration to shift one's eyes away from the commotion of the official spectacle toward the sly genius of disobedience in the everyday, like the daring black stocking with intentional rips, or the fancy brass placard stolen from the public rose garden – *Dark Lady, 1991* – casually emerging from a pot of sedum in the chipped paint courtyard of the low rent apartment complex. Perhaps to truly use a poem meant, at most, stopping before a wreath made of white feathers that had fallen into a gutter. The wind, the air, and accident sponsored that vision, but it was in the tradition of poetry that someone knew to marvel at a halo in a sewer.

Wherever there have been humans, there have always been those who partook of poetry's special impossibility, whether they wrote poems or not. These were the ones who in their daydream minutes conjured new worlds made of out of the nearly gossamer non-substance of imagination. They did not build petrol stations, erect sculptures, cook lavish meals, touch linseed oil to canvas, project political nightmares into networks of wires and glass. Yet making practically nothing out of the least solid of any materials, they created a tradition that is substantial enough to describe, ancient enough that its origin is lost, familiar enough that anyone can recognize it, free enough that anyone can partake of it. Deforming nothing but the crude requirements of materiality itself, they made limitless worlds out of the common realm of a single world. They left an impression but made no defacing marks. And somehow, these creations were more durable than the others, more durable even than skyscraper or submarines. No armies could storm invisible palaces, no rivals could burn down fantasy houses, no villains could slaughter imaginary flocks. A poem could never melt into the noxiousness of a plastic bag in an incinerator.

Some claimed that these people – the poets, and those like them – brought to the surface of human perception the feelings and conditions that everyone else once preferred stay repressed. As Freud pointed out, "the daydreamer carefully conceals his fantasies from other people because he feels he has reason to be ashamed of them." The poets were those who had overcome this modesty. Freud suggested the creative writer pays the price of sharing daydreams through the aesthetic bribe of form-finding. This was the toll of beauty, paid by the one who smuggles to the surface a permission to the entire species: you, too, might dream while still awake, or revisit your dreams, and you may do so, finally, in common, socially, discarding the daydream's nonsense veneer of shame.

The universal history of creativity is, in fact, a double history, at least in so far as the poetic has a special place in it, because poetry is the history of the human creation that has no blueprint, no patent, and no price. Poetry stood, as always, slightly apart

in a world which more and more understood itself
to be a creative one, as this creativity suited the
perpetual revolution of the capitalist, technocratic
economy. Having been there at the beginning – what
was once considered the only truly creative art in
the ancient taxonomies of art, and for this reason,
the most suspect one – in industrial modernity
poetic creativity then posed a curious and
unsettling problem. Poetry made nothing and made
nothing happen. It was useless, archaic. It wasn't
even *reasonable*. It's claims – like *"I am a cloud in
trousers"* – were easily disproved. I am not a cloud
in trousers. I am a person writing at a computer, but
that I am a cloud wearing clothes is also not untrue.
Poetry was a form of thought that did not follow
the plodding path of rationality. It was a mode of
sociality that evaded, too, the grim calculations of
the marketplace. The poetic suggested something
else, something rival, something beyond what the
contemporary cult of creativity had left behind.

This began as a history, but in truth, I have written
this essay to gesture toward the open secret about
what our species might do, something less grim and
destructive than what we are up to now. All of us are
poets, at least in sleep, and to dream is the night
mandate of all humans. There is no sleeping class.
There is no professional sleep. We are all, equally,
amateur sleepers, and all, in our sleep, exempt. The
prayer of sleep is the vegetable prayer. To sleep
is return to a vegetable Eden. It is to become, as
it were, as adorable as a fern again, or to be, for a
time, like a small puddle of lichen on a hard rock.
That is, to dream is to become gloriously without
utility. It is to excuse oneself, necessarily, from the
anxious press of the productive. The poem, the
dream, the daydream, the poetic moment – these
stand starkly against the expensive vertiginousness
of highspeed trains, air-tight storage containers,
work hours, and luxury handbags. The poetic
imports the night's worth into the daylight hours,
and in this it is the better part of nothing, both from
nothing and always moving toward it, full of fiction
yet bearing its serious truth.

Anne Boyer is an American poet and essayist. She is the author of
among others *Garments Against Women* (2015) and *The Undying:
Pain, Vulnerability, Mortality, Medicine, Art, Time, Dreams, Data,
Exhaustion, Cancer and Care* (2019), for which she won the Pulitzer
Prize in General Nonfiction.

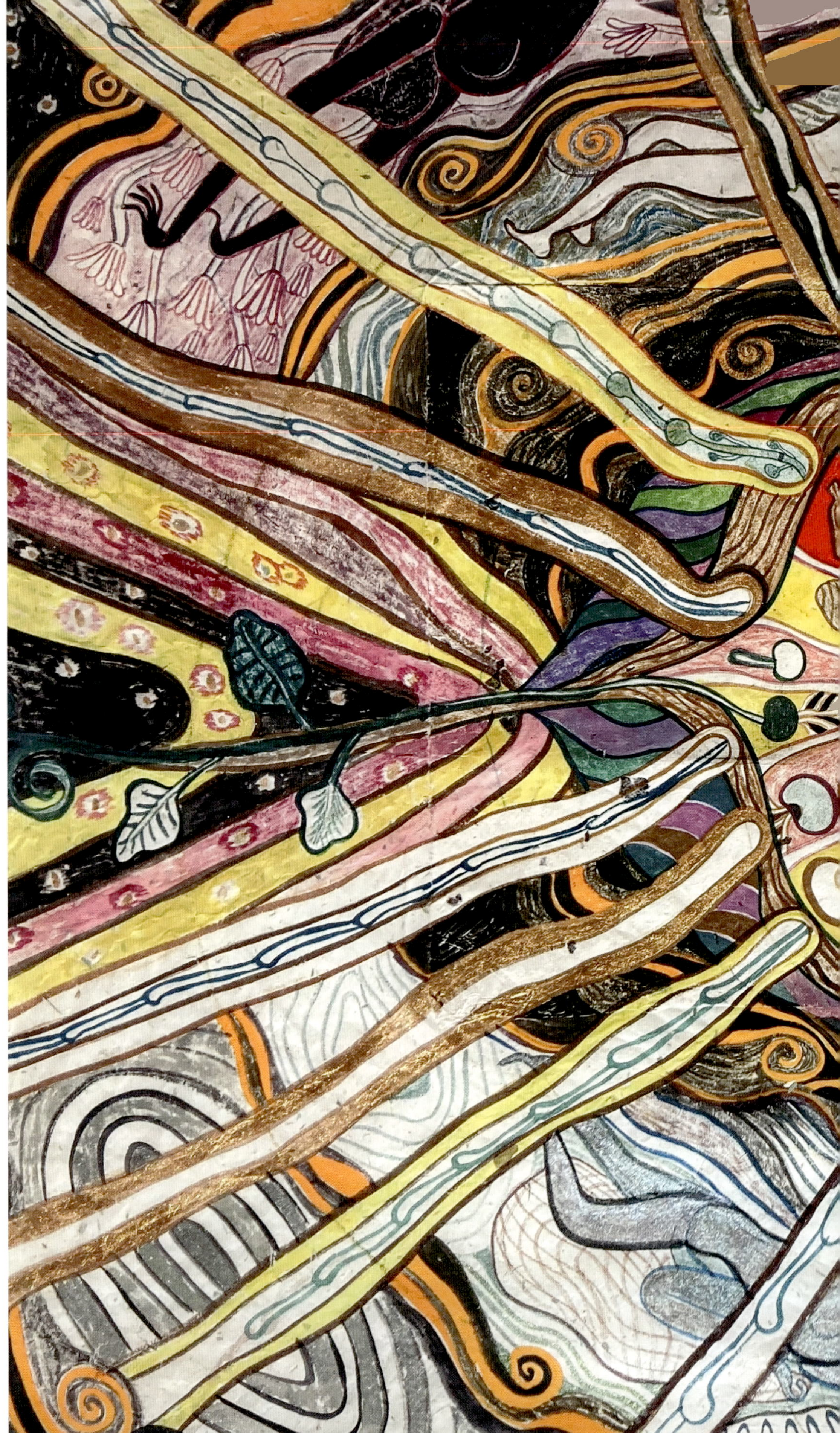

Emma Talbot
*Is All Human Production Just
Dreams and Ideas?*, 2023.
Study for *Seeds Grow in Fertile
Ground*, 2023

Next spread:
Jumana Manna
Still from *A Magical
Substance Flows Into Me,* 2016

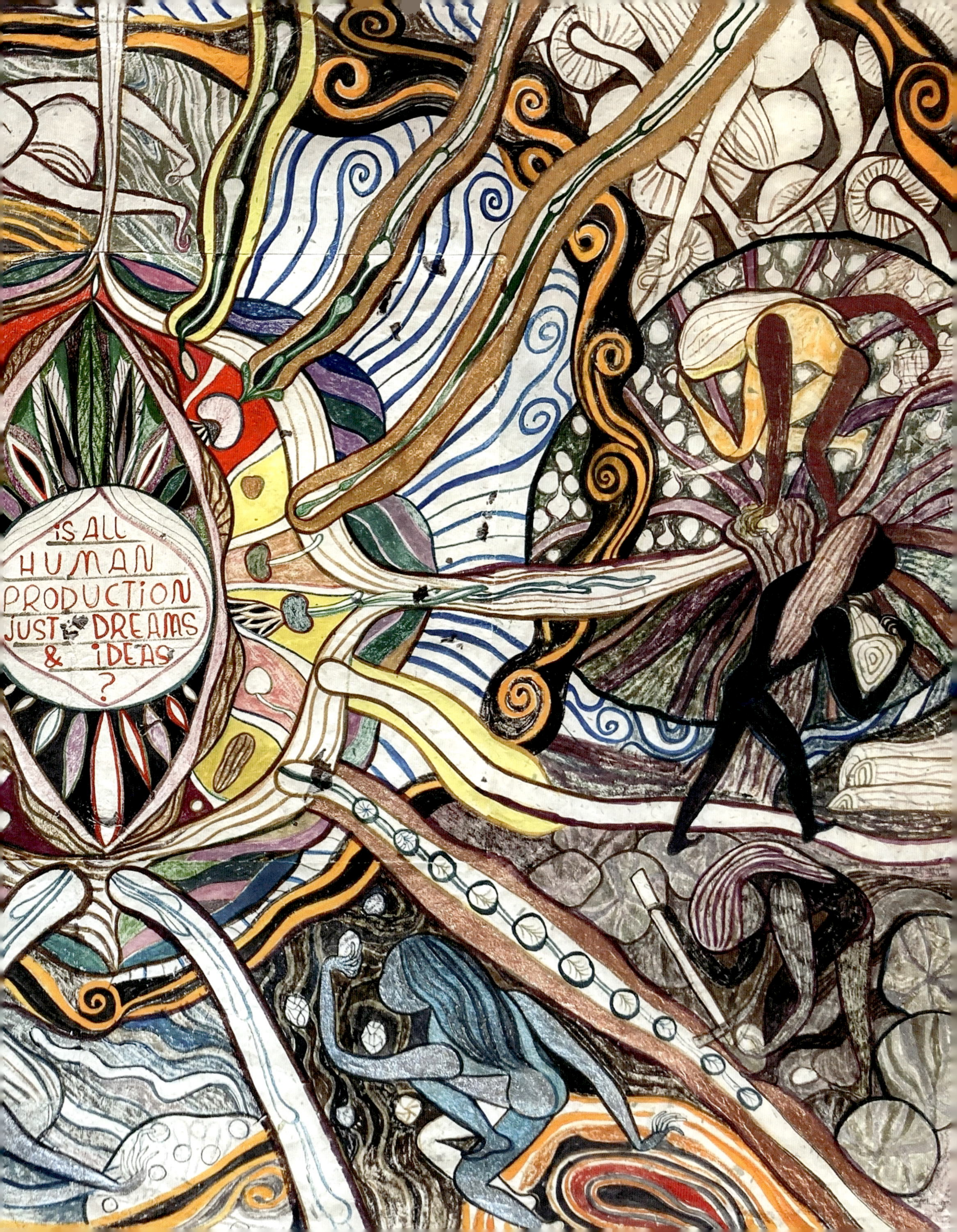

IS ALL
HUMAN
PRODUCTION
JUST DREAMS
& IDEAS
?

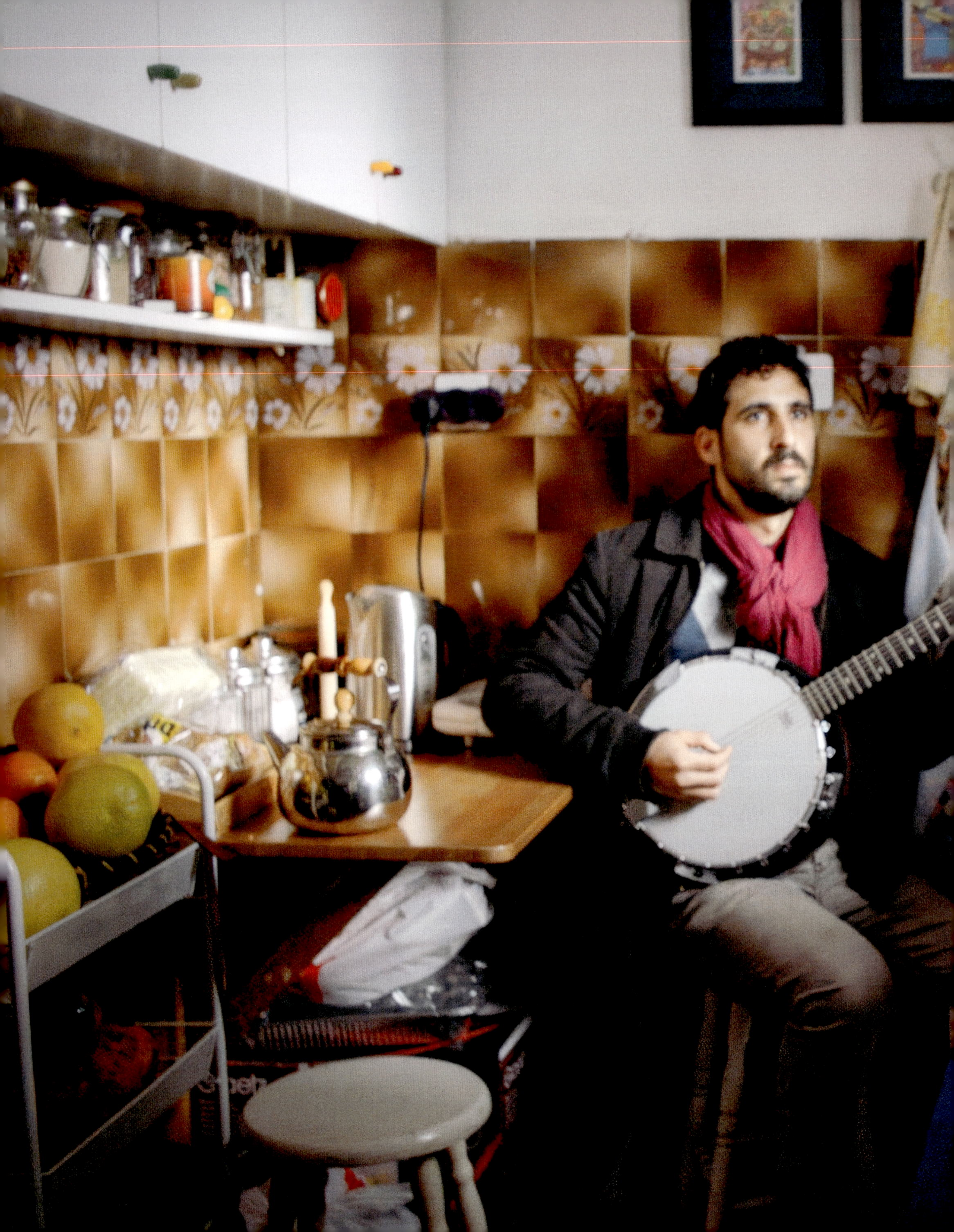

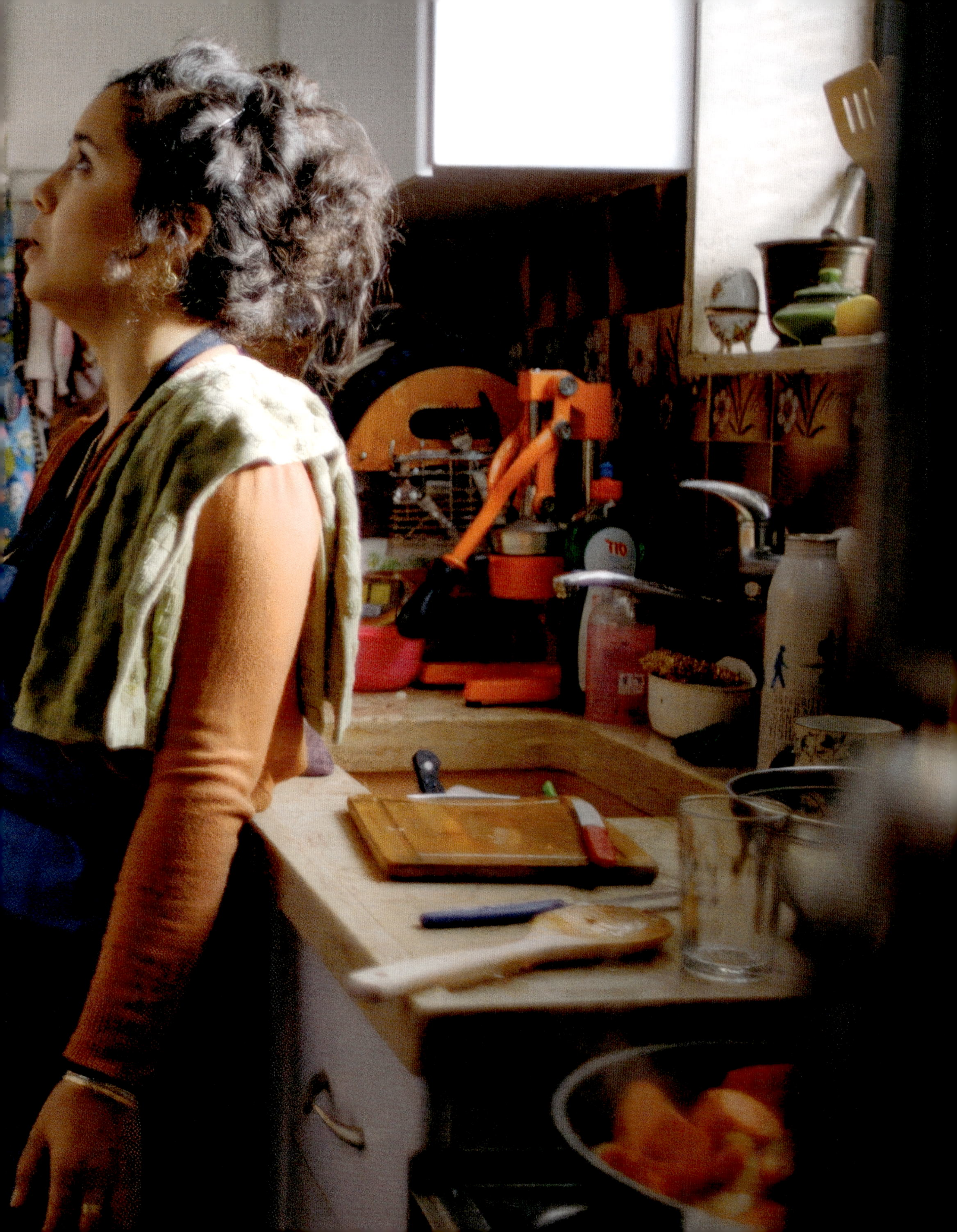

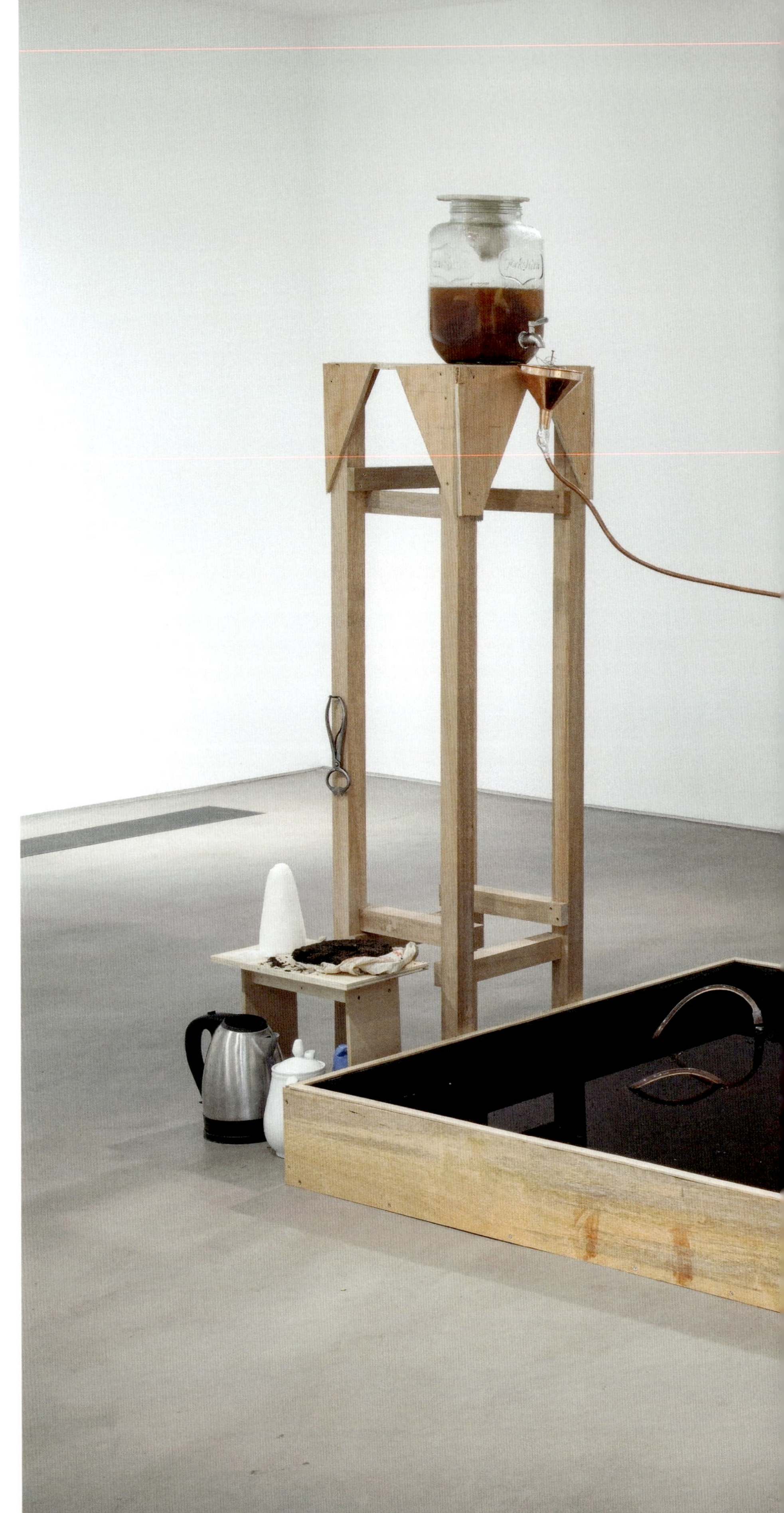

Candice Lin
System for a Stain, 2016

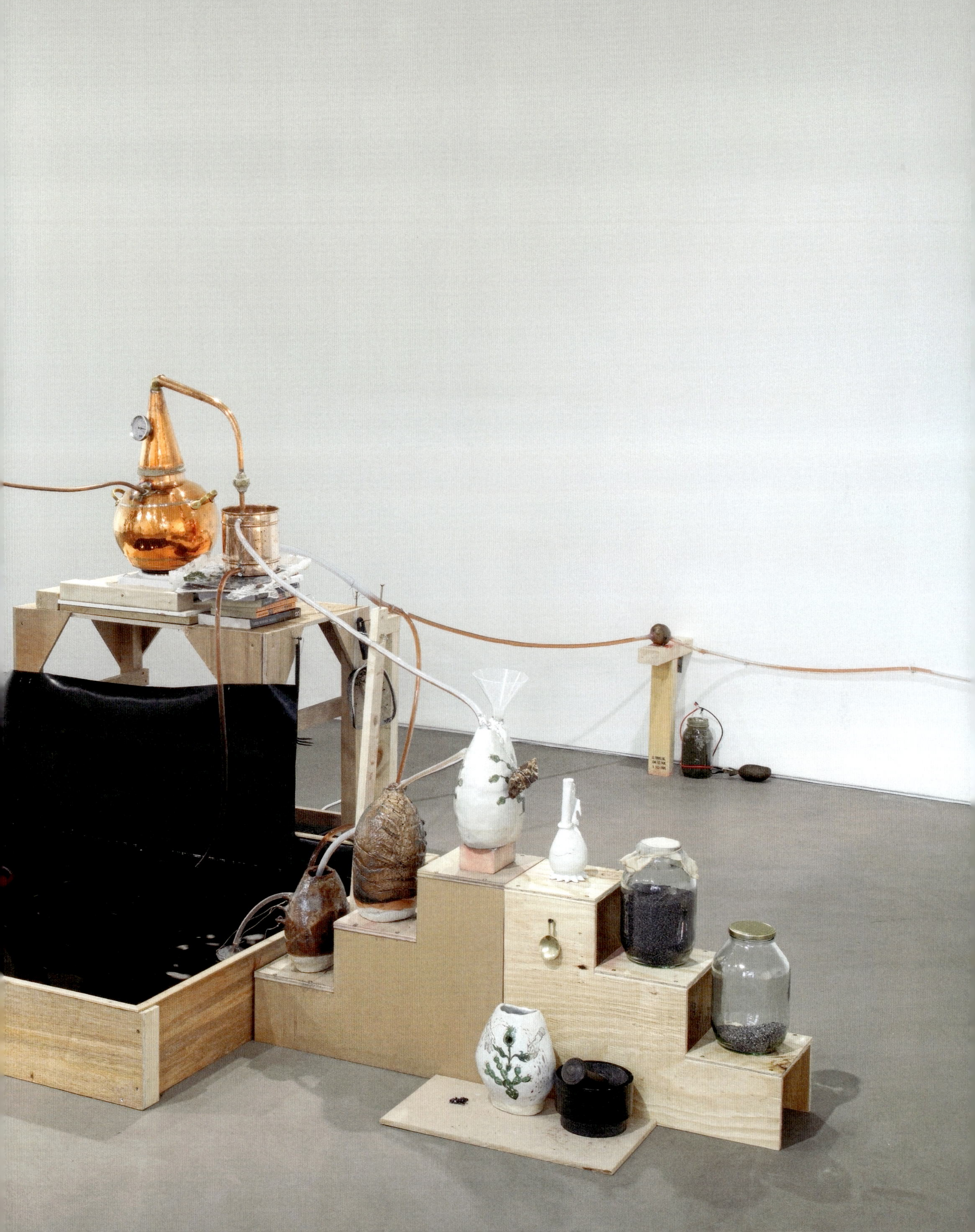

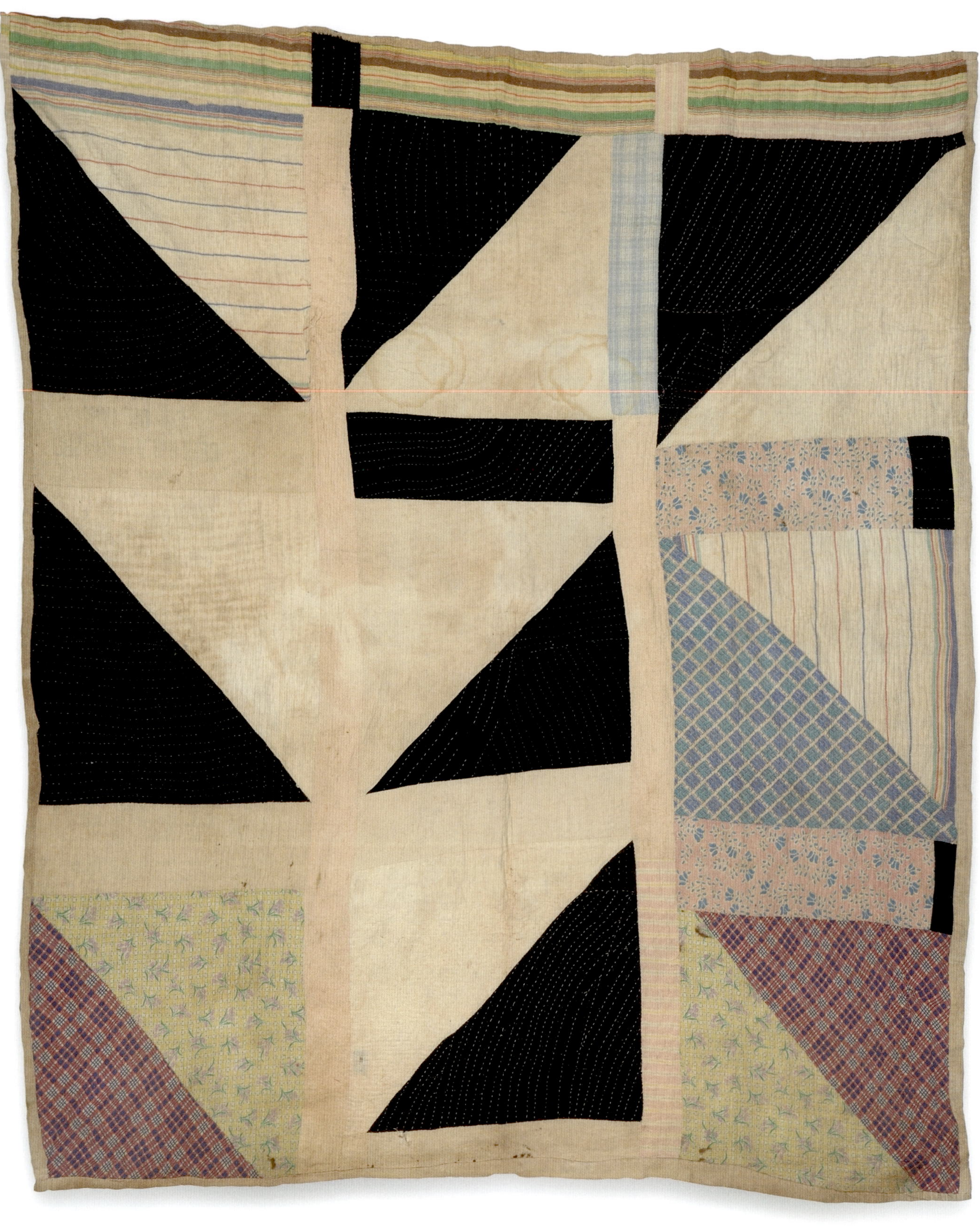

Martha Pettway
Half Squares, 1930s

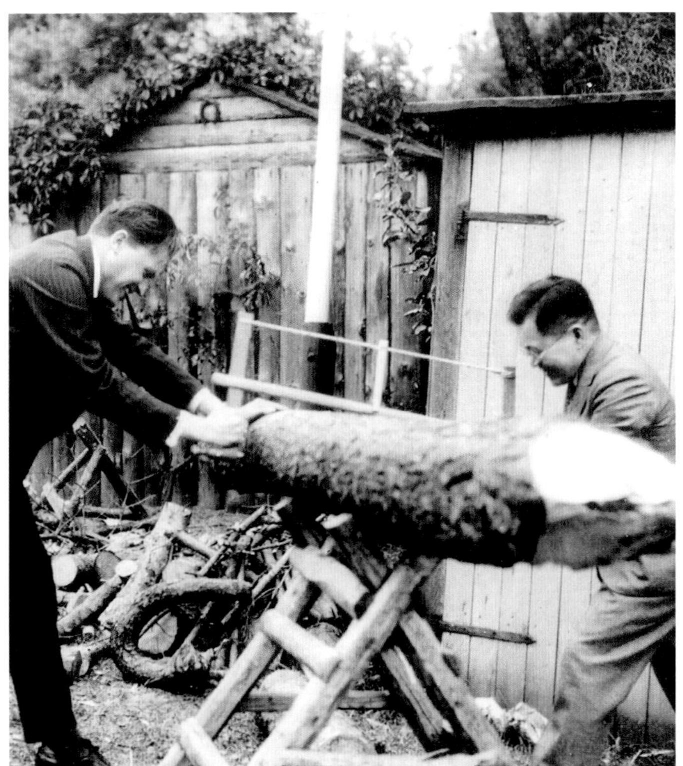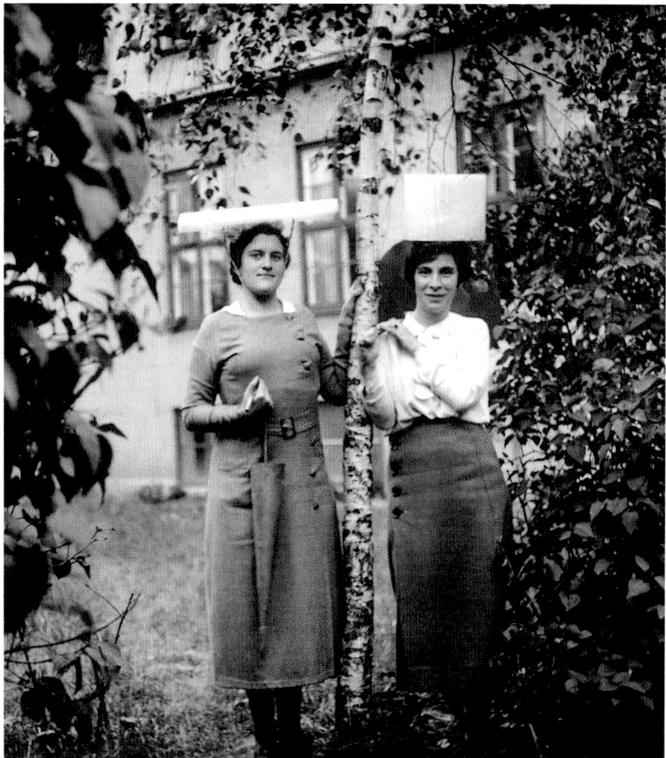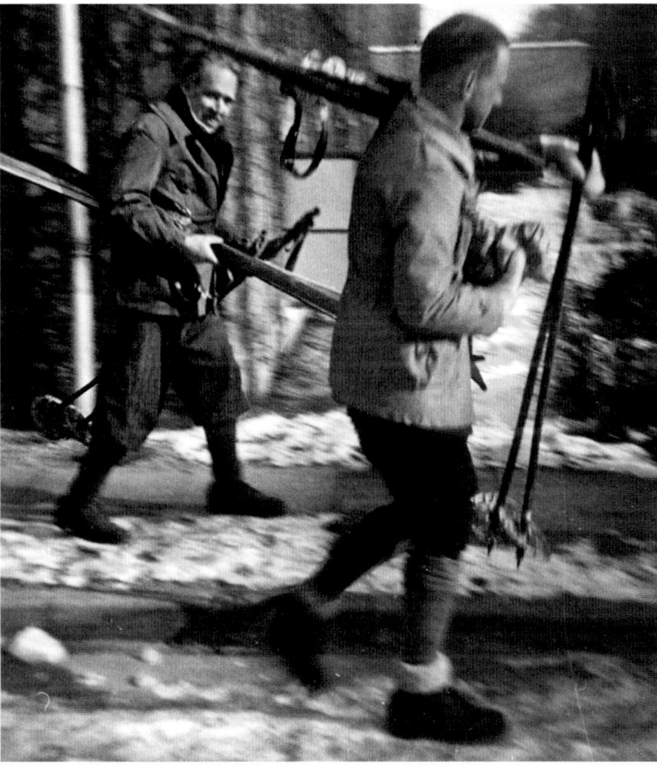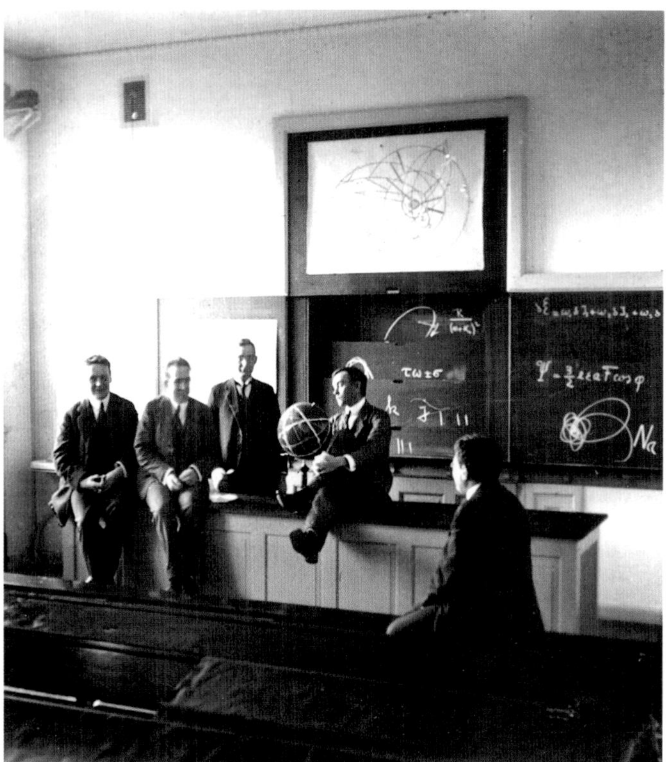

International collaboration: Svein Rosseland and Yoshio Nishina at Bohr's vacation house, Tisvilde, Denmark, 1924
Fun at Niels Bohr Institutet: Piedad de La Cierva Viudes and Hilde Levi from the photo album made on the occasion of James Franck's travel to USA, 1935
Cross country skiing and quantum physics: Werner Heisenberg and Bohr outside Niels Bohr institutet on their way to skiing at Fælledparken, Copenhagen, 1932
The original core of Niels Bohr Institutet: H.M. Hansen, Niels Bohr, Hendrik Kramers, Svein Rosseland and Paul Ehrenfest in Auditorium A. Niels Bohr Institutet, 1922

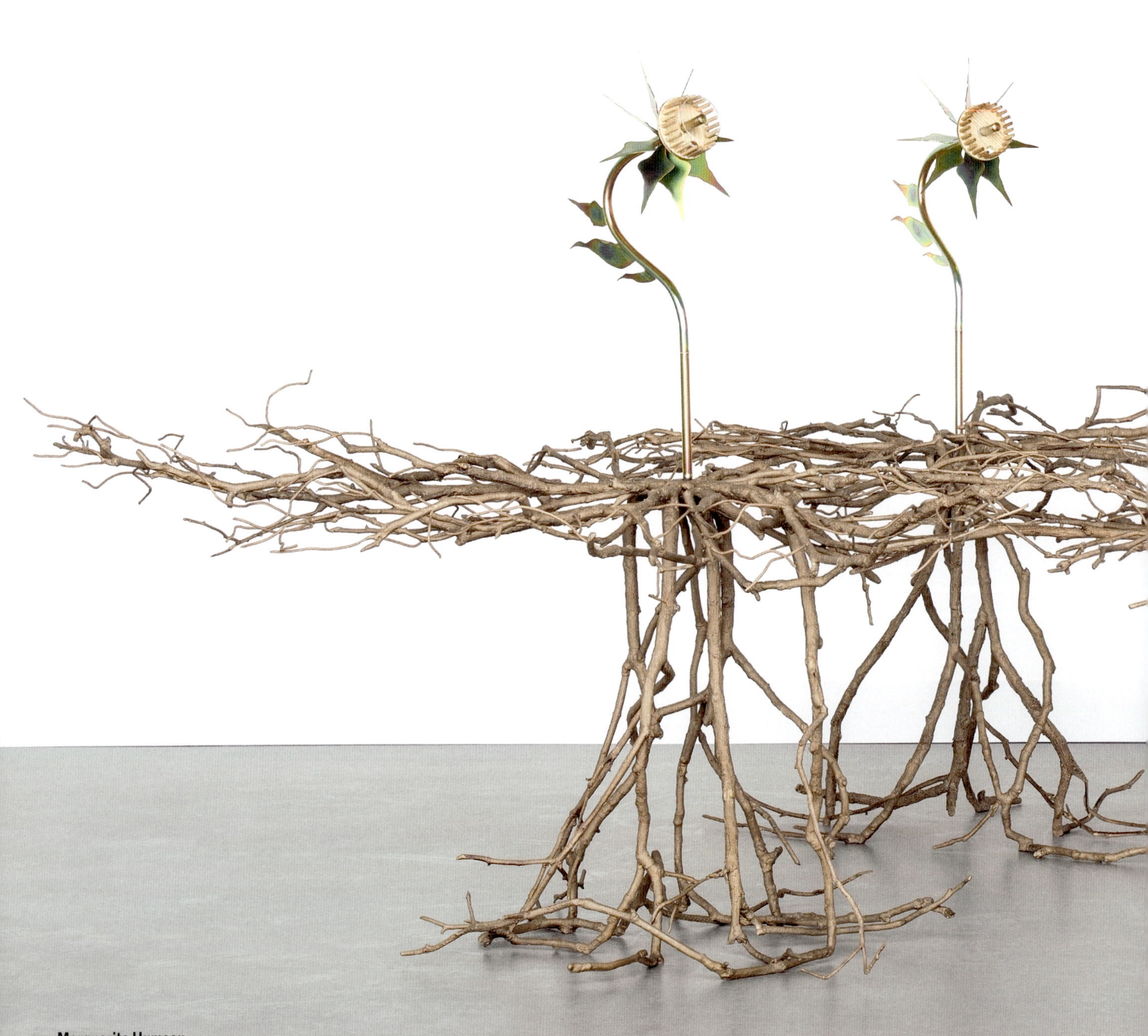

Marguerite Humeau
Russian Thistle Spins, 2023

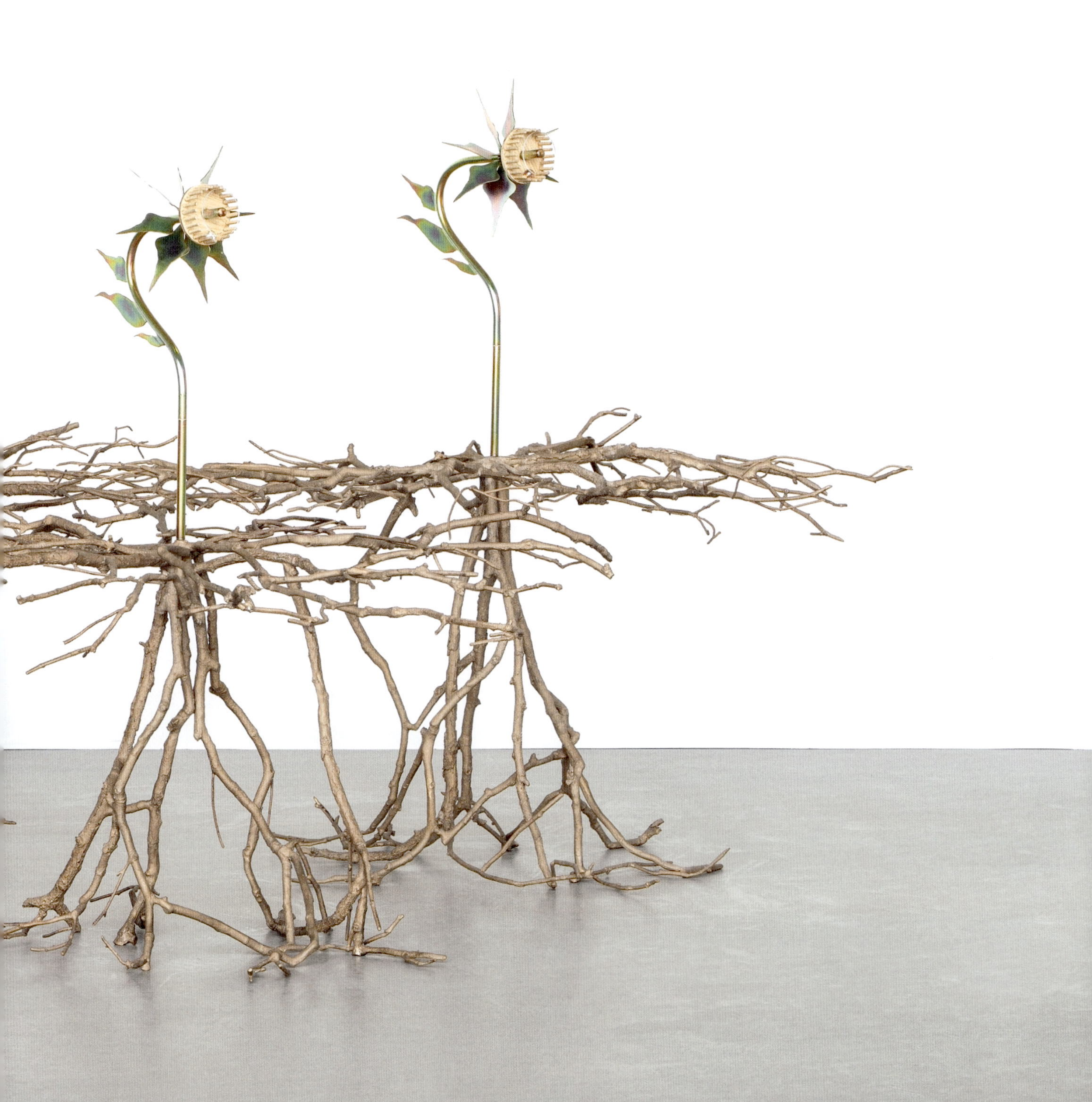

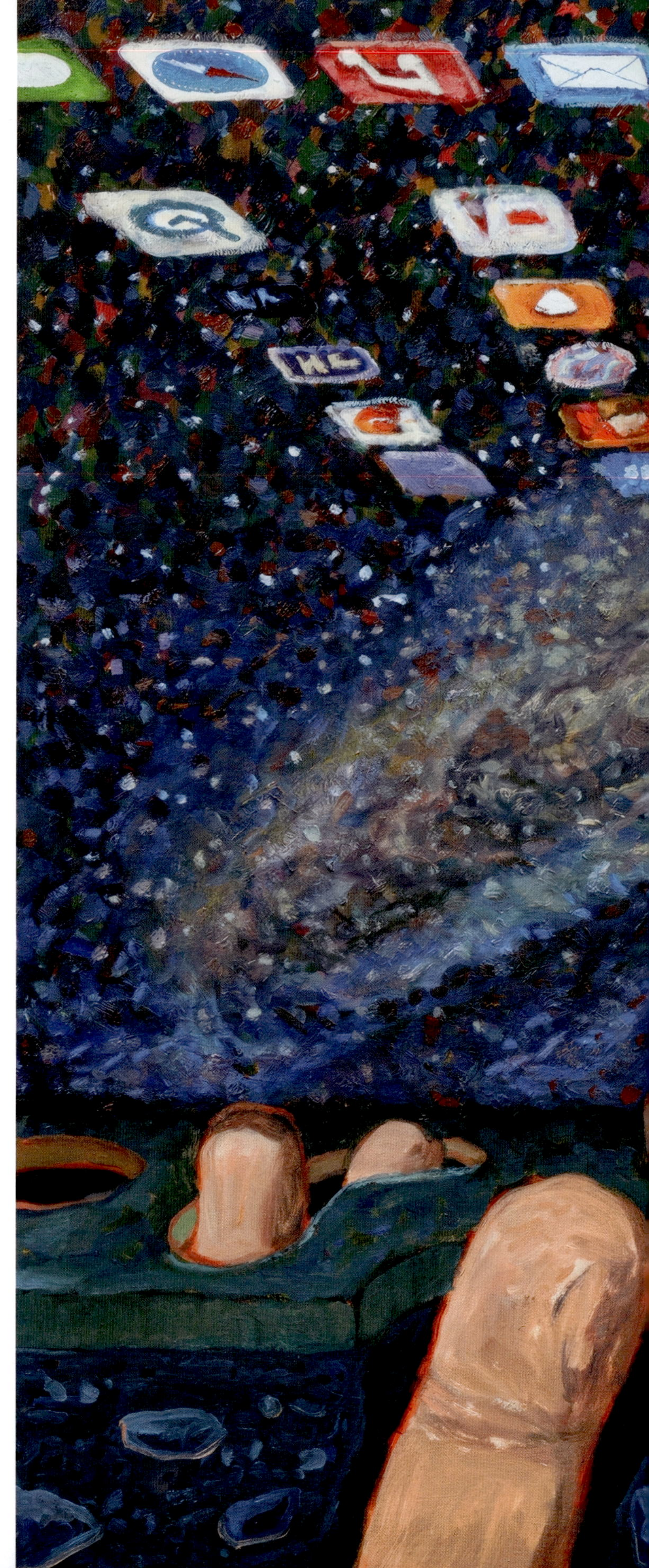

Trisha Baga
Fingerings, 2023

Next spread:
Tavares Strachan
Detail of *Six Thousand Years*, 2018

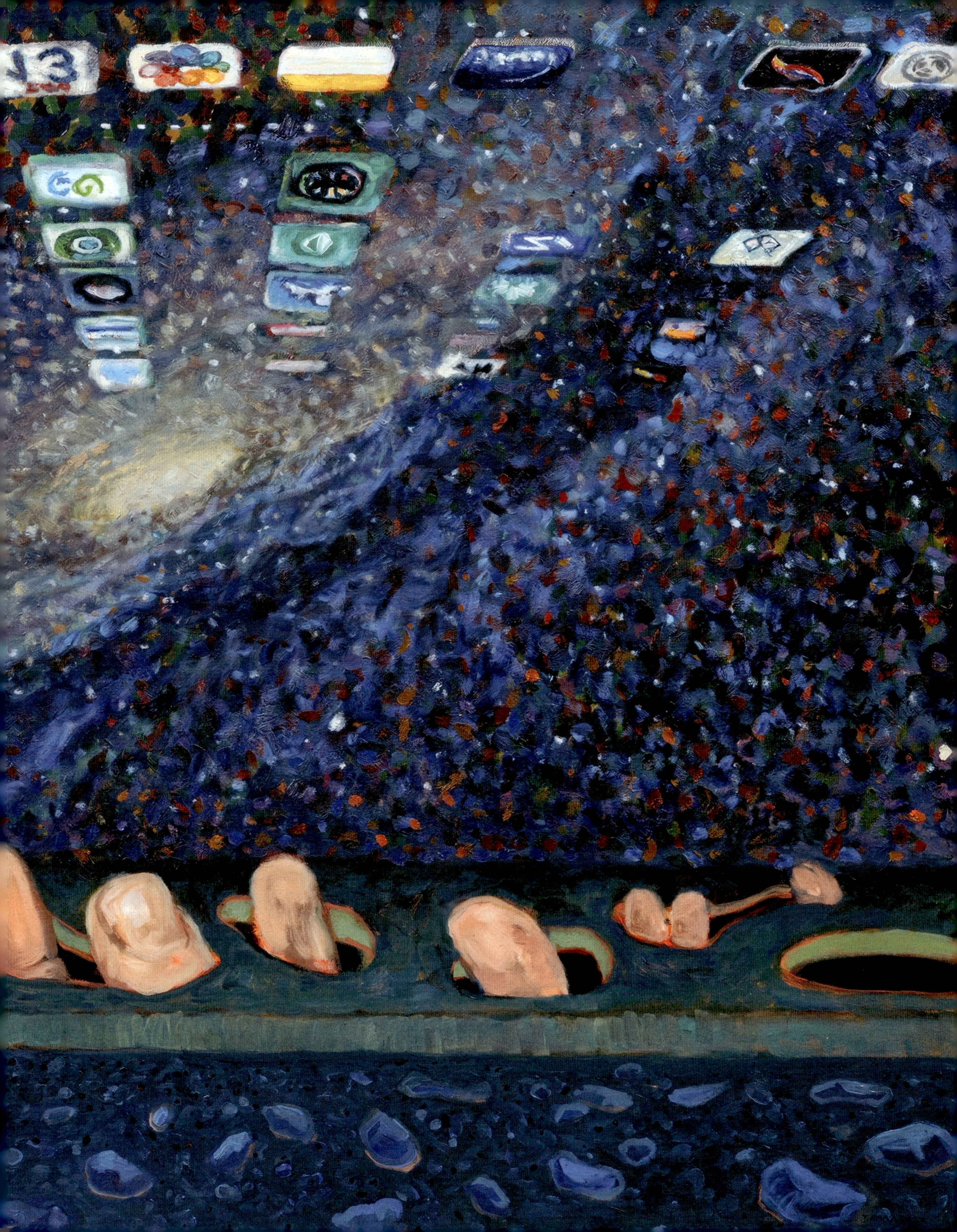

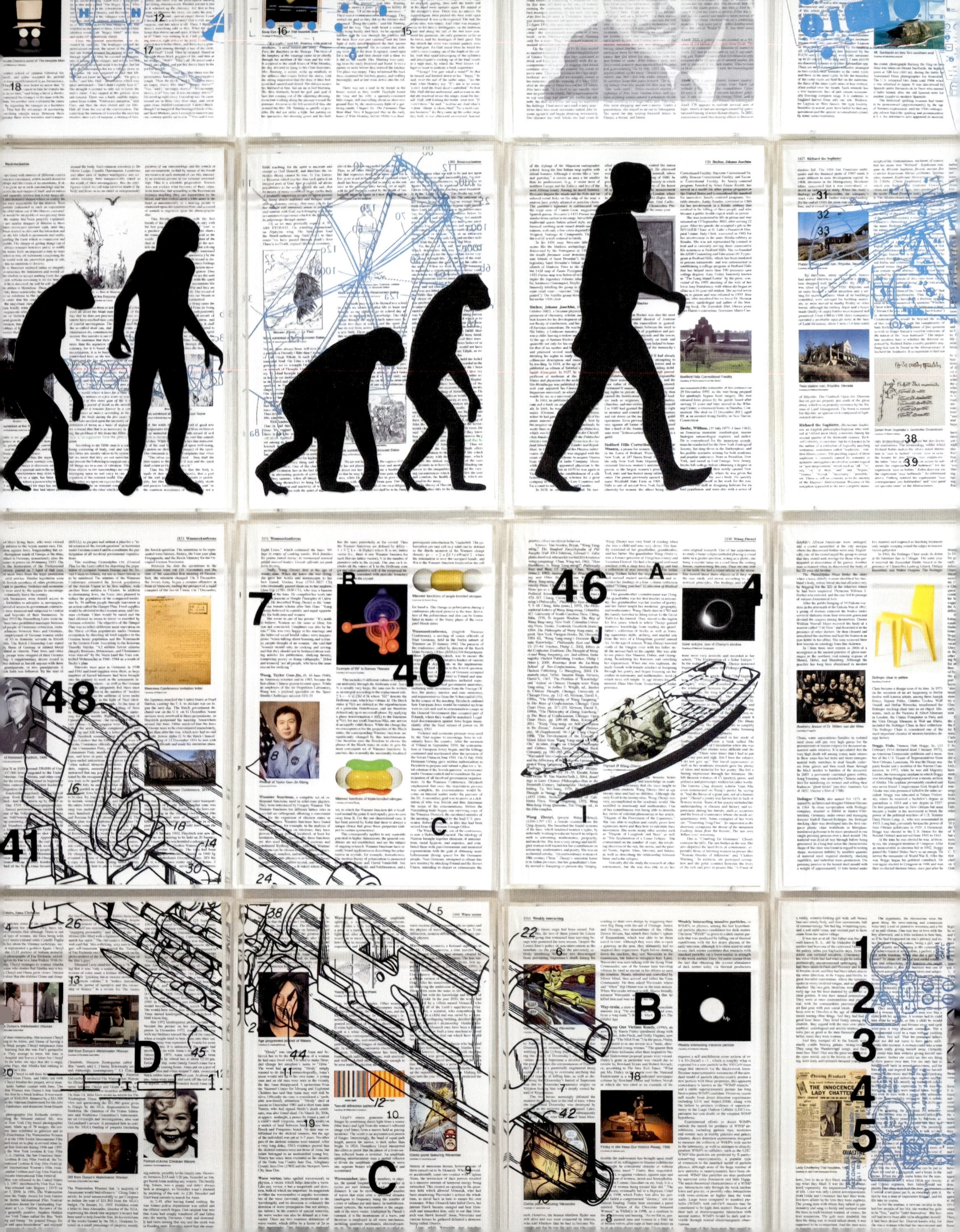

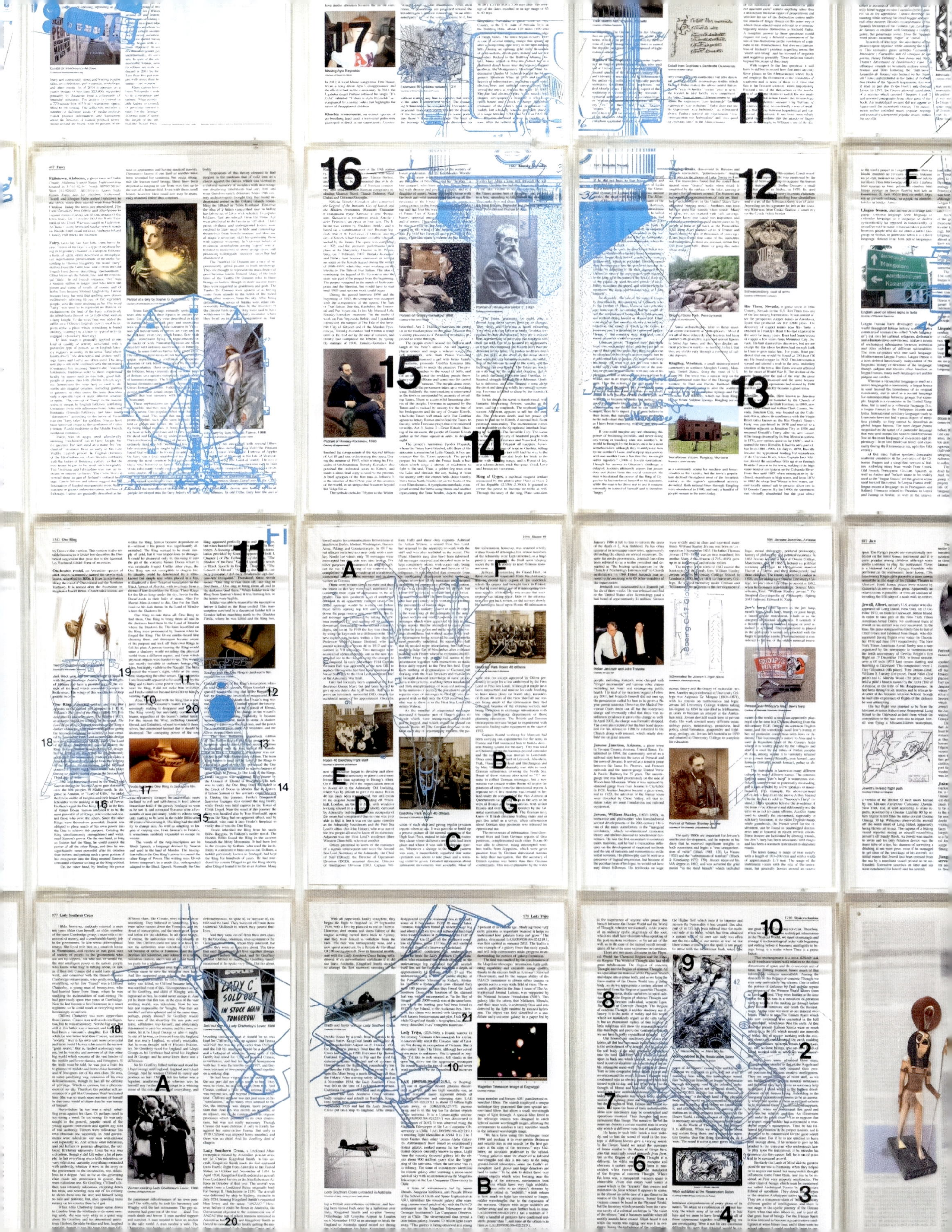

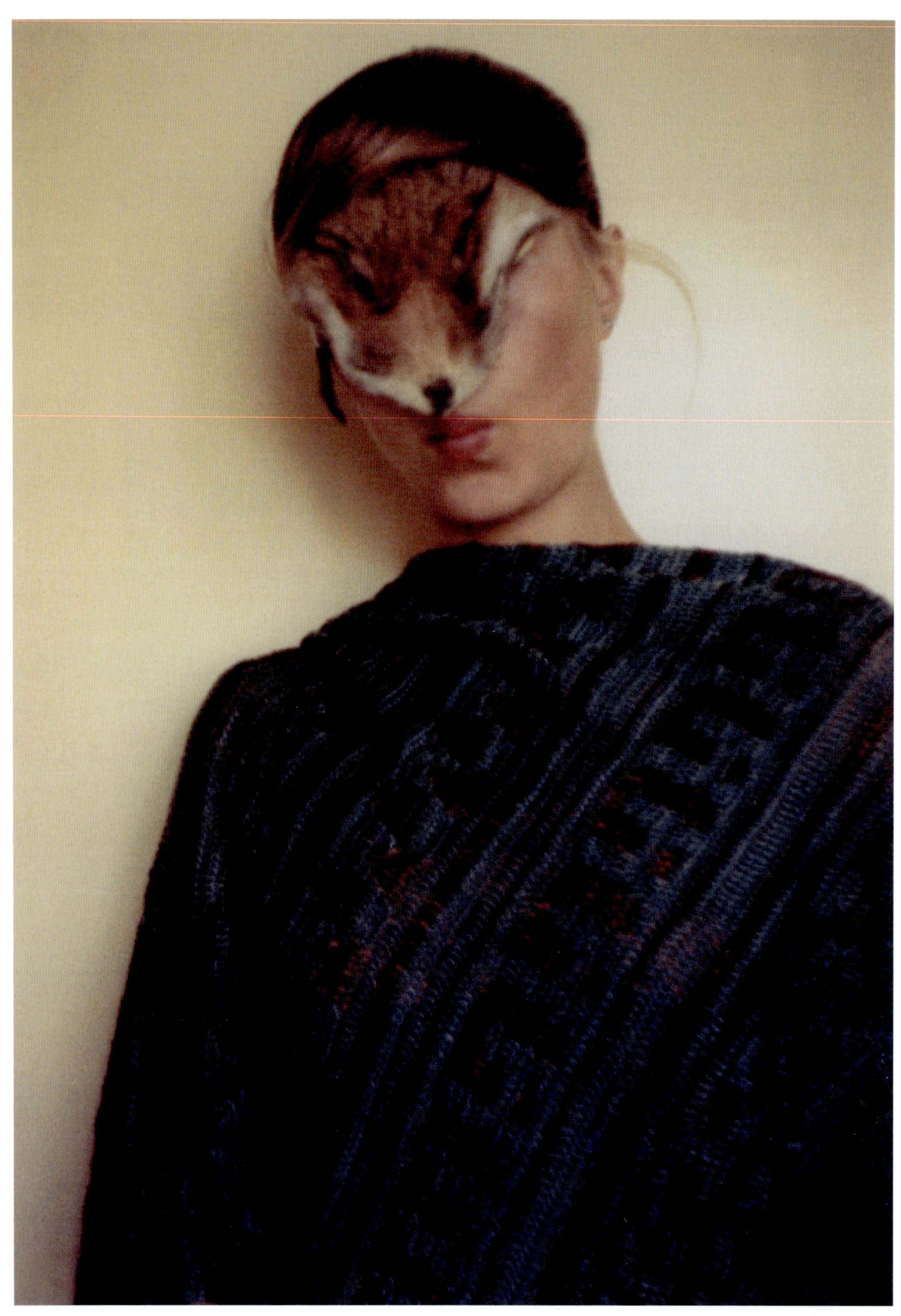

Birgit Jürgenssen
Ohne Titel (Selbst mit Fellchen) (Untitled (Self with Little Fur)), 1974/2011

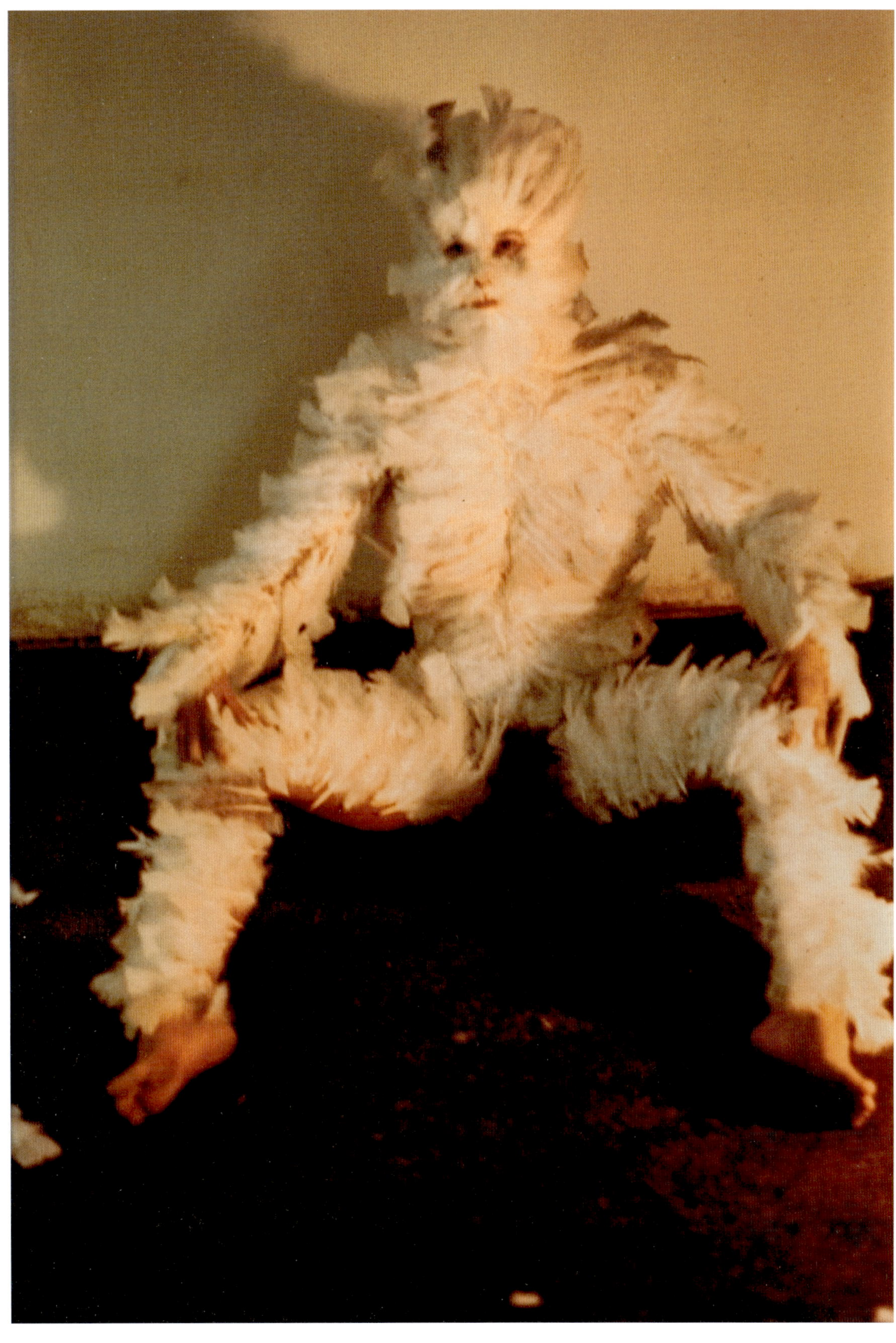

Ana Mendieta
Bird Transformation, 1972

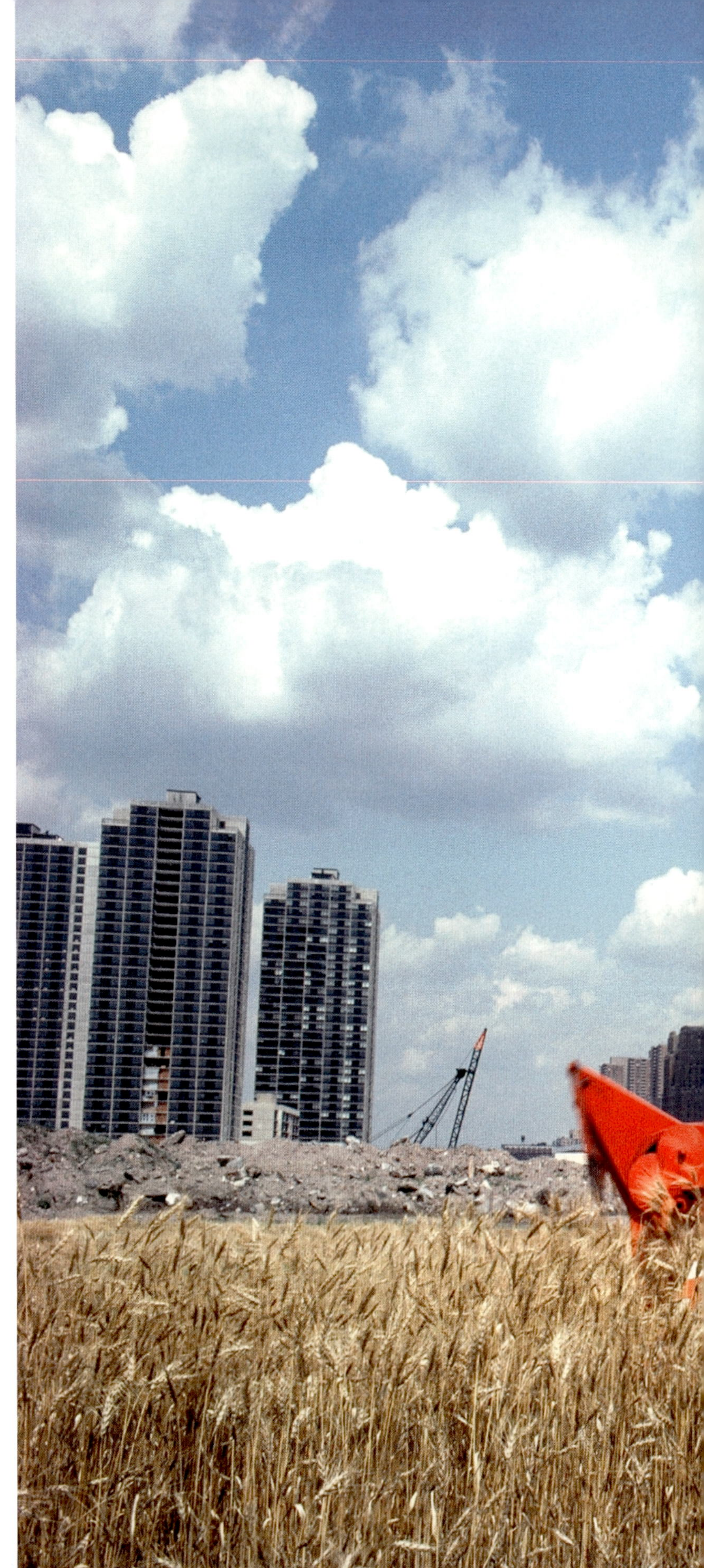

Agnes Denes
Wheatfield – A Confrontation: Battery Park Landfill,
Downtown Manhattan – The Harvest, 1982

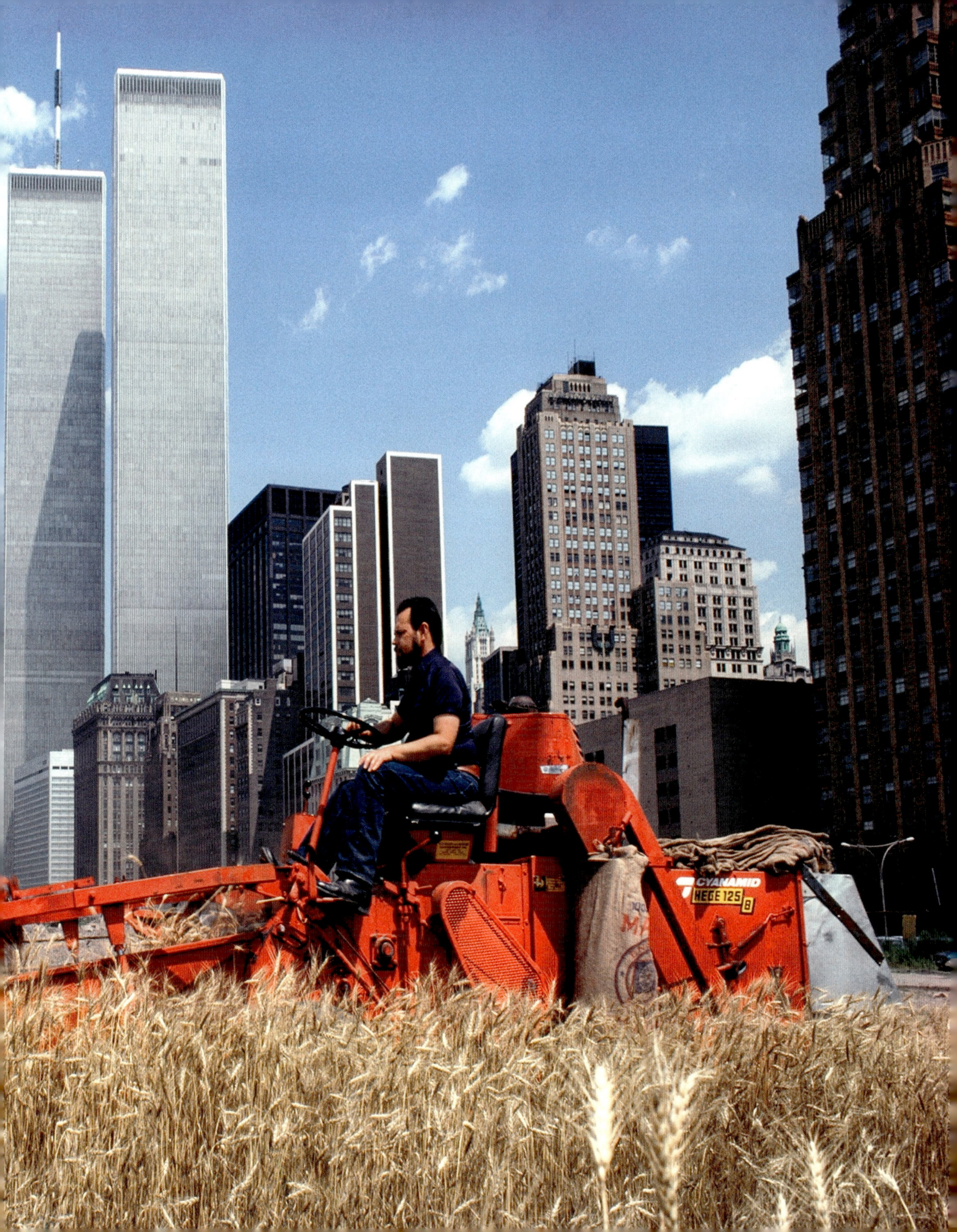
CYANAMID
HEGE 125 B

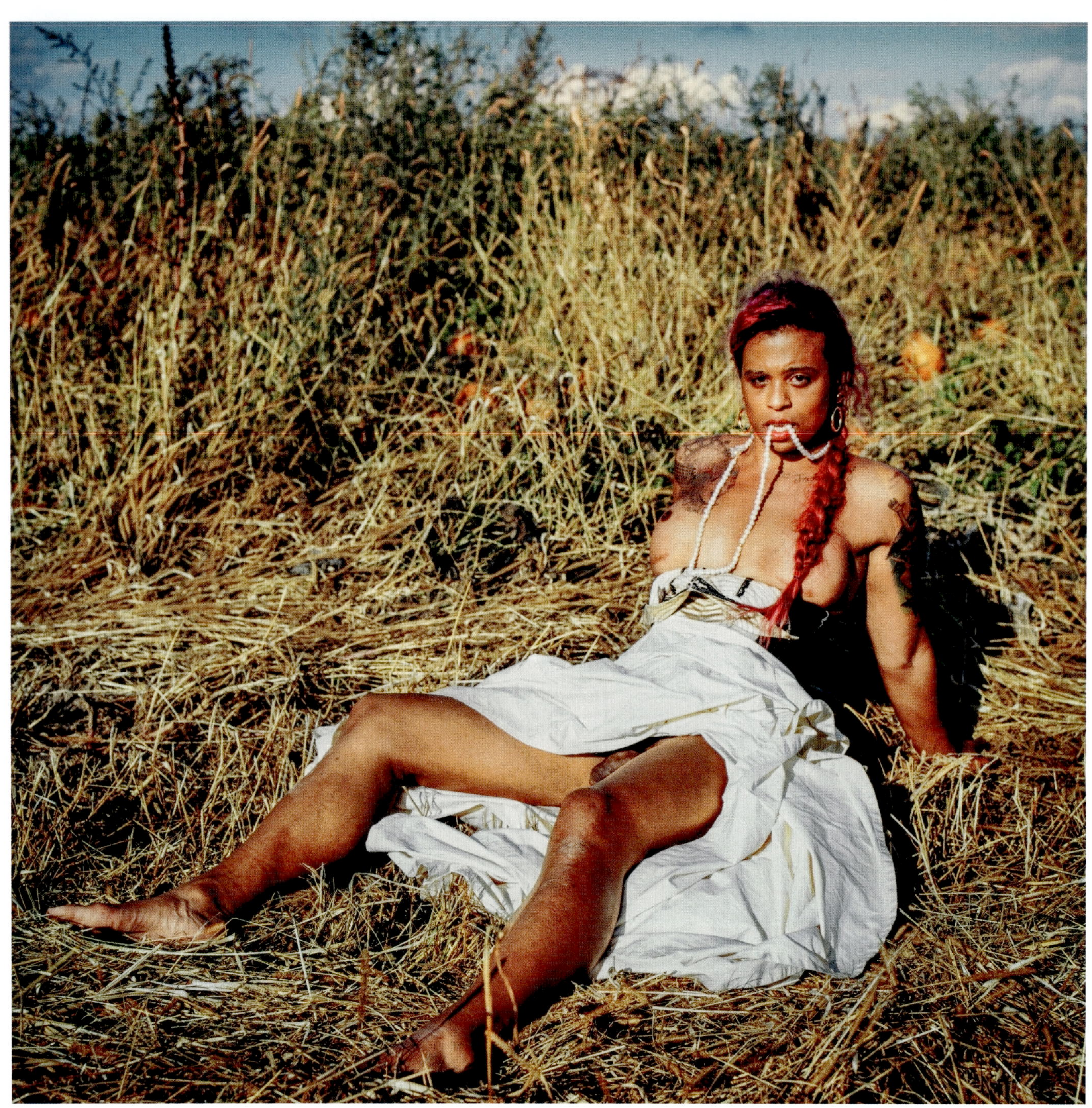

Tourmaline
Swallowtail, 2020

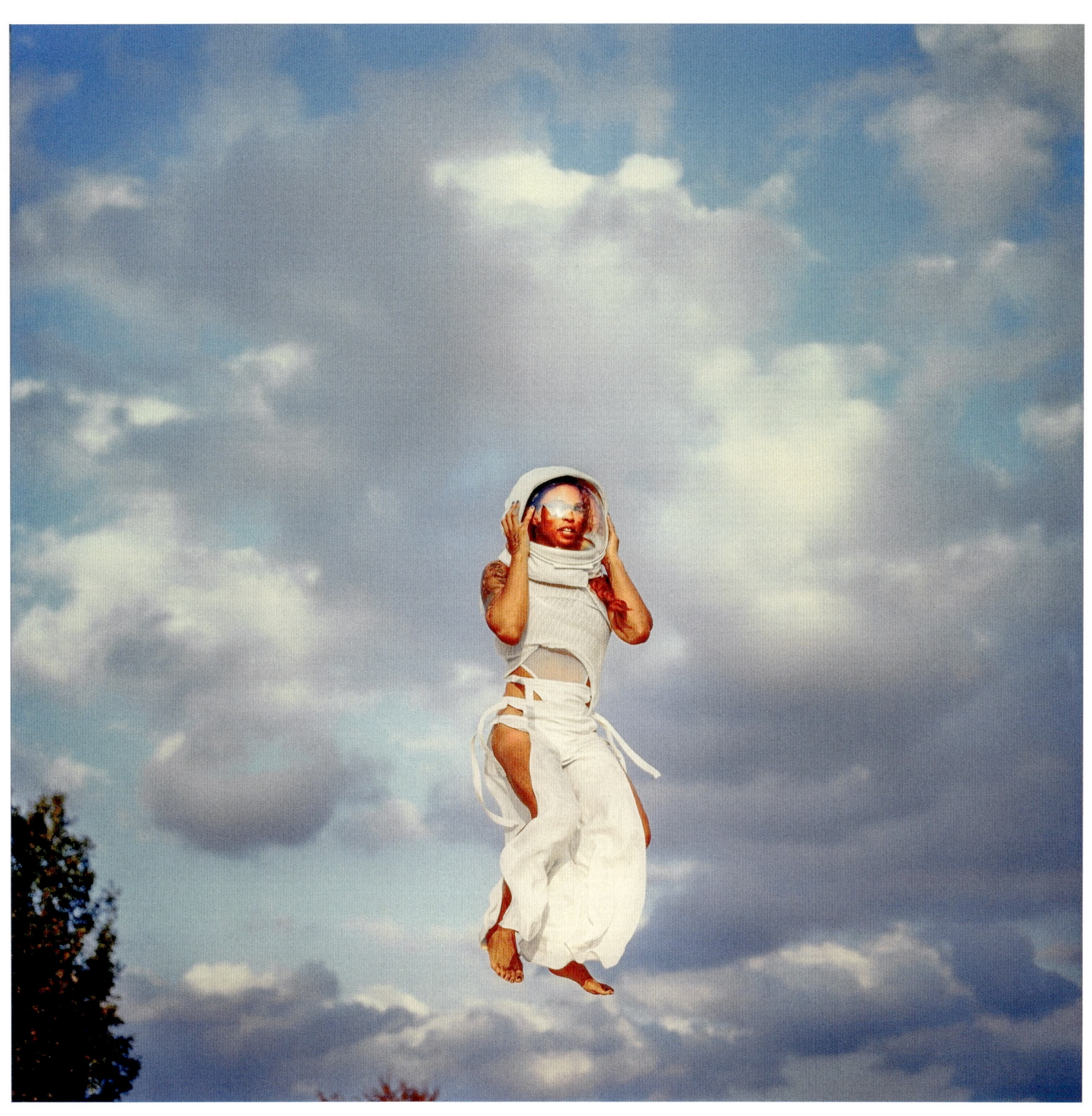

Tourmaline
Summer Azure, 2020

Olga Ravn
<u>One of the Ways She Walks</u>
Where does inspiration come from?
In this text, Danish writer Olga Ravn
writes poetically about the world of
experience behind working with words.

I never knew how to talk about my childhood in a way that could make it come across like a complete story or add up to a portrait. The memories I had couldn't be reached with words, would not be mastered sufficiently to be shared. Whenever I tried, a discomfort would arise and those stories would return to me as distorted as a cultivated field reflected by so many mirrors it comes to resemble a photograph taken from a speeding car, printed on a cheap scarf. Anyway, I hadn't been able to read for some time, but when Midsummer came round the skill came back and I seemed to stumble upon all the right books then, an amazing feeling, and with reading the memories seemed to return, this being something that's happened increasingly over the last couple of years, maybe because I've been satisfactorily treated for my mental illness, or maybe simply because I'm becoming adult; in any case, it appears as if I'm now increasingly able to accommodate my own childhood and it comes swimming towards me in the shape of small complete pictures, a bit like conclusions, that have been working away inside me somewhere, waiting for me to have the strength to look at them. One of the first I remember was the insight that from when I was six to when I was eight I had a best friend called Louise. The way I remembered things, I never had any friends as a child, but then Louise appeared and there we were walking along underneath the chestnut trees in front of the houses, the same way to school and home again every day, expanding on each other's proposals for inventions, and only now, thirty years on, am I able once again to feel that elation completely, the elation I felt with Louise; only now, perhaps, because afterwards, when we got older and everything became more complicated, I felt shame at having disengaged, but now I understand that love between female friends isn't just a romantic dream but something I was once fully and completely immersed in, it's incredible! What an amazing friendship! Something else I understood that came to me just now, which is why I'm writing it down –

I'm sitting in a shopping mall drinking a very expensive cup of coffee and it just came to me, though it's been bothering me the last couple of days, a memory like the one about Louise, a sort of a pond inside what's me, and I'm crossing the moor and there's an incredible ecosystem down there – is to do with my mum's four-track tape recorder, the one she uses to record demos on, and this is in the living room in autumn or winter, because the living room had a creamy feel to it then like thick writing paper, and it's not just one time but several, maybe I even took the tape recorder with me upstairs to my room; in any case, I've been instructed in how to use it and I think there's a little hand-held mic, because I seem to remember the metallic-smelling mesh against my lips. And was it my mum who encouraged me to tell a story? I don't remember anyone else being there, but the situation isn't what's important, it's the depth that opens up, cone-shaped like the mic, once I get started. It's a fairy tale I'm telling, possibly *The Princess on the Glass Hill*, only quite soon it alters, because I can't really remember how that fairy tale goes, what's important is that I discover that the story is a movement, a wandering, that keeps opening out in new ways, like a constantly shifting dream reveals infinity, the boundless potential that resides in the story being able to go wherever it wants, in any direction, and at the same time the way the words supersede each other, every progression calling for the next, without the girl knowing where the girl is going, it's like discovering an aptitude for kicking a ball, I was so psyched, it was my first encounter with writing, the telling of that story. Why am I writing about it now? I want to write about it. I want briefly to sing the praises of elation before the earth succumbs, I want to put out an anchor before I fly away.

Translated by Martin Aitken

Olga Ravn is a Danish poet and novelist, known for *The Employees* (2018) and *My Work* (2020). Her other interests include witchcraft and natural dyeing of clothes, and in 2023 she made her debut as a playwright with the play *Hex* at the Royal Danish Theatre.

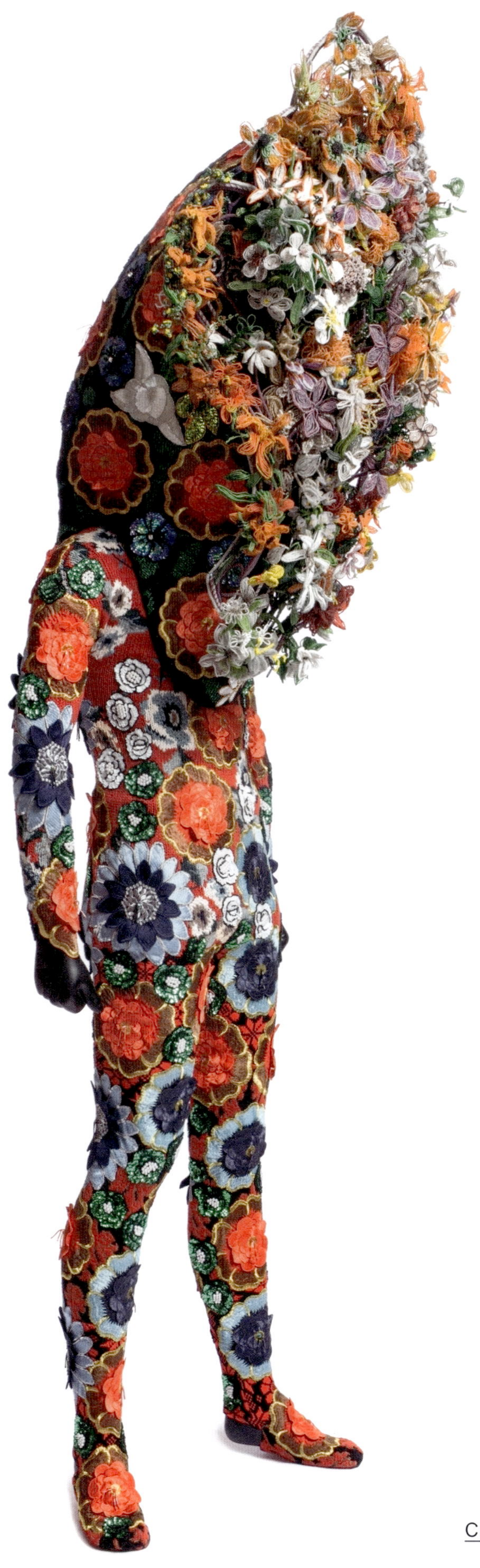

Nick Cave
Soundsuit, 2006

Paulo Freire, Françoise Vergès, Thomas Mann, Audre Lorde and Mladen Stilinović
The Irreplaceable human in literature

Although the word "creativity" did not gain widespread use in English before the 1940s and 1950s, related concepts such as "creation", "inspiration", "genius" and "invention" can be traced as far back as we have written sources. Ideas have not always been understood as originating in the individual; in ancient Greece, for example, inspiration was often ascribed to the muses. In the following, we have selected excerpts from texts by five writers and thinkers who relate to creativity in different ways. Brazilian educator and philosopher Paulo Freire (1921-1997) criticises traditional educational systems for creating passive recipients who cannot develop their creativity. French-Algerian historian Françoise Vergès (born 1952) explores how different types of work are valued differently; the dialectical relation between the white male performing body (e.g. office workers); and the racialised female exhausted body (e.g. performing cleaning and care work). In German Thomas Mann's (1855-1975) classic novel *Doctor Faustus*, composer Adrian Leverkühn sells his soul to the devil in exchange for artistic genius. The the essay by American writer and theorist Audre Lorde (1934-1992) is a defence of the creative potential of difference. And Croatian conceptual artist Mladen Stilinović (1947-2016) writes about laziness as an artistic necessity.

Paulo Freire
Pedagogy of the Oppressed (1968)

[A traditional educational system] turns [students] into "containers", into "receptacles" to be "filled" by the teacher. The more completely she fills the receptacles, the better a teacher she is. The more meekly the receptacles permit themselves to be filled, the better students they are.

Education thus becomes an act of depositing, in which the students are the depositories and the teacher is the depositor. Instead of communicating, the teacher issues communiques and makes deposits which the students patiently receive, memorize and repeat. This is the "banking" concept of education, in which the scope of action allowed to the students extends only as far as receiving, filing and storing the deposits. They do, it is true, have the opportunity to become collectors or cataloguers of the things they store. But in the last analysis, it is the people themselves who are filed away through the lack of creativity, transformation, and knowledge in this (at best) misguided system. For apart from inquiry, apart from the praxis, individuals cannot be truly human. Knowledge emerges only through invention and re-invention, through the restless, impatient, continuing, hopeful inquiry human beings pursue in the world, with the world, and with each other.

Paulo Freire, *Pedagogy of the Oppressed,* 1968, trans. Myra Bergman Ramos, Continuum, 2005, p. 72.

Françoise Vergès
Capitalocene, Waste, Race, and Gender (2019)

Every day, in every urban center of the world, thousands of black and brown women, invisible, are "opening" the city. They clean the spaces necessary for neo-patriarchy, and neoliberal and finance capitalism to function. They are doing dangerous work: they inhale toxic chemical products and push or carry heavy loads. They have usually travelled long hours in the early morning or late at night, and their work is underpaid and considered to be unskilled. They are usually in their forties or fifties. A second group, which shares with the first an intersection of class, race and gender, go to middle class homes to cook, clean, and take care of children and the elderly, so that those who employ them can go to work in the places that the former group of women have cleaned. Meanwhile, in the same early hours of the morning, in the same big metropoles of the world, we can see women and men running through the streets, rushing to the nearest gym or yoga center. They follow the mandate to maintain healthy and clean bodies of late capitalism; they usually follow their run or workout with a shower, an avocado toast and a detox drink before heading to their clean offices.

Meanwhile, women of color try to find a seat for their exhausted bodies as they return on public transit from cleaning those gyms, banks, insurance offices, newspaper offices, investment companies, or restaurants and preparing meeting rooms for business breakfasts. They doze off as soon as they sit, their fatigue visible to those who care to see it. The working body that is made visible is the concern of an ever growing industry dedicated to the cleanliness and healthiness of body and mind, the better to serve racial capitalism. The other working body is made invisible even though it performs a necessary function for the first: to clean spaces in which the "clean" ones circulate, work, eat, sleep, have sex and perform parenting.

Françoise Vergès, "Capitalocene, Waste, Race, and Gender", *e-flux journal 100*, May 2019.

Thomas Mann
Doctor Faustus (1947)

He: "[…] We are in league and in business – with your blood you have certified it and promised yourself to us and are baptized ours – this visit of mine is intended merely for confirmation. From us you have taken time, genius time, high-flying time, a full twenty-four years *ab dato recessi*, which we set as your bound. And when they are over and their course run, the which cannot be foreseen, and such a time is likewise an eternity – you shall be fetched. In recompense of which we will meanwhile be subject and obedient to you in all things, and hell shall profit you, if you but renounce all who live, all the heavenly host and all men, for that must be."

I (blown hard by utter cold): "How? That is new. What would this clause say?"

He: "It would say renounce. What else? Do you think jealousy is at home only in the heights and not in the deeps as well? You, fine creature well-created, are promised and betrothed to us […]. Your life shall be cold – hence you may love no human. What can you be thinking? The illumination leaves your intellect's powers unsullied to the last, indeed at times enhances them to dazzling rapture – what in the end should be its object but the sweet soul and the precious life of the affections? […] We want you cold, till scarcely the flames of production shall be hot enough for you to warm yourself in them. You shall flee into them from the coldness of your life …."

I: "And out of the fire back into the ice. It is evidently an anticipated hell you prepare now for me on earth."

He: "It is extravagant existence, the only one that will suffice for a proud mind. Your arrogancy would truly never wish to exchange it for a lukewarm one. Do I have your hand on it? You shall enjoy it for the work-filled eternity of a human life."

Thomas Mann, *Doctor Faustus*, 1948, trans. John E. Woods, Vintage, 1999, p. 264.

Audre Lorde
The Master's Tools Will Never Dismantle the Master's House (1979)

Interdependency between women is the way to a freedom which allows the "I" to "be", not in order to be used, but in order to be creative. This is a difference between the passive "be" and the active "being".

Advocating the mere tolerance of difference between women is the grossest reformism. It is a total denial of the creative function of difference in our lives. For difference must be not merely tolerated, but seen as a fund of necessary polarities between which our creativity can spark like a dialectic. Only then does the necessity for interdependency become unthreatening. Only within that interdependency of different strengths, acknowledged and equal, can the power to seek new ways to actively "be" in the world generate, as well as the courage and sustenance to act where there are no charters.

Within the interdependence of mutual (non-dominant) differences lies that security which enables us to descend into the chaos of knowledge and return with true visions of our future, along with the concomitant power to effect those changes which can bring that future into being. Difference is that raw and powerful connection from which our personal power is forged.

As women, we have been taught either to ignore our differences, or to view them as causes for separation and suspicion rather than as forces for change. Without community, there is no liberation, only the most vulnerable and temporary armistice between an individual and her oppression. But community must not mean a shedding of our differences, nor the pathetic pretense that these differences do not exist.

Those of us who stand outside the circle of this society's definition of acceptable women; those of us who have been forged in the crucibles of difference; those of us who are poor, who are lesbians, who are Black, who are older, know that *survival is not an academic skill*. It is learning how to stand alone, unpopular and sometimes reviled, and how to make a common cause with those other identified as outside the structures, in order to define and seek a world in which we can all flourish. It is learning how to take our differences and make them strengths. *For the master's tools will never dismantle the master's house.* They may allow us temporarily to beat him at his own game, but they will never enable us to bring about genuine change. And this fact is only threatening to those women who still define the master's house as their only source of support.

Audre Lorde, "The Master's Tools Will Never Dismantle the Master's House", 1979, in *This Bridge called my Back: Writings by Radical Women of Colour*, eds. Cherríe Moraga and Gloria Anzaldúa, Kitchen Table: Women of Color Press, 1981, p. 99.

Mladen Stilinović
In Praise of Laziness (1993)

As an artist, I learned from both East (socialism) and West (capitalism). Of course, now that the borders and political systems have changed, this type of experience will be no longer possible. But what I have learned from that dialogue stays with me. My observation and knowledge of Western art has recently led me to the conclusion that art cannot exist in the West anymore. This is not to say that there is not any. Why can art not exist anymore in the West? The answer is simple. Artists in the West are not lazy. Artists from the East are lazy; whether they will stay lazy now that they are no longer Eastern artists remains to be seen.

Laziness is the absence of movement and thought, dumb time – total amnesia. It is also indifference, staring at nothing, non-activity, impotence. It is sheer stupidity, a time of pain, of futile concentration. Those virtues of laziness are important factors in art. Knowing about laziness is not enough, it must be practiced and perfected.

Artists in the West are not lazy and therefore not artists, but rather producers of something. Their involvment with matters of no importance, such as production, promotion, the gallery system, the museum system, the competition system (who is first), their preoccupation with objects – all that drives them away from laziness, from art. Just as money is but paper, a gallery is but a room.

Artists from the East were lazy and poor because the entire system of insignificant factors did not exist. Therefore, they had time enough to concetrate on art and laziness. Even when they did produce art, they knew it was in vain, it was nothing.

Artists from the West could have learned about laziness, but they did not. Two major 20th century artists dealt with the question of laziness, in both practical and theoretical terms: Marcel Duchamp and Kazimir Malevich.

Duchamp never really discussed laziness, but rather indifference and nonwork. When asked by Pierre Cabanne what had brought him most pleasure in life, Duchamp said, "First, having been lucky. Because basically I've never worked for a living. I consider working for a living slightly imbecilic from an economic point of view. I hope that some day we'll be able to live without being obliged to work. Thanks to my luck, I was able to manage without getting wet."

Malevich wrote a text entitled "Laziness – The Real Truth about Mankind" (1921). In it he criticized capitalism, because it enabled only a small number of capitalists to be lazy, but also socialism, because the entire movement was based on work instead of laziness. To quote: "People are scared of laziness and persecute those who accept it, and it always happens because no one realizes laziness is the truth; it has bees branded as the mother of all vices, but it is in fact the mother of life. Socialism brings liberation in the unconscious, it scorns laziness without realizing it was laziness that gave birth to it; in his folly, the son scorns his mother as a mother of all vices and would not remove the brand; in this brief note I want to remove the brand of shame from laziness and to pronounce it not the mother of all vices, but the mother of perfection."

Finally, to be lazy and conclude: there is no art without laziness.

"Work is a disease."
-Karl Marx

"Work is shame."
-Mladen Stilinovic and Vlado Martek

Mladen Stilinović, "The Praise of Laziness", 1993, *Moscow Art Magazine*, no. 22, 1998, pp. 25-26.

List of Works

5 signs/posters from the Danish
national teachers' lockout in 2013
Dimensions variable
Arbejdermuseet, Copenhagen

Bertille Bak
Mineur Mineur, 2022
Dimensions variable
Video installation with 5
synchronized videos
Duration: 15:23 min.
Co-production: Bertille Bak, La
Fondation des Artistes, Institut
Français et La Criée Centre
d'art contemporain, Rennes
Courtesy of the artist, Xippas
Galleries (Paris, Geneva & Punta
del Este) and The Gallery
Apart, Rome

Brian Belott
*Rhoda Kellogg Mandala
(exhibition copy),* 2019
Dia.: 180 cm
Courtesy the artist

Joost Conijn
*Siddieqa, Firdaus, Abdallah,
Soelayman, Moestafa, Hawwa en
Dzoel-kifl,* 2004
Duration: 41:37 min.
Video
Courtesy of the artist

Rineke Dijkstra
*Ruth Drawing Picasso, Tate
Liverpool,* 2009
Duration: 6:36 min.
Single-channel HD video
Louisiana Museum of Modern Art
Acquired with funding from The
Augustinus Foundation

David Douglas Duncan
*Paloma posant devant l'objectif
avec le dessin qu'elle vient de
réaliser,* 1957
Paloma Posing in front of the
Camera with the Drawing She
Just Made
35.3 × 28 cm
Gelatin silver print
Private collection

David Douglas Duncan
*Paloma dessinant pendant que
Picasso grave une plaque de
linoléum,* 1957
Paloma Drawing while Picasso
Carves a Linocut
20.2 × 12.7 cm
Gelatin silver print
Private collection

David Douglas Duncan
*Paloma dessinant devant le
regard observateur de son père,*
1957
Paloma Drawing under Her
Father's Observant Gaze
16.1 × 24 cm
Gelatin silver print
Private collection

David Douglas Duncan
*Picasso, Claude et Paloma au
travail,* 1957
Picasso, Claude and Paloma
at Work
39.7 × 30 cm
Gelatin silver print
Private collection

David Douglas Duncan
Villa La Californie, Cannes, 1957
24.5 × 35.5 cm
Gelatin silver print
Private collection

Froebel Archive for Childhood
Studies, University of
Roehampton
Archive material:
Friedrich Fröbel
Gift 1-6, c. 1900,
Gift 7 A,C,D,E,F, 1930s,
Gift 13, 1952,
Gift 14, c. 1930s
Dimensions variable and
mixed media
and various photographic and
documentary material from
Froebel Educational Institute,
1880s-1919

Flavia Gandolfo
Los alumnus, 1996-1998
The Students
Series of 3, each 54.5 × 44.5 cm
Inkjet print
Courtesy of the artist and
CRISIS galeria

Tetsuya Ishida
Mebae, 1998
Awakening
145.6 × 206 cm
Acrylic on panel
Collection of Shizuoka
Prefectural Museum of Art

Rhoda Kellogg
*Books, hand drawn taxonomies
and scribble drawings,*
1950s-1975
Dimensions variable and
mixed media
Rhoda Kellogg Child Arnt
Collection, courtesy of Golden
Gate Kindergarten Association

Martin Kippenberger
Kaputtes Kind, 1985
Broken Child
130 × 120 cm
Dispersion, plastic, varnish
and stickers on canvas
Kunsthaus Zürich, Vereinigung
Zürcher Kunstfreunde, Gruppe
Junge Kunst, 1989

Isamu Noguchi
*Swings, Jungle Gym and Slide,
Playground Equipment for Ala
Moana Park,* 1940
Dimensions variable and
mixed media
The Isamu Noguchi Foundation
and Garden Museum, New York;
gift of Linda Tatti Beck and Steven
Beck from the collection of the
Alexander Tatti Family, 2006

Isamu Noguchi
4 Study models, c. 1965-1968,
c. 1980
Dimensions variable and
mixed media
The Isamu Noguchi Foundation
and Garden Museum, New York

Pablo Picasso
Enfants dessinant, 1954
Children Drawing
91.8 × 73 cm
Oil on canvas
Private Collection, courtesy of
Nahmad Collection

Aura Rosenberg
John Baldessari/Carmen, 1996
116.8 × 91.4 cm
Inkjet print
Courtesy of the artist

Aura Rosenberg
Jutta Koether/Karla, 1996
116.8 × 91.4 cm
Inkjet print
Courtesy of the artist

Aura Rosenberg
Ann Craven/Chelsea, 1996-1998
116.8 × 91.4 cm
Inkjet print
Courtesy of the artist

Aura Rosenberg
Gerald Jackson/Toni, Ti,
1996-1998
116.8 × 91.4 cm
Inkjet print
Courtesy of the artist

Aura Rosenberg
Mike Kelley/Carmen (crying),
1996-1998
116.8 × 91.4 cm
Inkjet print
Courtesy of the artist

Aura Rosenberg
John Miller/Joe (Homer),
1996-1998
116.8 × 91.4 cm
Inkjet print
Courtesy of the artist

Aura Rosenberg
Jim Shaw/Joe, 1996-1998
116.8 × 91.4 cm
Inkjet print
Courtesy of the artist

Aura Rosenberg
Laurie Simmons/Lena, 1996-1998
116.8 × 91.4 cm
Inkjet print
Courtesy of the artist

Aura Rosenberg
Mike Smith/Bogyi, 1996-1998
116.8 × 91.4 cm
Inkjet print
Courtesy of the artist

Aura Rosenberg
Fred Tomaselli/Desi, 1996-1998
116,8 × 91.4 cm
Inkjet print
Courtesy of the artist

Aura Rosenberg
Dan Graham/Carmen, 2000
116,8 × 91.4 cm
Inkjet print
Courtesy of the artist

Aura Rosenberg
Christopher Williams/Bram, 2007
116,8 × 91.4 cm
Inkjet print
Courtesy of the artist

Lily van der Stokker
*All kind of good advice
(Happy Childhood),* 2004-2023
100 × 320 cm
Acrylic paint on wall
Courtesy Gallery Air de Paris

Banner, Clog workers' division
in Solbjerg, Denmark: *"8 hours'
labour, 8 hours' recreation, 8
hours' rest"*
147 × 118 cm
Arbejdermuseet, Copenhagen

Tony Cokes
Evil.35: Carlin / Owners, 2012
Duration: 7:56 min.
HD video, colour and sound
Courtesy the artist and Greene
Naftali, New York

Jeremy Deller
*Motorola WT4000 Wearable
Terminal,* 2013
10 × 14 × 64 cm
Plastic and electronics
Courtesy of the artist and The

Modern Institute, Toby Webster
Ltd, Glasgow

*Park Green Mill Double Dialled
Longcase,* c. 1810
Metal, paint and wood
On Loan from the Science
Museum Group

Jeremy Deller
*Hello, today you have day off
(New Version),* 2023
317 × 210 cm
Fabric banner
Courtesy of the artist and The
Modern Institute, Toby Webster
Ltd, Glasgow

Simon Denny
Document Relief 27, 2020
30 × 21 × 13 cm
Inkjet print on archival paper,
glue and custom metal wall mount
Courtesy of: Monika Schnetkamp
Collection

Simon Denny
Document Relief 28, 2021
30 × 21 × 13 cm
Ink jet print on archival paper,
glue and custom metal wall mount
Courtesy of: Monika Schnetkamp
Collection

Simon Denny
*Amazon delivery drone patent
drawing as virtual Rio Tinto
mineral globe,* 2021
180 × 178 × 150 cm
Base: 77 × 68 × 42 cm
Powder coated aluminum, steel,
fiberglass, resin, paint, iOS
Augmented Reality Interface
Courtesy of: Monika Schnetkamp
Collection

Simon Denny
*Document Relief 37 (Amazon
Worker Cage Patent),* 2023
29.7 × 21 × 11 cm
Inkjet print on archival paper,
glue and custom metal wall mount
Courtesy of the artist and Petzel
Gallery, New York

Ryan Gander
Chronos Kairos, 88.88, 2023
Stainless steel
Courtesy of the artist and
Lisson Gallery

Ryan Gander
School of Languages, 2023
125 × 340 × 230 cm
Animatronic gorilla, audio,
desk, fan
Courtesy of the artist and
Lisson Gallery

Ben Grosser
ORDER OF MAGNITUDE, 2019
Duration: 47:15 min.
HD video with stereo sound
Courtesy of the artist

Andreas Gursky
Nha Trang, 2004
295.7 × 207 × 6.6 cm
Chromogenic colour print,
Diasecmumok - Museum
moderner Kunst Stiftung Ludwig
Wien, Acquired 2004

Huang Po-Chih
Production Line - Denim Shirt,
2014
Denim shirts and paper
Courtesy of the artist and
Taipei Fine Art Museum

Huang Po-Chih
*Blue Elephant-Mother, "Wanting
falls around me. Heavy garment,
but I can be a floating elephant in
my dream.",* 2018 (2023)
140 × 160 cm
Giclée on Canson Infinity Baryta
Photographique II Matt
Courtesy of the artist

Huang Po-Chih
You are a blue elephant, 2021
21 × 29.7 cm
Pencil on paper
Courtesy of the artist

Tetsuya Ishida
Untitled, 1997
103 × 145.6 cm
Acrylic on panel
Collection of Shizuoka Prefectural
Museum of Art

Josh Kline
*Universal Early Retirement (spots
#1 & #2),* 2016
Duration: 3 min.
HD video with sound
Courtesy of the artist and
47 Canal, New York, NY

Pilvi Takala
The Stroker, 2018
Duration: 14:26 min.
Video
Courtesy the artist, Carlos/
Ishikawa, London; and Stigter Van
Doesburg, Amsterdam

Lee Wan
*Proper Time: Though the Dreams
Revolve with the Moon,* 2017
30 selected clocks
Sound via headphones
Courtesy of the artist

Clip from MODERN TIMES by
Charles Chaplin, 1936
©1936 Roy Export S.A.S.
Renewed ©1963 Roy Export
S.A.S. All Rights Reserved

Television clips from various
press conferences with Danish
Prime Minister Mette Frederiksen
concerning work

Ian Cheng
Something Thinking of You, 2015
Dimensions variable
Live simulation: infinite duration
and sound
Louisiana Museum of Modern Art
Acquired with funding from
Museumsfonden af 7. december
1966

Josh Kline
*By Close of Business (Maura/
Small-Business Owner),* 2016
58.4 × 71.1 × 99.1 cm
3D-printed plaster, inkjet
ink, cyanoacrylate, foam and
polyethylene bag
Astrup Fearnley Collection, Oslo,
Norway

Josh Kline
Unemployed Journalist (Dave),
2018
53.3 × 63.5 × 104.1 cm
3D-printed sculpture in acrylic-
based photopolymer resin, foam
and polyethylene bag
Danjuma Collection

Agnieszka Kurant
A.A.I., 2017
6 objects (different colours)
Dimensions variable
Termite mounds built by colonies
of living termites from coloured
sand, gold and crystals
Courtesy of the artist

Agnieszka Kurant
Errorism, 2019
Dia.: 75 cm
Hologram, 3D animation,
artificial intelligence algorithms
GPT-3 GPT-2
Courtesy of the artist

Agnieszka Kurant
Aggregated Ghost, 2020
61 × 35.6 × 1 cm
Back-printed ink on acrylic
mounted on dibond
Courtesy of the artist

Mismatch Media
Nothing, Forever, 2022-
AI generated television show
streaming on Twitch, 24/7, 365
days a year
Brian Habersberger and Skyler
Hartle/Mismatch Media

Henrik Olesen
"A.T.", 2019
141 × 99.5 cm
Inkjet print on paper
Louisiana Museum of Modern Art
Acquired with funding from The
Augustinus Foundation

Henrik Olesen
"A.T.", 2019
141 × 99.5 cm
Inkjet print on paper
Louisiana Museum of Modern Art
Acquired with funding from
The Augustinus Foundation

Trevor Paglen
*The Treachery of Object
Recognition,* 2019
38 × 32 cm
Dye sublimation on
aluminum print
Courtesy of the artist, Altman
Siegel Gallery, San Francisco
and Pace Gallery

Trevor Paglen
From 'Apple' to 'Abomination',
2023
5 × 27 m
Prints, pins, labels
Courtesy of the artist, Altman
Siegel Gallery, San Francisco and
Pace Gallery

Yuri Pattison
Open Stacks, 2023
Dimensions variable
Installation, video
Courtesy the artist

Yuri Pattison
clock speed (the dead),
2019-2022
22" Samsung 1:1 ratio monitor,
video, software, single board
computer
Variable duration
Courtesy the artist

Yuri Pattison
clock speed (the exanimate),
2022-2023
22" Samsung 1:1 ratio monitor,
video, software, single board
computer
Variable duration
Courtesy the artist

Yuri Pattison
clock speed (the erased),
2022-2023
22" Samsung 1:1 ratio monitor,
video, software, single board
computer
Variable duration
Courtesy the artist

Jon Rafman
Counterfeit Poast, 2022
Duration: 39:53 min.
4K stereo video
Courtesy the artist and
Sprüth Magers

robotlab
manifest, 2008
360 × 240 cm
Industrial robot, writing desk,
computer, pen tool, paper and
software
Courtesy the artist

Tega Brain and Sam Lavigne
Synthetic Messenger, 2021/2023
Dimensions variable
Assorted screens and computers,
astroturf, custom bot software,
website
Courtesy the artists

Andrea Büttner
3 Phone Etchings, 2015
Each: 195 × 112 cm
Etchings
Courtesy the artist and Hollybush
Gardens, London

Chicks on Speed & collaborators
Sleep Synthesis, 2013/2023
Installation supported by
*Artistic Research project Real
Time Telematic Audiovisual
Improvisation, Norwegian
Directorate for Higher Education
and Skills and Trondheim
Academy of Fine Art, Norwegian
University of Science and
Technology* containing:

- Bruce Sampson/NTNU (Photo),
Liz Dom (Grafic Design), Annett
Busch (Sloganeering), *Artistic
Entrepreneur-Ship,* 2023,
Photography, Courtesy of
the artists
- Alex Murray-Leslie (Photo by
Nanna Klith Hougaard, ©Alex
Murray-Leslie), 2017, *Freeing
Time: Talking about Dreams,*
2017, Polysomnography, St Olavs
Hospital Sleep Lab, Norwegian
University of Science and
Technology, with thanks to Assoc.
Prof. Morten Engstrøm, Prof.
Ingvild Saksvik-Lehouillier &
ARTEC (Art & Technology Task
Force/NTNU), Photography,
Courtesy of the artist
-Alex Murray-Leslie, *Colour
Tuning feat.* The Lycra Ladies
and Billy Lime with a text by
Andrew Mueller, 2023 (2013),
Photography, Courtesy of
the artist
-Leslie Johnson, *Less Time –
Timeless,* 1995, Etched zinc and
wood, Courtesy of the artist
-Douglas Gordon, *Burnt shirt,*
2023, Private collection
-David Rych, *Untitled (práce je*

*nemoc), after Mladen Stilinović:
Umetnik na delu (Artist at work),*
2023, Courtesy of the artist
-Mladen Stilinović, *Práce je
nemoc,* 2005, Work is a disease,
Silkscreen print on cotton T-shirt,
Private collection
-Peter Weibel, *Sessel, Aus der
Serie: Scanned Objects,* 1991,
Chair, From the series: Scanned
Objects, Plexiglass, varnished
old wooden chair, Private
Collection, Berlin
-"TV timeline" selected by Chicks
on Speed, edited by Mohammad
Bayesteh
Artists: Liz Dom, Hedvig
Aannestad Iost, Klas Barbrosson,
Unnur Andrea Einarsdóttir,
Gustav O. Gunvaldsen,
Mohammad Bayesteh, Silke Briel,
Annett Busch, RTAI, Shared
Campus & UkrainaTV

Chicks on Speed: Alex Murray-
Leslie & Melissa E. Logan
COLLABORATORS:
Peter Weibel
Shannon Williamson
Mladen Stilinović
Sam Ferguson
Kathi Glas
Morten Engstrøm
Ingvild Saksvik-Lehouillier
Leslie Johnson
Douglas Gordon
Mohammad Bayesteh
Sophia Efstathiou
Joshua Dekia
KANGELATROMOKRATISCH
Annett Busch
Jacob Jessen
Ayodele Arigbabu
Catarina Gartner
Giulia Timis
Sahar Tarzi
Bruce Sampson
Liz Dom
David Rych
Anneli Røros
Vilde Stokke
Diana Lindbjerg
Sofia Reznichenko
Gleb Dovzhuk
Hedvig Aannestad Iost
Ania Kepka
Tina Frank
Panja Göbel
Klas Barbrosson
Unnur Andrea Einarsdóttir

Jeremiah Day
Alia Mascia / XEROX.ED
Roman Dziadkiewicz
UkrainaTV
Ksenia Mirgorodska
Gustav O. Gunvaldsen
Mar Carnet
Varvara Guljajeva
Sebastian Meal
Krõõt Juurak
Federico Visi
Silke Briel
Sayo Oto
Gabrielle Gerber
Sabela Peinado Casal
Rui Han
Branca Peixoto Vasconcelos
Qi Fang Huang
Ming Mengmeng
Max Kibardin
Andrew Mueller
Nanna Klith Hougaard
Orkun Tunc/ Armageddon Turk

"Sleep Synthesis" is a reversion of "Sleep Symphony" (2013) and made possible with the generous support of: SymbioticA, Centre for Excellence in Biological Arts, Center for Sleep Science, The University of Western Australia, Feedback Studios Vienna, Dr. Ralf Haensel/401Contemporary Berlin, Sleep and Chronobiology laboratory, St Olavs Hospital, Trondheim, Norwegian University of Science & Technology, ARTEC, Prof. Andrew Ferguson, Creativity & Cognition Studios, The University of Technology Sydney, Trondheim Academy of Fine Art (NTNU), Mark Feary, Sabine Breitwieser, Branka Stipančić, Shared Campus, RTAI & Norwegian Directorate for Higher Education and Skills. Heartfelt thanks to Louisiana Museum, Mathias Ussing Seeberg and team for the trust & immense support to make this version of "Sleep Synthesis" a reality. Chicks on Speed & collaborators "Sleep Synthesis" installation supported by Artistic Research project Real Time Telematic Audiovisual Improvisation, Norwegian Directorate for Higher Education and Skills and

Trondheim Academy of Fine Art, Norwegian University of Science and Technology

Tacita Dean
Portraits, 2016
Duration: 16 min.
16 mm film, colour and sound
Louisiana Museum of Modern Art
Acquired with funding from
Museumsfonden af 7. december
1966

Mia Edelgart
Sov, 2020
Sleep
Duration: 31:31 min.
Still, video
Courtesy of the artist

Jenny Holzer
In a dream you saw a way to survive..., 1984
14 × 24.1 cm
Text: Survival (1983-85)
Text on cast aluminum plaque
Courtesy of the artist and
Sprüth Magers

Tetsuya Ishida
Untitled, 1995
72,8 × 103 cm
Acrylic on panel
Collection of Shizuoka
Prefectural Museum of Art

Roman Opalka
1.252.561 - 1.255.562, 1965
Paper size: 33 × 24 cm
Ink on paper
Louisiana Museum of Modern Art
Donation: The Riklis Collection of
McCrory Corporation

Roman Opalka
1.255.563 - 1.258.489, 1965
Paper size: 33 × 24 cm
Ink on paper
Louisiana Museum of Modern Art
Donation: The Riklis Collection of
McCrory Corporation

Dawn Parsonage
Boring Miriam – Time Perception,
2019
244.5 × 291 cm
Photography, wall-paper
Courtesy of the artist

Dawn Parsonage
Boring Found Photographs, 2019
30 × 30 × 2.7 cm
14 found photographs
Courtesy of the artist

Dawn Parsonage
Boring Electrocution Box, 2019
14 × 16 × 16 cm
Wood and electronics
Courtesy of the artist

Nastja Säde Rönkkö
6 months without, 2018-2019
Dimensions variable
Selection of letters and HD videos
(camera: Magda Fabianczyk, edit:
Magda Fabianczyk and Heli Kota)
Duration: 40:20 min.
Produced by Somerset House
Studios, The Finnish Institute in
London and Wysing Arts Centre
Supported by The Finnish Cultural
Foundation and The Kordelin
Foundation

Qiu Shihua
Untitled, 2013
228.5 × 299 cm
Oil on canvas
Louisiana Museum of Modern Art
Acquired with funding from The
Augustinus Foundation

Mladen Stilinović
Artist at Work, 1978
8 photographs, each 30 × 40 cm
Black-and-white photographs,
polyptych consisting of eight
photographs
Courtesy by Branka Stipančić,
Zagreb

Mladen Stilinović
Ich habe keine Zeit, 1983
I have no time
17.3 × 12.6 cm
Artist's book, offset, hardcover,
106 pages, Edition Dacić,
Tübingen
Courtesy by Branka Stipančić,
Zagreb

Pilvi Takala
The Trainee, 2008
Duration: 13:52 min.
Video, power point presentation,
keycard and welcome letter
Courtesy the artist; Carlos/
Ishikawa, London and Stigter Van
Doesburg, Amsterdam

Hourglass (St. Laurentii Church,
Kerteminde, Denmark), 1681
41 × 24 × 10 cm
Gilded and painted wood, glass
with sand, gilded and painted iron
National Museum of Denmark

CROSS-POLLINATION

Yuji Agematsu
zip: 02.01.07 … 02.28.07, 2007
Original cellophane cigarette
wrappers, each: 6.3 × 5.3 × 2.5
cm, mixed media and shelving unit
Siska Bulkens

Yuji Agematsu
zip: 02.01.13 … 02.28.13, 2013
Original cellophane cigarette
wrappers, each: 6.3 × 5.3 × 2.5
cm, mixed media and shelving unit
Siska Bulkens

Trisha Baga
Fingerings, 2023
122 × 153 × 4 cm
Oil on canvas
Courtesy the artist and private
collection, Lund, Sweden

Louisiana Bendolph
"Housetop" Medallion, 1974
193 × 183 cm
Cotton and corduroy
Courtesy of Souls Grown Deep
Foundation, Atlanta, Georgia

Niels Bohr Archive,
Niels Bohr Institute, Copenhagen
Various objects and photographs

Nick Cave
Soundsuit, 2006
182.9 × 76.2 × 76.2 cm
Found sequined and beaded
materials, hand sewn, mannequin
and armature
Collection of Carol McCranie and
Javier Magri

Minder Coleman
*"Four Patch" / "Nina Patch"
variation,* 1956
208 × 208 cm
Cotton and corduroy
Courtesy of Souls Grown Deep
Foundation, Atlanta, Georgia

Tony Conrad
Music and the Mind of the World,
1976-1982
Piano recordings
Courtesy of the Estate of Tony
Conrad, the Tony Conrad Archive,
Greene Naftali, New York and
Galerie Buchholz, Cologne/
Berlin/New York

Agnes Denes
*Wheatfield – A Confrontation:
Battery Park Landfill, Downtown
Manhattan,* 1982
*The Harvest
With Statue of Liberty in the
Large Field
Ocean Liner Passing Wheatfield
on the Hudson
Green Wheat
With New York Financial Center
Aerial View 2
Close Up of Agnes Denes in
the Field*
Each: 40.64 × 50.8 cm
Chromogenic colour print
Courtesy Leslie Tonkonow
Artworks + Projects

Ryan Gander
*2000 year collaboration (The
Prophet),* 2018
19.4 × 24 × 28.2 cm
Mouse: 4 × 4 × 5 cm
Animatronic mouse, sound
Museum Voorlinden, Wassenaar,
The Netherlands

Felix Gonzalez-Torres
"Untitled" (Passport #II), 1993
20.3 cm (at ideal height) x 76.2 x
61 cm (original size)
Each bound booklet, 12 pages:
each 15.2 × 10.2 cm (original size)
Print on paper, endless copies
Courtesy Sammlung Goetz,
Munich

Marguerite Humeau
Russian Thistle Spins, 2023
Wind, zinc-passivated recycled
steel, glass, hand-carved
hardwood, bronze
Pinwheel 1: 110 × 129 × 125 cm
Pinwheel 2: 110 × 140 × 135 cm
Pinwheel 3: 110 × 160 × 110 cm
Pinwheel 4: 105 × 130 × 115 cm
Courtesy of the artist and
C L E A R I N G New York/
Brussels/Los Angeles

Birgit Jürgenssen
Ohne Titel (Selbst mit Fellchen),
1974/2011
Untitled (Self with Little Fur)
17.5 × 12.5 cm
Colour photograph
Louisiana Museum of Modern Art
Acquired with funding from The
Augustinus Foundation

Birgit Jürgenssen
Notebook, Early 1990s
24.6 × 17.6 × 1 cm
Courtesy of Estate Birgit
Jürgenssen and Galerie
Hubert Winter

Candice Lin
System for a Stain, 2016
Dimensions variable
Wood, glass jars, cochineal, poppy
seeds, metal castings, water,
tea, sugar, copper still, hot plate,
ceramic vessels, mortar and
pestle, Thames mud, microbial
mud battery, plastic tubing and
vinyl floor
Courtesy of Candice Lin and
François Ghebaly Gallery

Jumana Manna
*A Magical Substance Flows Into
Me,* 2016
Duration: 1:6 min.
HD video
Courtesy the artist and Hollybush
Gardens, London

Ana Mendieta
Bird Transformation, 1972
39.8 × 31 × 3.1 cm
Colour photograph, vintage print
Louisiana Museum of Modern Art
Acquired with funding from
Museumsfonden af 7. december
1966

Martha Pettway
"Half Squares", 1930s
203 × 185 cm
Cotton
Courtesy of Souls Grown Deep
Foundation, Atlanta, Georgia

Martha Jane Pettway
*"Housetop" - nine-block Half-Log
Cabin variation,* c. 1945
183 × 183 cm
Corduroy
Courtesy of Souls Grown Deep
Foundation, Atlanta, Georgia

Pope.L
*The Polis or the Garden or Human
Nature in Action (Louisiana
Version),* 1998/2023
Painted onions, glass mirrors,
wood shelf
Courtesy of the artist and
Mitchell-Innes & Nash, New York

Tavares Strachan
*Encyclopedia of Invisibility
(White),* 2018
Book: 39,. × 34 × 12.7 cm
Table: 139.7 × 91.4 × 52.4 cm
Leather, gilding, archival paper,
maple, felt and acrylic
Courtesy the artist and Marian
Goodman Gallery

Tavares Strachan
Six Thousand Years, 2018
Each: 20.3 × 27.9 × 5.4 cm,
832 panels in total
Inkjet print, pigment, enamel,
vinyl, graphite, Mylar, spray paint,
cut
Courtesy the artist and Marian
Goodman Gallery

Emma Talbot
Seeds Grow in Fertile Ground,
2023
494 × 761 cm
Acrylic on silk
Courtesy the artist, Galerie
Onrust and Petra Rinck Galerie

Tourmaline
Coral Hairstreak, 2020
75.1 × 76.2 cm
Dye sublimation print
Courtesy of the Artist and
Chapter NY

Tourmaline
Summer Azure, 2020
75.1 × 76.2 cm
Dye sublimation print
Courtesy of the Artist and
Chapter NY

Tourmaline
Swallowtail, 2020
75.1 × 76.2 cm
Dye sublimation print
Courtesy of the Artist and
Chapter NY

Irene Williams
"Bars" variation, c. 1965
213 × 201 cm
Wool knit, linen, polyester double
knit, cotton, drapery material
Courtesy of Souls Grown Deep
Foundation, Atlanta, Georgia

*'Biological networks and their
fragility'*
Data from ongoing project
Bo Dalsgaard, Globe Institute,
University of Copenhagen,
Denmark
Xingfeng Si & Wande Li, East
China Normal University, China
Chen Zhu & Ping Ding, Zhejiang
University, China
Funding: Independent Research
Fund Denmark (grant/award
number 0135-00333B),
National Natural Science
Foundation of China

Ryan Gander
Detail of *School of Languages,* 2023

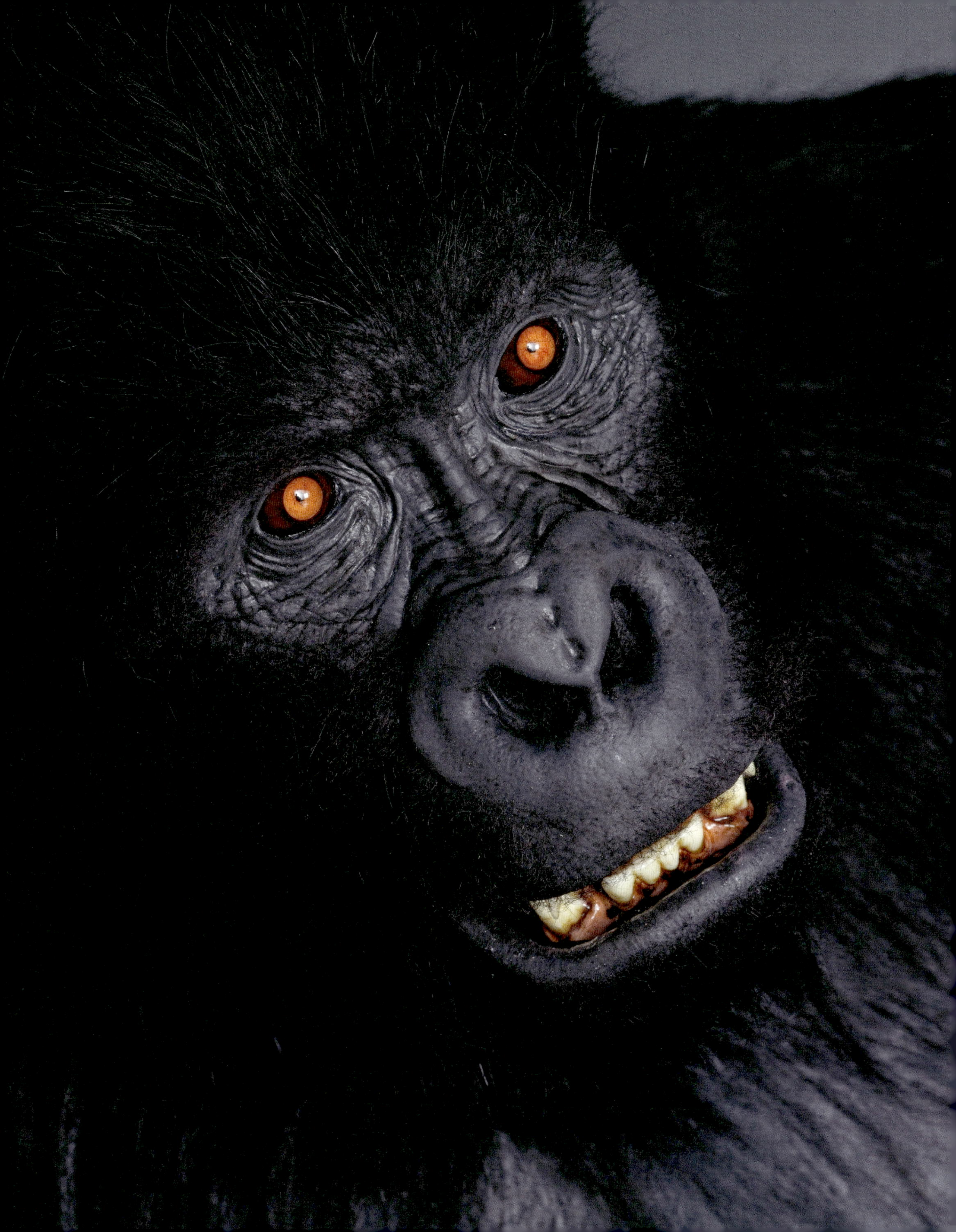

The Irreplaceable Human – Conditions of Creativity in the Age of AI

© 2023 Louisiana Museum of Modern Art & the contributors

Edited by Lærke Rydal Jørgensen, Mathias Ussing Seeberg, Lise Villemoes Grønvold and Malou Wedel Bruun
Graphic Design: Marie Lübecker
Photo Editor: Grethe Røndal Christensen, Kim Hansen
Translations: Adam King (foreword), Glen Garner (Mathias Ussing Seeberg)
Proofreading: Henry Broome
Parts of Amy F. Ogata's essay are adapted and revised from the book *Designing the Creative Child* published by the University of Minnesota Press, 2013
Olga Ravn's text was originally commissioned by TIFA (Toronto International Festival of Authors)

Cover, front: Josh Kline: *Productivity Gains (Brandon/Accountant)*, 2016
3D-printed sculpture, 55 × 69 × 140 cm
Installation view from the exhibition *Antibodies*, 2020, Astrup Fearnley Collection, Oslo, Norway
Photo: Christian Øen
Cover, back: Huang Po-Chih: *Blue Elephant-Mother, "Wanting falls around me. Heavy garment, but I can be a floating elephant in my dream."*, 2018 (2023)
Giclée on Canson Infinity Baryta Photographique II Matt, 140 × 160 cm
Courtesy of the artist
Endpapers, front and back: Emma Talbot: Details from *Seeds Grow in Fertile Ground*, 2023
Acrylic on silk, 494 × 761 cm
Courtesy the artist, Galerie Onrust and Petra Rinck Galerie
Endpapers, front: Ryan Gander: *2000 year collaboration (The Prophet)*, 2018
Animatronic mouse, sound, 19.4 × 24 × 28.2 cm, mouse: 4 × 4 × 5 cm
Museum Voorlinden, Wassenaar, The Netherlands
Photo: Antoine van Kaam
Endpapers, back:
Candice Lin: Detail of *System for a Stain*, 2016
Photo: Andy Keate

Litho/Print: Narayana Press
ISBN: 978-87-93659-76-6
Printed in Denmark 2023
www.louisiana.dk

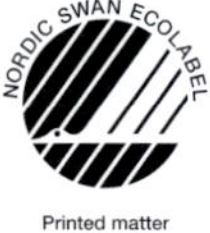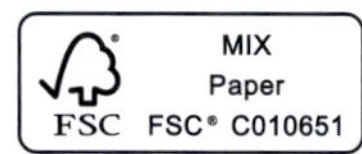

The catalogue is published on the occasion of the exhibition
The Irreplaceable Human – Conditions of Creativity in the Age of AI
Louisiana Museum of Modern Art, Humlebæk, Denmark
23 November 2023 – 1 April 2024

Curator: Mathias Ussing Seeberg
Assistant Curators: Lise Villemoes Grønvold, Amalie Marie Laustsen
Curatorial Coordinators/Registrars: Marie Mose Hyllested, Marianne Ahrensberg
Exhibition Architects: Mia Frykholm, Brian Lottenburger
Conservator/Exhibition Producer: Jesper Lund Madsen
Graphic Design: Maria Hviid Bengtson, Marie Lübecker and Thomas J. Winther

The exhibition is supported by

A. P. Møller og Hustru Chastine Mc-Kinney Møllers Fond til almene Formaal

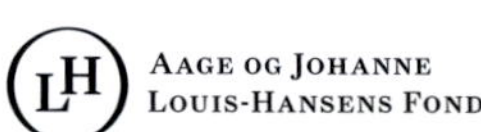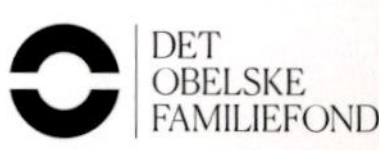

Main Corporate Partner

FRITZ HANSEN

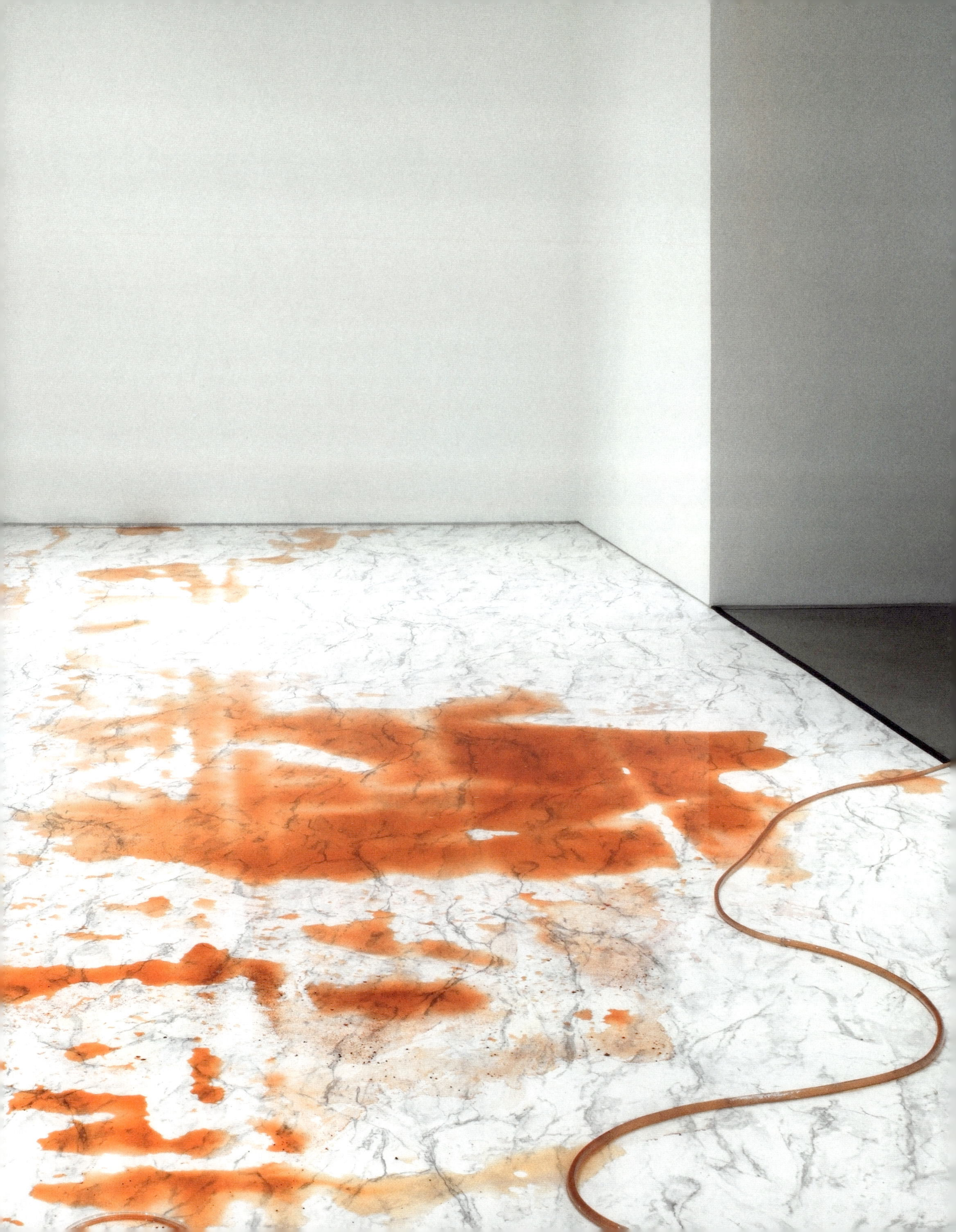

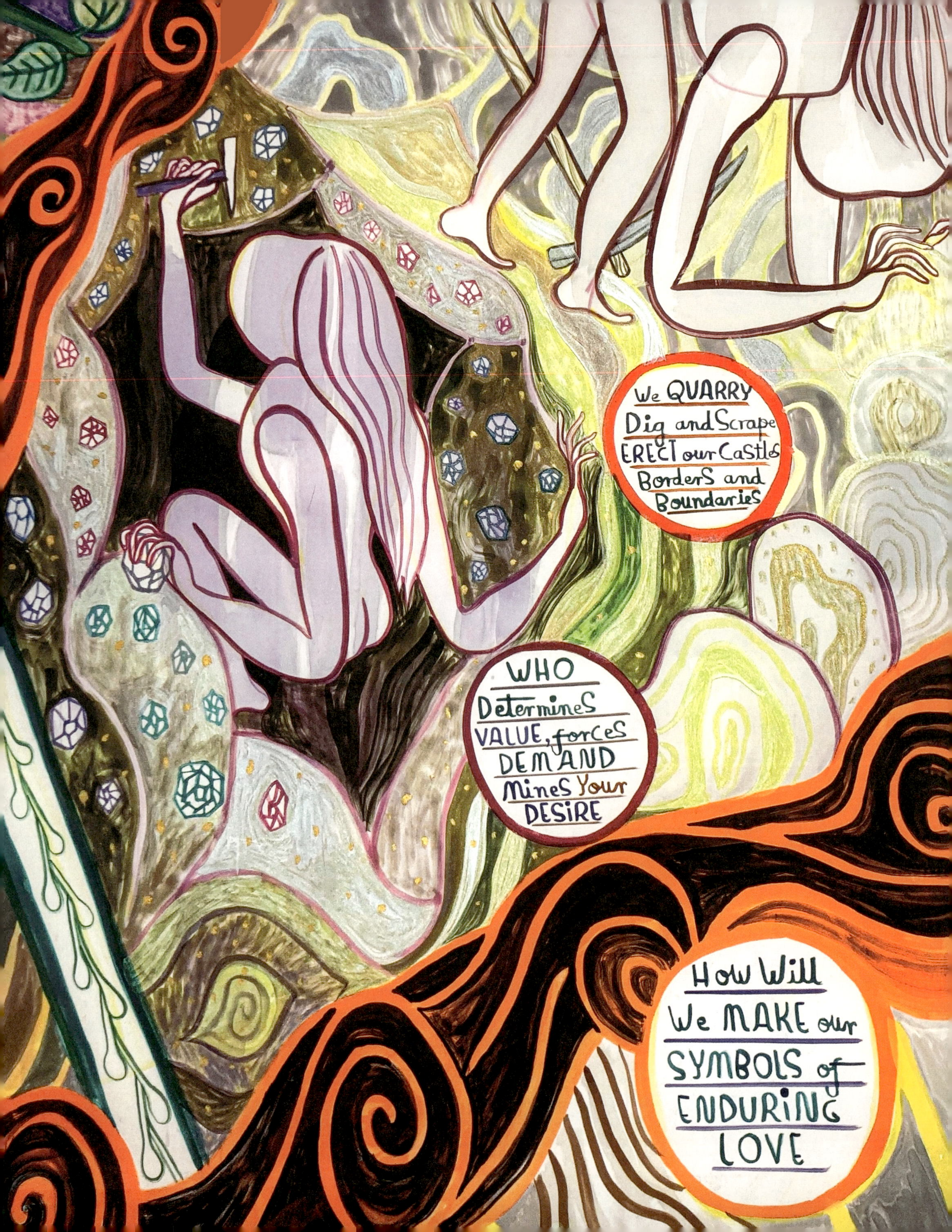

We QUARRY Dig and Scrape ERECT our Castles Borders and Boundaries
WHO Determines VALUE, forces DEMAND Mines Your DESIRE
How Will We MAKE our SYMBOLS of ENDURING LOVE